PRAISE FOR

TORN

"In TORN, Justin Lee blends simplicity, clarity, humility, honesty, and vulnerability in a gracious and eye-opening way. The book brings fresh perspectives to old and polarized debates, and it offers a wise and faithful way forward for pastors and other Christian leaders, parents, and other family members, not to mention gay men and women themselves. This is **the** book that *every* Evangelical, Charismatic, and Roman Catholic Christian should read on the question of homosexuality."

> —**Brian D. McLaren,** author of *Why Did Jesus, Moses, the Buddha, and Mohammed Cross the Road? Christian Identity in a Multi-Faith World* (brianmclaren.net)

"Justin didn't leave the church when he realized he was gay…he has been too determined to show them how much he loves them. This is not the story of how a gay man has reconciled his sexuality inside his Southern Baptist upbringing. This is the story of how one Christian man's faith taught him to accept himself, serve others who are in need, and bridge the gap for those who do not always understand."

> —**Jennifer Knapp,** singer/songwriter, founder of InsideOutFaith.org

"In TORN, Justin Lee speaks for so many other gay and lesbian persons' unspoken experiences. This book is not about politics, but a life. I hope people read this book and realize the journey of faith and sexuality is a reality—a reality that the church, whether they agree or not, must face as a legitimate expression of how LGBT people unnecessarily feel torn between two worlds."

> —**Andrew Marin,** author of the award-winning book *Love Is an Orientation* (www.themarinfoundation.org)

"So many gay, lesbian, bisexual, and transgender people give up on Christianity because they cannot reconcile with who they are, with what they were brought up to believe that the Bible teaches about sexuality. Here is a wonderfully told story of a brave young homosexual man who has struggled to hold on to his faith while still affirming himself as gay. This is a must-read."

> —**Tony Campolo,** Eastern University

"Justin Lee has been put through the ringer by the church. Yet, unlike so many others of his generation, he hasn't given up on the church. Instead, he's put a great deal of effort into reforming the church, and he's done so with a virtue that so many lack: hope. If the Christian church is ever to treat LGBT persons the way that Jesus would treat them, then we need to pay close attention to the pages of TORN."

—Tony Jones (tonyj.net) theologian, author of The New Christians

"The most important book I've read in years, and the first I'd recommend to anyone interested in bridging the divide between the LGBT community and the church. Justin has given us a precious gift with this story. May we receive it with the same courage and faith with which it was delivered."

—Rachel Held Evans, blogger, author of Evolving in Monkey Town
and A Year of Biblical Womanhood

"Justin Lee's TORN is a wise, informative book that's nothing short of a gift. Through both theological and personal lenses, Lee tears the masks off of the gays vs. Christians 'culture war.' An important read for all Christians, TORN shines a bright light on how this polarizing topic is affecting people, the church, and the Gospel of Christ."

—Matthew Paul Turner, author of Churched and Hear No Evil

"TORN sheds light on one of the most important and divisive issues facing the church. If you're looking for a deeper understanding on this or are just trying to make sense of the whole debate, this is the book."

—Jay Bakker, pastor of Revolution Church NYC, author of Faith, Doubt, and Other Lines I've Crossed, Fall to Grace, and Son of a Preacher Man

"I talk with young believers who know they're gay and wonder how to live with that reality while holding on to their faith. Many of these friends are confused and questioning—and haven't received a clear word from their churches about how (or if) they are welcome and what form their discipleship ought to take. I know Justin Lee as a compassionate, thoughtful leader at the forefront of ministry to these gay Christians, and this book tells the story of that ministry. As a celibate gay Christian myself, I wish I could make this courageous, truth-telling book mandatory for every pastor and church member I know."

—Wesley Hill, author of Washed and Waiting: Reflections on Christian Faithfulness and Homosexuality

"With gracious spirit, intelligent sense of proportion, and, above all, prayerful and rigorous honesty in pursuing a deeply biblical perspective, Justin Lee engages the churches' latest sad assault against folks they still have failed to hear. What he's lived and learned and written needs to be received with gratitude and given prayerful reflection—not to agree or disagree with this or that, but to listen with the love that fulfills the law and the prophets."

—Dr. Ralph Blair, psychotherapist, founder of
Evangelicals Concerned, Inc.

TORN

◆

RESCUING THE GOSPEL FROM THE GAYS-VS.-CHRISTIANS DEBATE

JUSTIN LEE

JERICHO
BOOKS ™

New York ● Boston ● Nashville

Unless otherwise indicated, Scriptures are taken from The Holy Bible, New International Version® NIV®. Copyright ©1973, 1978, 1984, 2011 by Biblica, Inc.™ Used by permission of Zondervan. All rights reserved worldwide. www.zondervan.com

The "NIV" and "New International Version" are trademarks registered in the United States Patent and Trademark Office by Biblica, Inc.™

Scriptures marked ESV are taken from The Holy Bible, English Standard Version® (ESV®), copyright © 2001 by Crossway, a publishing ministry of Good News Publishers. Used by permission. All rights reserved.

Scriptures noted TNIV® are taken from the Holy Bible, Today's New International Version™ TNIV®. Copyright © 2001, 2005 by International Bible Society®. All rights reserved worldwide.

Scriptures noted KJV are taken from the King James Version of the Bible.

Jericho Books
Hachette Book Group
237 Park Avenue
New York, NY 10017

www.JerichoBooks.com

Printed in the United States of America

RRD-C

First edition: November 2012
10 9 8 7 6 5 4 3 2 1

Jericho Books is a division of Hachette Book Group, Inc.
The Jericho Books name and logo are trademarks of Hachette Book Group, Inc.

The Hachette Speakers Bureau provides a wide range of authors for speaking events. To find out more, go to www.HachetteSpeakersBureau.com or call (866) 376-6591.

The publisher is not responsible for websites (or their content) that are not owned by the publisher.

Library of Congress Cataloging-in-Publication Data
Lee, Justin, 1977-
  Torn : rescuing the Gospel from the gays-vs.-Christians debate / Justin Lee. -- 1st ed.
      p. cm.
  Summary: "A loving and biblically-based response to the controversy that pits the church against the LGBT community and that divides Christians from each other"--Provided by the publisher.
  ISBN 978-1-4555-1431-1
  1. Homosexuality--Religious aspects--Christianity. 2. Church work with gays.
3. Gays--Religious life. I. Title.
  BR115.H6L44 2012
  261.8'35766--dc23
2012014250

To my parents. Your love, faith, and encouragement made me who I am today. I love you both with all my heart.

CONTENTS

AUTHOR'S NOTE

This book is about a controversial subject that touches many people's lives.

In order to best address the human side of the issue, I've chosen to use a number of personal stories from my own life. The events described are all real, and I've worked hard to ensure the accuracy of the details, relying not only on my own memory but also on hundreds of pages of saved emails, journal entries, and other documents.

I have changed some names and personally identifying details to protect the privacy of individuals I've written about, and in some cases I have altered event sequences or other minor details for the sake of brevity and clarity. Everything else is exactly as I remember it.

TORN

CHAPTER 1

BATTLE OF THE CENTURY

A few years ago, a call came into the Christian ministry where I worked.

The woman on the other end of the phone was in tears. Every so often, she would gain her composure, get a few more sentences out, and then dissolve into sobs once more.

I encouraged her to take her time in explaining the situation.

Her name was Cindy. She was the mother of a fifteen-year-old son. He was her only child, her pride and joy. He was, she explained to me, a good kid. The best kid. Kind, loyal, honest. A good student. Active in the church youth group. A committed Christian. She and her husband couldn't have been prouder.

And then the unthinkable had happened.

Late one night, their precious son had confessed to them that he had realized he was gay.

In the two weeks since, the loving parents had been through a wide range of emotions, wondering what they'd done wrong and what to do next. They'd read and reread the relevant Bible passages, scoured the internet for information, and had numerous conversations with their son, hoping for some sign that he wasn't gay after all. Much to their chagrin, he kept insisting that he was.

More than anything else, Cindy was afraid for her son. She was afraid for his soul and for his future. She had thought about what this would mean for his prospects of having a family, and she had thought about the dangers of AIDS and hate crimes. But of all the things on her mind, there was one she kept coming back to over and over in our conversation.

Most of all, it seemed, she was afraid of their church.

The family had long been members of a rural, conservative evangelical church. "It's a wonderful church," she assured me. "They're wonderful people. But this—if they found out about this, they would never treat him the same way again. I know it."

It was the threat of this Christian rejection following him for the rest of his life that shook her up the most. She knew that America was filled with many churches like theirs and many Christians like the ones she knew. This was the world her son would soon be venturing out into, and for the first time, she found that troubling.

Whatever mistakes her son might make in life, Cindy was sure God would have mercy on him. The church, she feared, might not.

A 2007 study by the Barna Group, a Christian research firm, asked 16- to 29-year-olds to choose words and phrases to describe present-day Christianity. Among the many choices available to them were positive terms like "offers hope" and "has good values" along with negative terms like "judgmental" and "hypocritical."

Out of all of it—good and bad—the most popular choice was "antihomosexual." Not only did 91 percent of the non-Christians describe the church this way, but 80 percent of *churchgoers* did as well.

In the book *unChristian,* Barna Group researchers David Kinnaman and Gabe Lyons describe the results of their three-year study of young Americans' views of the church:

> In our research, the perception that Christians are "against" gays and lesbians…has reached critical mass. The gay issue has become the "big one," the negative image most likely to be intertwined with Christianity's reputation. It is also the dimension that most clearly demonstrates the unChristian faith to young people today, surfacing a spate of negative perceptions: judgmental, bigoted, sheltered, right-wingers, hypocritical, insincere, and uncaring. Outsiders say our hostility toward gays—not just opposition to homosexual politics and behaviors but disdain for gay individuals—has become virtually synonymous with the Christian faith.[1]

Growing up in a conservative Christian home, I knew that we disapproved of homosexuality in general, but I never thought we had "disdain for gay individuals." Now, however, I'm convinced that Kinnaman and Lyons are right: The church's "antihomosexual" reputation isn't just a reputation for opposing gay sex or gay marriage; it's a reputation for *hostility to gay people.* And that leaves Christian moms like Cindy afraid of their own churches.

This is disturbing news for all of us in the Christian community. Jesus wasn't known for his *disdain* for people; he was known for his unconditional love for everyone, especially outcasts and sinners. One of the charges Jesus' opponents had against him was that he was "a glutton and a drunkard, a friend of tax collectors and sinners."[2] Surely the faith he founded should never be known for looking down on *anyone.* After all, isn't the whole message of the gospel that all of us are sinners and fall short of God's glory and that that's why Jesus had to die for us and why we so need grace?[3]

In one of Jesus' parables, a king forgives a servant's massive debt.

The servant then goes out to find a fellow servant who owes *him* a much smaller sum and demands that he pay immediately or be thrown in prison. When the king finds out, he is angry and has the first servant thrown in prison instead.[4] Jesus' message is clear: We've been shown so much grace from God that we must be gracious to others.

In another parable, Jesus tells of two people who go to the temple to pray. One, a devoutly religious man, prays, "God, I thank you that I am not like other people—robbers, evildoers, adulterers—or even like this tax collector. I fast twice a week and give a tenth of all I get." The other prays only, "God, have mercy on me, a sinner."[5] It is the second man, the sinful and ostracized tax collector, who goes home justified before God. Why, then, do so many people think Christians sound more like the first guy?

Part of the issue is that sexual morality is a big deal to Christians, and the majority of Christians believe that sex between two men or two women is immoral. This view by itself creates a certain amount of conflict with the gay community. But that's not the whole story. Whatever views they might hold on homosexuality, I don't know any Christians who want *that* to be the primary thing the church is known for. If it is, that suggests that something somewhere has gone horribly wrong.

Yet that's exactly what we're seeing. Throughout American society, and especially among young people, there is growing discomfort with what is widely perceived as a nasty culture war between gays and Christians, with Christians having fired the first shot.

Images of this war are easy to find. Two days after the horrifying 9/11 terrorist attacks, influential preacher Jerry Falwell blamed gays in part for what he viewed as a sign of God's wrath on America, saying, "I point the finger in their face and say, you helped this happen."

"Well, I totally concur," televangelist Pat Robertson responded. Both men later said they regretted the exchange.

Then there's perhaps the most visible symbol of the Gays-vs.-Christians culture war: the controversial Westboro Baptist Church, a hate group famous for picketing events like gay pride marches and funerals of gay-bashing victims, carrying signs that read "God hates fags" along with various Bible verses.

On the other side of the fence, the perception that Christians are decidedly anti-gay has left many gay people more hostile to Christianity than ever. In 2010, popular gay columnist Dan Savage—himself the child of Christian parents—lashed out at the Christians he viewed as responsible for a rash of gay teen suicides:

> The dehumanizing bigotries that fall from lips of "faithful Christians," and the lies that spew forth from the pulpit of the churches "faithful Christians" drag their kids to on Sundays, give your straight children a license to verbally abuse, humiliate and condemn the gay children they encounter at school. And many of your straight children—having listened to mom and dad talk about how gay marriage is a threat to the family and how gay sex makes their magic sky friend Jesus cry himself to sleep—feel justified in physically attacking the gay and lesbian children they encounter in their schools. ...
>
> Oh, and those same dehumanizing bigotries that fill your straight children with hate? They fill your gay children with suicidal despair. And you have the nerve to ask *me* to be more careful with my words.[6]

The truth is far more complex than these images suggest. Teen suicide devastates us all. The Westboro protesters are few in number, and many Christians rightly denounced Falwell's remarks as inappropriate. But these illustrations still resonate in our culture as extreme examples of a conflict that shows up on a smaller scale in a thousand different ways, from the pulpit to the ballot box. There is undeniable tension in our country between the gay community and the Christian community, and, increasingly, it feels like a full-scale fight to the death.

Ladies and gentlemen! Get your tickets now for the Battle of the Century! Gays vs. Christians! Who will control the future of our culture?

As people pick sides in this epic Gays-vs.-Christians match, each camp has an unflattering image of the other to promote. To those who sympathize with the gays, Christians are ignorant, homophobic bigots, trying to force their outdated religious views down everyone else's throats. To their opponents in the Christian community, the gays are "homosexual activists," seeking to undermine the family and the moral fabric of our society, all in the name of their selfish, perverse, and unhealthy sexual lifestyles.

And with the battle lines drawn, the fight is on.

Political groups on each side frantically raise funds to battle over issues like same-sex marriage and hate crimes legislation, each using scare tactics to warn their supporters that if they don't raise enough money and the other side wins, *their* rights will be taken away and the country will go down the tubes. They battle over court decisions, media messages, and school curricula, agonizing over each shift in public opinion. According to both sides, this is a life-or-death situation; the outcome of these battles will determine the safety of our youth and the future of our country.

The political issues being fought over are real, and some of them are very important. But in the midst of the polarized and often vicious political fight between the gays and the Christians, a lot of real people are getting caught in the crossfire.

Take Cindy, that Christian mom with a gay son. The anti-gay messages she had heard in her church—not just about sexual behavior, but about gay *people*—had left her feeling too afraid even to talk to her pastor about her son's revelation. She was afraid her son would be condemned rather than loved. It was the first time in her life that she felt she couldn't count on her church for something, and that realization was crushing.

I'm sure her pastor never intended to come across that way. Whatever he may have said from the pulpit, and whatever attitudes toward homosexuality might exist in the congregation, surely no one intended them to be directed at Cindy and her son. Regardless of the intent, though, she was convinced that her church was now an unsafe place for her son and, by extension, for her whole family.

Cindy is not alone. As you read these words, Christian parents all across the country are wrestling with the discovery that their children are gay, torn between their unconditional love for their children and their deep desire to follow God at all costs. If the things their churches tell them about gay people don't match what they know from their own children, who are they supposed to believe?

It's not just parents. The church pews are filled with Christians wrestling with these questions in many different ways. Perhaps a friend, a relative, a co-worker, or even a spouse has come out to them, and they don't know how to respond. Some are struggling with their own sexuality. Some self-identify as gay. Some think the church has gotten this whole thing wrong, while others believe the problem is focusing too much on one sin and emphasizing it above all else. Whatever the case, as more people come out as gay, that leaves more Christians who know them with questions about how to truly be loving in a culture that views Christianity as anti-gay.

Sadly, today's churches are all too often unprepared to help people with these sensitive and complex situations. In their zeal to take a strong moral stand on sexuality, they have said and done things that only alienate the people who most need their support.

Meanwhile, as Christians question the hard-line approach they've seen so many churches take, many are rejecting the church's traditional approach to sexuality, leading to splits within denominations and congregations. Even there, the fights can quickly become polarized and harsh.

Americans on both sides are becoming increasingly frustrated with the tone of the debate, and many are calling for more loving ways of handling the differences of belief.

In an opinion piece for *USA Today,* evangelical author Jonathan Merritt writes, "Now is the time for those who bear the name of Jesus Christ to stop merely talking about love and start showing love to our gay and lesbian neighbors. It must be concrete and tangible. It must move beyond cheap rhetoric."[7]

If only it were that simple. Unfortunately, without communication or understanding between the camps, proposals that one side views as compassionate and loving are not necessarily perceived as such by the other side.

Merritt's own well-intentioned words are no exception. A few days after his article, *USA Today* ran responses under the headline, "Behind message of 'love,' an anti-gay agenda."

"Merritt's message of being nice to gay people…is just a way for the religious right to soften their image and to make bigotry acceptable," wrote one critic, noting that Merritt believes gay relationships to be sinful. Meanwhile, Southern Baptist bloggers took Merritt to task for the opposite reason, arguing that he was failing to take a strong enough stand against sin.

Not everyone agrees that it's time for more compassion on this issue. But even among those who do, there's no widespread agreement on what that ought to look like.

Some Christians suggest offering ministries to "heal sexual brokenness" as a compassionate alternative to anti-gay rhetoric in the church. The gay community balks at this idea, calling it offensive and ineffective. Some in the gay community seek to bridge the gap through pro-gay religious leaders and reinterpretations of Scripture; this, however, does not fly with many Christians. Members of both communities have suggested a live-and-let-live approach, but this has largely proved unsatisfactory on both sides.

If we can't compromise, then, what's the answer? Will one side have to wipe the other side out? There are some on both sides who seem to think this is the case. As long as such culture-war attitudes prevail, people will continue to be hurt.

Some have managed to stay insulated from the conflict by surrounding themselves only with those who agree with them, and they're often surprised to learn what a big issue this continues to be for others. "Haven't we settled this question already?" they ask. "How do *those people* still not 'get it'?"

Several years ago, I was discussing this topic with a not-too-religious acquaintance from California. "I don't think it's really much of an issue anymore, is it?" he said. "It certainly isn't here. Out here, we just live and let live. Gay people, straight people—no one cares who you're sleeping with." He was completely dumbfounded a year later, when Proposition 8 passed, banning same-sex marriage in California. In spite of the state's reputation as a liberal, gay-friendly locale, clearly many Californians don't see things the way he does.

It works the other way, too. I've met a number of pastors and families over the years who had always thought this "gay" thing was confined to some other group of people—nothing to do with good Christians like them—until someone they loved came out, often the last person they ever would have expected. A study by the research firm Christian Community found gay-identified teens in virtually every congregation they surveyed, even those with the most negative things to say about homosexuality. Not surprisingly, the kids had often not told any adults at the church about their sexuality.[8]

America is still far more polarized on this than many of us realize, and the United States is only one of the many countries dealing with this conflict on the world stage. The Church of Sweden—the largest Christian denomination in that country—made headlines in 2009 for voting to begin performing same-sex wedding ceremonies, a decision other Swedish denominations opposed. That same year, Christian leaders in Uganda backed a bill to execute gay people, a move sparking international outrage and criticisms that worldwide Christian groups were slow to condemn the bill and may even have been unwittingly instrumental in its formation. In 2011, the son of a family I know in Northern Ireland came out as gay—and was promptly disowned by his Christian parents, who now refuse to have any contact with him. His own mother won't even talk to him.

These issues are varied and complex. Underlying all of them, however, is the essential question of how we Christians, having traditionally condemned homosexuality, should respond to a world that is increasingly accepting of it. Some say that the growing acceptance of homosexuality is further evidence of our world's fallen nature, and that we Christians must hold fast to God's truth in the face of the winds of change. Others say that we Christians have made a terrible mistake in unequivocally condemning homosexuality, and that a more complete understanding of human sexuality and the Bible's cultural context should move us to repent and reevaluate our stance. Either way, if we answer this question incorrectly, will we have committed one of the greatest tragedies in the history of the church?

Families and congregations alike are torn over these issues. But if we continue to disagree, is there really any hope of ending the culture war? Is there a more compassionate approach? What would that look like, in practical terms?

Such questions matter to people like Cindy. They matter to the gay people whose lives this is all about. And they ought to matter just as much to all of us who call ourselves Christians and claim to represent Jesus.

Today's young people have gay friends whom they love. If they view the church as an unsafe place for them, a place more focused on politics than on people, we just might be raising the most anti-Christian generation America has ever seen, a generation that believes they have to *choose* between being loving and being Christian.

Over the last fifteen years, God has taken me on an incredible, often painful, but ultimately inspiring journey through precisely these questions. I could tell you what I think, but when it comes to this debate, opinions are a dime a dozen.

Instead, I'd like to share with you what I've experienced and how it radically altered my approach to an issue I thought I knew everything about.

And it all started with the kid in high school who called me "God Boy."

CHAPTER 2

GOD BOY

Hey God Boy, I have a question for you."

Sean grinned at me from across the lunch table in our high school cafeteria. We were sixteen-year-old high school sophomores, at that wonderful age when you think you know everything.

Okay, to be fair, as a teenager I *hated* it when adults made jokes about "teenagers who think they know everything." It sounded condescending and rude. I didn't actually think I knew *everything*, and my most recent history test had just proved it.

However, I did think I was pretty smart, and (that last history test excepted) my academic record bore that out. I was a straight-A student taking challenging, top-level classes at a challenging, top-rated high school for the academically gifted. My bookshelf at home held a collection of math and computer competition trophies I had won over the years, and while I didn't brag about my academic achievements, I tended to be the kid in several of my classes who messed up the curve by doing "too well" on tests.

Yeah, I was *that* kid.

Learning had taught me that, as smart as I was, there was always more to know. But if there was any area where my teenage know-it-allness came out in full force, it was when it came to my faith.

I was a committed Christian, and everybody knew it. If I didn't have a Bible in my backpack, I at least had a church bulletin and some tracts about salvation. I was ready to witness to anybody, anywhere, at the drop of a hat. More than anything in the world, I wanted to represent my God well, and I prayed every day for the wisdom and opportunities to do so. I was confident in my knowledge of my faith and always eager to explain some minor point of theology to my friends and classmates.

Yeah, I was *that* kid too.

Sean was a friend of a friend who sometimes joined my friends at lunch. He had teasingly nicknamed me "God Boy," and he took special pleasure in trotting out the nickname whenever he was going to ask me about a controversial religious or political issue of the day. He wasn't particularly religious himself, but he enjoyed coming up with hypothetical moral quandaries to pose to me, just to see how I'd handle them.

For my part, I enjoyed the challenge. I had studied the Bible from a young age, and I knew it well. Whenever Sean called me "God Boy," I knew he was challenging me to express my faith intelligently. *Bring it on,* I silently thought. *I'm ready for you.* As I saw it, debates with Sean were a way to hone my rhetorical skills and share the truth of Christianity with a non-Christian. I knew I wanted to do ministry work in the future, so being forced to defend my faith seemed like great practice.

On this particular occasion, Sean had a gleam in his eye as he considered his question. Either he thought it would be tough, or he had other reasons for wanting to hear my response.

I put down my sandwich and met his gaze. The challenge was on. "Okay, what's the question?"

"What do you think about this big gay controversy? Whose side are you on?"

"Ah," I said. The question didn't come as a surprise. The whole school had been buzzing about it for the last few days.

It had all started when some students anonymously taped up a poster in the school hallway. Titled "A Call to Arms," the poster broached the topic with all the subtlety and compassion of an angry bull.

"Attention all heterosexual students," it began. "Many of us have come to realize that we are in the presence of faggots and dykes!" It continued predictably into vicious hate speech, urging straight students to band together against their gay peers.

The poster was pulled down by the administration as soon as they saw it, but it had already been seen by hundreds of students, leading to ripple effects throughout the school. Some laughed; some trembled; others dismissed it as irrelevant. But everyone was talking about it.

That evening, six students got together to write up a response. The next morning, they were distributing pamphlets of their own. The pamphlets mocked the language of the original poster and called for tolerance and understanding of gay students. The principal, likely seeking to avoid controversy, created one instead by suspending the six students who were pleading for tolerance.

It turned out that there was an old rule on the books that forbade distribution of literature without prior administrative approval. The poster, with all its hate speech, had been anonymous. But the six students calling for tolerance had put their names on their work. They hadn't known—none of us had—that it would be against the rules for them to pass out something they had written in an attempt to do good.

The local media had a field day with the event. It was a juicy story: Students who wanted to combat hate speech with compassion had been suspended for their efforts! It also raised disturbing questions for many parents about homosexuality among high school students. Now, even those of us who hadn't been talking about the poster were really talking about it all.

The student body was divided. Many of us didn't know, or didn't think we knew, anyone gay. A lot of us opposed homosexuality in principle—some out of prejudice; others for religious reasons. On the other hand, this was also a free speech issue, and American high school students *hate* having their free speech curtailed.

It was the perfect storm of moral outrage and indignation on all sides. Sean took great pleasure in raising the subject just to see how God Boy would weigh in on it all. What could be more controversial than the much-hyped cultural battle of Gays vs. Christians?

LOVE THE SINNER...

As far as I was aware, I had never met a gay person. I had seen them on TV and I had read about them in the newspaper, but I didn't know any personally. If there were gay people at our school, I had no idea who they were.

As a Christian, though, I did know a thing or two about homosexuality. For one thing, I knew that the Bible said it was a sin. I didn't have the passages memorized, but I remembered that it was called an abomination, and I knew that it was outside of God's design for our sexuality. God had created men and women for each other, and sex was supposed to be part of their lifelong bonding in marriage. I thought of sex like fire: Used properly, it was a beautiful and awesome thing. Used carelessly, it could create all manner of destruction—including unwanted pregnancies, sexually transmitted diseases, and psychological hurt. It wasn't just about calling things "sin" for the sake of it. God had created sex, He understood its power, and He had good reasons for giving us boundaries.

Homosexuality was outside of those boundaries. That didn't

mean that God *hated* gay people; on the contrary, I was sure that God loved them! I was also sure, however, that God didn't want them to be gay. If homosexuality was a sin, why would God *make* people homosexuals? It didn't make any sense. I was pretty sure that meant people weren't "born gay."

This is why I, like many Christians, was concerned about the growing acceptance of homosexuality in our culture. Adolescence is a confusing time; I knew that well as a sixteen-year-old. Suppose other teenagers like me—teens who didn't have a strong faith like I did—heard people say that being gay was normal and acceptable; I worried that might lead them to declare themselves gay just because of a momentary same-sex thought or some other insecurity, and then the rest of their lives would go down a sinful path that could have been easily avoided. I saw it as my responsibility to speak up and warn people that the pro-gay messages they were hearing on TV were wrong, that no one was born gay, and that God had something better in store for them.

I knew some people would call this view "homophobic." But I didn't hate or fear gay people; my whole point was wanting to love them the way God loved them. Loving people doesn't always mean agreeing with them. Sometimes you show your love for people by telling them what they need to hear instead of what they want to hear.

I considered how to apply this understanding to the situation at hand.

I hadn't seen the "Call to Arms" poster, but based on the descriptions of it I had heard from other students, I was disgusted by it. As a Christian, I have always opposed bullying and hate speech in any form. It's simply wrong. Yes, I had moral objections to homosexuality, but I would never, ever support calling people nasty names or threatening them. I was proud of the six students for standing up against that kind of hate speech.

But I had mixed feelings about the pamphlet they were distributing. I worried about the impact of their message, which was that it was okay and normal to be gay. I didn't believe that either.

I answered Sean with what I thought was the perfect Christian response: loving, compassionate, nuanced, and, above all, biblical.

"I think the words on that poster were wrong," I said. "God loves everyone, gay people included. There's no need for nasty language like that. But—"

"Here it comes," Sean interrupted.

"*But* it's still a sin," I said. "The Bible's clear on that. It's not God's best for us. But even though it's a sin, that doesn't mean God hates gay people. God loves us, and that's why He gives us rules to live by—so that we can have the abundant lives He's called us to."

"So basically, love the sinner, hate the sin?"

"Exactly!" I said. I smiled.

He didn't.

At the time, I thought that conversation had gone exceptionally well. I felt good about defending the truths of Scripture in a way that was loving, not hateful. I was proud of myself for taking an unpopular stand in the face of a culture that was becoming more and more accepting of homosexuality. In short, I was sure that this was just how God wanted me to respond to a question like this. I imagined that even Jesus, though surely more eloquent than I, would have responded in a similar fashion. It was the only reasonable Christian approach.

Today, I'm embarrassed when I look back on that conversation. I recognize that my motives were good, and I still approach the issue as a Bible-believing Christian. But after everything I've been through, I now see many things about that situation that I didn't see at the time.

I'm ashamed to realize how my youth and pride blinded me to so much: The complexities of the question. The motives of the questioner. The unintentional callousness of my response. I thought I was sharing the gospel that day, when in fact I was probably only confirming Sean's negative views of Christians. A wiser Christian would have responded much differently.

Neither of us knew I was about to have a crash course in just how wrong I'd gotten things, a series of experiences that would transform me into a nationally recognized authority on this very subject, with a mission to forever alter the way Christians think about gay people.

God Boy's life was about to be turned upside down.

CHAPTER 3

THE STRUGGLE

For all my confidence on the issue, there was one thing I couldn't tell Sean that day.

God Boy had a secret.

It was, I thought, the worst secret in the world. It was the deepest, darkest secret I could ever imagine having, one that I could never tell anyone, not even my parents or best friends. It was the secret I would take with me to my grave.

Years earlier, when I had first hit puberty and all my male friends were starting to "notice" girls, I was having the opposite experience: I was starting to "notice" other guys.

I wasn't a late bloomer; my young sex drive was kicking in right along with theirs, bringing with it all the mysterious feelings of attraction to classmates who had previously been only friends on the playground. But in my case, it was guys, not girls, who triggered this strange reaction.

At first I had simply ignored the feelings. Puberty is a confusing time, after all, so I assumed these attractions to guys were just some sort of weird phase I had to pass through as I matured. I'd heard Christian authorities such as radio host Dr. James Dobson say that young teenagers sometimes went through a period of sexual confusion, and this seemed to be the proof. All of this only reinforced my view about the importance of opposing the normalization of homosexuality. What if someone else experienced feelings like these? They might think they were gay! Thank goodness I knew better.

I waited patiently to grow out of this phase. In the meantime, all I had to do was stay focused on the important things: my relationship with God, my schoolwork, my church, and my family. In time, this would pass. Of that I had no doubt.

But as I got older, I began to notice that none of my guy friends seemed to be going through the same sort of phase. More and more, their attentions turned toward girls, and a note of sexual tension was evident in their voices when they talked about them.

As kids, we had joked about who "liked" whom, but it had all been full of childish innocence. As teenagers, my guy friends had become interested in girls in a different way, and they talked eagerly about their eyes and lips and breasts and legs. I avoided these conversations, telling myself that the reason I didn't lust after women was that I was a good Christian boy. Lust was a sin, so I convinced myself I just didn't objectify women the way some of my friends did. That wouldn't have been Christlike, after all.

The truth, however, was that I didn't feel any of the things they did. I wasn't overcoming some great moral struggle to avoid lusting after women; in actuality, I didn't have any sexual feelings toward women at all. My sex drive was in full swing, but it was directed at guys, not girls, and I didn't know how to change it.

I was just beginning to recognize all of this when my best friend asked me about it one day on the way to class. "You never talk about girls, Justin. What's up with that?"

I panicked, terrified he would discover my secret. "I just want to be a gentleman, so I don't talk about them like that." It was true, but not the whole truth.

"Well yeah," he persisted, "but isn't there any girl you like?"

My mind raced. I thought about all the girls we knew. One in particular popped into my head, a girl I considered a good friend. "Suzanne," I said. "But don't tell anybody."

"Ah!" He seemed thrilled to be my confidant. "What do you like about Suzanne?"

What did I like about her? I didn't know. I had just picked her so I'd have someone to name. "I dunno," I said. "She's nice."

Apparently this was the wrong answer. "Well sure, but what about physically? Don't you think she's pretty?"

Pretty? The thought had never occurred to me.

It was an awkward conversation, but it was also a relief to finally have a girl I "liked." I began to talk about Suzanne more and more with my friends, secretly hoping that if I talked and thought about girls more, my natural attractions for them would eventually develop and I'd begin to feel what all the other guys felt.

My dad and I had a close relationship, and I had always felt like I could tell him anything. So one evening, during some private father–son time over a game of pool, I decided to broach the subject of Suzanne. I mentioned that there was a girl at school I was interested in.

"Tell me all about her!"

"Well, she's really nice…" I began, but then realized I didn't know what else to say about her.

"What does she look like?" he asked.

I didn't know how to describe her. I really hadn't thought much about her looks.

"For instance, what color hair does she have?" he offered helpfully.

"Blonde," I said.

"Ooh, a blonde!" he said with a sly grin. "Blondes do have a certain allure, don't they?"

It was just the sort of conversation a father and son are supposed to have. And yet, for the first time in my life, I felt something I couldn't say to my dad. How could I tell him what I was really feeling, that I didn't care that she was blonde, or what she looked like at all, that I never thought about any girls like that, but that there *was* a blond boy I couldn't get out of my head—a classmate with a shy smile and cute dimples and bright green eyes? Argh! How could I even think such things about a boy?

Still, I was convinced this was just a phase. It was going to be my deep, dark secret until I grew out of this period of sexual confusion, and then I'd fall in love with a beautiful girl, and we'd get married and have kids and I'd live my life in service to God. I just knew that was how things would go.

◇

I dated girls in high school, and even though I wasn't physically attracted to them, I was sure that those feelings would develop in time.

What concerned me more was that my feelings for guys weren't going away. They were just getting stronger and stronger as I matured. I found myself struggling to concentrate on my schoolwork and my faith, trying my best to avoid thinking about attractive guys. Even if I could keep my mind off of guys during the day, though, I'd go to sleep at night and have dreams about guys. I'd wake up in the morning feeling sick and disgusted with myself. Something was really wrong with me, but I couldn't tell anyone. I was too ashamed of my own feelings.

Night after night, I cried myself to sleep, begging and pleading with God to take away my sexual attractions to other guys. "Please don't let me feel this anymore," I'd pray over and over, sure that God would take the feelings away eventually, but wanting it to be soon. I hated myself for what I felt, and I was desperate to be rid of it.

On the outside, I was the kid every parent wanted their kid to be: a good student, active in the church youth group, trustworthy, independent, and a smiling friend to anyone who needed one. Inside, I was falling apart.

My senior year of high school, I met a girl named Liz, and we became fast friends. She was a gymnast, a committed Christian, and an overall fun person to be around. We would go to church youth events, hang out at the mall, and go for walks in the park. The more we did together, the more I realized that she was everything I wanted in a girl. She was funny, spontaneous, cheerful, honest, and, above all, a Christian. We spent so much time together that our friends started to joke that we were going out "by default," since I had never actually asked her out.

Wanting to be romantic, I asked her out for the first time on Valentine's Day, but making ourselves officially "a couple" didn't really change our relationship at all. I enjoyed the innocent friendship-based relationship we had, and I was in no hurry to move on to anything physical. I did the things a boyfriend was supposed to do—holding doors for her, paying for meals, putting my arm around her at the movies—but there was never any physical aspect to the relationship. I just didn't think of her in that way. My friends told me she was "hot," and one in particular was drooling over her, but to me she was just someone I enjoyed hanging out with. I didn't see her as physically attractive, but I was sure that I would...someday.

I felt kind of awkward cuddling with her, but I did it happily because I cared about her and I wanted to be a good boyfriend to her. Still, the romantic part of me wanted to save our first kiss for a time when I really felt the urge to kiss her. After months of dating, including the prom, I still hadn't done any more than kiss her on the cheek.

Things seemed to be going well, until the night I took Liz to see a concert by two of my favorite Christian artists, Michael W. Smith and Jars of Clay.

The evening was beautiful and the music was powerful. We sat there entranced, holding hands and swaying to the melodies. For a moment, my life seemed perfect.

Then out of the blue, I noticed a face in the crowd. He was another young guy, there to see the concert, walking past us to rejoin his group. I only saw him for an instant, but I couldn't help noticing his attractive features, and suddenly I found my thoughts and emotions rushing toward him. I wanted to know everything about him. Who was he? Who had he come with? Where was he going? Where did he go to school? I wanted to meet him, to talk to him, to get to know him, to spend time with him. I think I would have been content just to sit near him and stare at him for the rest of the night.

I knew nothing about this guy, but just seeing him gave me feelings unlike anything I had ever felt around a girl. He intrigued me, tempted me, attracted me. For an instant, my head was filled with thoughts of him.

And then I suddenly caught myself. Here I was, holding hands with the most wonderful girl in the world, a girl whom I loved dearly and who loved me, my girlfriend whom I even would have been willing to marry someday, and yet all I could think about was some guy I happened to glimpse in a crowd. What was wrong with me? Why did I still have these feelings, after so many years of trying to be rid of them? Wasn't God hearing the urgent prayers I had cried for so long, asking not to have these horrible, perverted, unwanted feelings for other guys?

The song playing was an emotional one, so no one noticed the tears trickling down my cheeks.

The rest of the concert was a blur for me. All I could think about was "What's wrong with me?" Liz noticed my mood on the way home, but I couldn't tell her the truth. I was too scared to let my secret out, and too worried that I would hurt her if she knew.

The experience disturbed me, but all I knew to do was to keep doing what I always did: praying about it and focusing on my schoolwork.

Then one night, everything changed.

I was online, chatting with some of my friends and other local students. One of the students, Brian, was a friend of a friend at another school. We didn't know each other well, but there was something about him that was different from the other boys I knew. Something about him seemed familiar, something I could connect with. But I couldn't put my finger on exactly what it was or why I found our connection so compelling.

On this particular occasion, Brian and I chatted late into the night. I needed to go to bed, but I couldn't tear myself away from the conversation. Something about this guy made sense to me in a way I couldn't explain. And the longer we chatted, the more keenly aware I became of just how similar he and I really were. Even though we hadn't broached the topic at all, I suddenly knew he was different in the same way I was different. And I needed to know what that was.

Brian seemed to feel it too. "There's something I should probably tell you," he finally admitted.

He paused. I caught my breath. This was it. He was going to tell me the thing that I had never been able to tell anyone.

"I'm bisexual," he typed.

And I burst into tears.

I cried more that night than I ever had in my life. For years, I had thought I was the only one in the world tormented by these feelings of attraction to other guys. Now, here was someone else with the same feelings, and he had a word for them: "bisexual." Finally, I wasn't the only one in the world. I wasn't alone. Someone else was like me.

I was…bisexual.

The word brought equal parts horror and comfort. It was like having suffered for years with strange medical symptoms no doctor could explain, only to finally be diagnosed with some rare illness. Even if the prognosis for the illness isn't good, there's something comforting about finally having a name for what you feel. Knowing that you're not the only one to have experienced the symptoms, that there's an explanation and a diagnosis for what is happening to you, is a powerful thing.

That's what the word "bisexual" was for me. It was a diagnosis. It was the word to describe what was wrong with me. Realizing that I was "bisexual" wasn't a way of establishing it as a core part of my being; that place belonged only to my faith. "Bisexual" was, in my eyes, just the name for the disease I had, and identifying it was the first step to finding a cure. Finally having that diagnosis, I felt hopeful about my sexuality for the first time in a long time.

There was only one problem with this. The word "bisexual" refers to people who are more or less equally attracted to males and females. The truth was that I *wasn't* equally attracted to males and females. Even though I was dating a girl and wanted desperately to be attracted to her, I had still never experienced even a moment of attraction for a woman, ever, in my life. All of my attractions were for other guys.

I didn't want to admit to myself that there was a different word for guys who are only attracted to other guys. That word was not "bisexual," but it was a word I was nowhere near ready to use for myself.

I confided my deep, dark secret in Brian that night, the first time I had ever admitted to anyone that I was attracted to other guys. I told him how confused I was, and how I didn't know what to do about it. He told me that he had found a boyfriend, and that he was very happy. I cried more, because I knew that was something I could never accept. Unlike him, I had to be rid of these feelings. My faith required it.

CHAPTER 4

THE TRUTH COMES OUT

At the time, I had no idea where these feelings came from or why I had them. In Chapter 5, I'll share some of the things I've learned since then that may shed some light on that question. Back then, it was still a complete mystery to me.

What I did know was that I was a Christian. Somehow I had to find a way to deal with this as a Christian. Encouraged by my discovery that I wasn't alone, but still terrified to tell anyone in my life what I was feeling, I turned to the internet for answers.

My first search brought only websites discussing why Christians should oppose homosexuality. I already knew that, but what were you supposed to do when the "it" you were opposing was inside of yourself? Another search brought more of the same, and a third search led me to the website of a church that claimed you could be a committed Christian in a same-sex relationship and that God would be okay with that. *Ludicrous,* I thought. *Clearly they haven't read their Bibles.*

Finally, I stumbled upon the website I was hoping for: a Christian ministry offering support to "Christians struggling with homosexuality." It was a simple website with precious few details, but I read them over and over. The site didn't offer any specifics about what sort of support they offered, nor did it give any physical address or phone number. I didn't care. Here was evidence that someone out there could help me.

The only contact information the site offered was an email address to write to for more information. With trembling hands, I slowly typed out my confession, that I was a Christian teenage male who was attracted to other guys, and that I didn't want to be. I took my time, chewing over each word, worrying the whole time about whether someone might somehow see this message and trace it back to me. I reassured myself that that couldn't happen, and sent the email. Now I just had to wait.

I went to bed that night happy. My troubles would soon be over.

At school the next day, I could barely concentrate. All I could think about was hearing back from the anonymous web ministry. When I got home, I raced to my computer, booted it up, and checked my email.

No response.

The next day was much the same. I doodled and daydreamed my way through class, able to focus on only one thing—hearing back from someone who would understand my situation. Alas, I returned to my computer that evening only to find an empty virtual mailbox.

This continued, day after day, for the next couple of weeks. With time, my hope of hearing from them vanished, and my hope of finding support vanished along with it.

I never did hear back from them.

With or without these strangers on the internet, I knew I couldn't continue to keep my struggles a secret. I was going to need the support of other Christians in my life to deal with this, and that meant I would have to tell the truth about what I was going through.

The idea terrified me. How could I tell others I wasn't straight when I could barely even admit it to myself? And yet, now that I *had* faced it myself, the need to talk to someone about it was growing every day. Plus, I thought, if having the support of other Christians meant that I could become straight faster, then I was willing to do it. To finally be rid of this burden, I was ready to do almost anything, however difficult it might be.

Just like that, my mind was made up. My deepest, darkest secret in the world, the secret I was sure I would take to my grave, was about to be a secret no longer. I was going to have to risk my reputation, the respect people had for me, and the relationships I had with friends and family, for the sake of being honest and finding a solution to the predicament I was in.

And I knew what that meant: I had to tell my girlfriend.

Liz already knew something was wrong. After the night at the concert, she hadn't pressed me for details, but she knew I was struggling with something stressful, and she wanted to help. I just didn't know how to tell the girl I'd been dating for months that I dreamed about guys instead of girls.

It had taken me years of dealing with my own feelings before I could admit them to myself, so I had no idea how anyone else would respond to the news without that time to process it. Telling Liz right away seemed too risky, so I needed to test the news out on someone else first. But who?

The answer came during a conversation with Brittany, a member of my church and a mutual friend of mine and Liz's. Brittany was a committed Christian and someone I trusted. Since she was a girl, I thought she might respond better than my guy friends.

Over the course of another tearful late-night internet chat, I confessed everything to Brittany. After swearing her to secrecy, I started typing and everything just spilled out: my years of struggle, my internet friendship with Brian, my desire to serve God, my fear about telling Liz. Brittany was shocked, but she offered to pray for me, and she encouraged me to tell Liz the truth. "I think she'll understand," she advised.

I broke the news to Liz while sitting on the curb outside my church after a youth event. It was the first time I had ever said the words out loud, and it proved to be much harder than typing them on a computer screen. With my voice constantly threatening to give out on me, I tried several times to work up to the revelation. In the end, the most I could get out was, "I'm not…straight." And then I was crying again.

She said it was okay. She told me she loved me. She said that no matter what, she'd always be there for me.

I didn't ask how she was doing. I was so caught up in my own pain and fear, it never occurred to me that my girlfriend was trying her best to mask her own sadness in order to support me.

I told her that I still wanted to keep dating if she wanted to, and that I just needed her prayers right now to help me overcome this temporary setback. I wasn't going to be "this way" forever; I just needed to get support and therapy and keep trusting God, and soon everything would be normal and I'd be rid of these horrible feelings.

I was sure of it.

BYE-BYE, BI

Once I'd told Liz, I felt better—for a little while. But the burden of this secret continued to weigh on me. So far only three people knew: a guy from the internet I'd never met, a girl from church I rarely saw, and *my girlfriend*. I needed to be able to talk about this with someone in person. Someone I could open up to and trust—who *wasn't* my girlfriend.

Hesitantly, I settled on the idea of sharing my struggle with a couple of close friends from school. Over a period of weeks, I worked up the courage to drop some hints with various friends and see how they responded. I'd gently bring up the topic of same-sex attractions in a vague, theoretical sense, and if a friend reacted negatively, I'd quickly change the subject and never bring it up again. But when a couple of my friends seemed understanding, I gradually moved the conversation from theoretical to reality: "What if someone you *knew* was like that? Could you still be friends with them?"

My friends promised to keep my secret, even though the subject seemed to make them uncomfortable.

Then one night, one of them asked the question I didn't want to face.

"How do you know you're bi?" he asked me.

"What do you mean?" I said. "I'm attracted to guys."

"What I mean is… how do you know you're not *gay*?"

"I'm not gay," I said indignantly. "I'm not anything like that. I love Liz. We're dating. I'm going to get married someday. I'm not gay."

"So you're telling me that you are equally attracted to both men *and* women?" he persisted.

"Yes," I lied.

"You have sexual feelings and fantasies toward women?"

"Well, I mean… I don't think that way."

"Okay, so when you see an attractive woman, is there a part of you that wants to imagine her with her clothes off?"

"No, but…"

"And you don't think that's odd?"

"But I'm a Christian, and I don't think about women that way. I *respect* them. I think that's how this whole trouble started. Maybe I just respect them so much that I didn't allow myself to think about them sexually, and my sex drive got a little confused or something."

He laughed.

"That's not funny!" I protested.

"I don't know, but I don't think it works that way. I respect women too, you know. But I have a daily struggle to keep from lusting after them, because that's what my sex drive naturally wants to do if I don't keep a rein on it. Do you have a daily struggle?"

"No," I admitted. I *did* have a daily struggle to keep from lusting after guys, though.

"Do you dream about women at night?"

"No. Not really."

"Respecting women doesn't turn off your sex drive, Justin. I don't think you're really bi."

"You can't see in my head," I countered, and changed the subject.

I didn't want to admit it, but he was right. I had never had a sexual thought or attraction for a woman in my life. The real reason I called myself bi was that it didn't sound so scary. If I was bi, all I had to do was get rid of my same-sex attractions and keep the opposite-sex ones. But if I was gay, things were going to be a whole lot harder than I had imagined.

That night, I put it out of my mind, but as time passed I began to realize the truth in what my friend had said. As scary as the label was, the truth was that I wasn't bi. I was gay.

Gay.

The word seemed to hold the weight of eternity within its single syllable.

As strange as it may seem, in all the years I had struggled with my sexuality, the idea that I could be gay had simply never crossed my mind. I was a Christian! That was my whole life! And Christians weren't gay.

I already had an image of what gay people were like. They were sinners who had turned from God and had an "agenda" to mainstream their perverse lifestyles. I didn't actually know any gay people, but I had seen them in video footage of Pride parades, where they were dressed in outrageous outfits or wearing next to nothing at all, and I knew that they engaged in all kinds of deviant sexual practices. I had nothing in common with people like that, so how could I be gay?

Even after realizing it was true, it was a long time before I could bring myself to breathe the word aloud.

I sat up late at night, after everyone else had gone to bed, trying to come to grips with what this word meant for my life. In my softest whisper, paranoid about being overheard by anyone, I tried to muster up enough courage to say to myself those two words: "I'm gay."

"I'm..." A pause. A deep breath.

"I'm..."

But the "g" word would never come. It was dark and frightening. I knew it was true, but I couldn't bring myself to say it, not even in a barely audible whisper alone in my room at night.

It's funny how our brains work. Once you become aware of something for the first time—a new vocabulary word, for instance—you begin to see it everywhere, and you wonder how you never noticed it before.

I had been feeling for a while that something was different about me, but I hadn't really understood what it was. Now that I knew, everything around me seemed to reinforce that I was a freak. Suddenly, it seemed that every guy I knew was talking nonstop about hot girls, with me only pretending to agree. "Fag" and "gay" had become ubiquitous insults overnight; I was sure they hadn't been before. Every TV show featured punch lines about a straight guy being mistaken for gay, resulting in raucous laughter from the audience. Every sermon at church was either about the goodness of marriage or the sinfulness of homosexuality.

Though none of them knew it, they were talking about *me*. Laughing at *me*. Condemning *me*. And it was getting to me.

I couldn't stay like this. I had to become straight. But how long would it take? Was it really fair for me to ask Liz to keep waiting indefinitely for me to feel something, someday, that I still didn't feel?

For her part, Liz had been doing her own research. The next time I saw her, she had a book in her hand.

"I checked this out for you," she said. "I don't know what the answers are, but I thought this might help." She passed the book to me.

I stared down at it, horrified. She had given me a book about gay Christians who had accepted themselves as gay, a book that seemed to suggest that God would be okay with same-sex partnerships.

Outwardly, I tried to be gracious. I knew she was only trying to help, and that this whole subject was as new to her as it was to me. Inwardly, I was fuming. How could she give me something like this? Didn't she know that homosexuality was contrary to God's will? Wasn't she supposed to be praying for God to heal me? Had she already given up hope? Was she really willing to violate God's Word, or encourage me to do so? What kind of Christian was she? Perhaps, I thought, I had been wrong to date her—not because of my lack of attraction to her, but because anyone who could possibly accept homosexuality couldn't be a serious Christian. I only dated *serious* Christians.

All of these thoughts ran through my head as I accepted the book. I took it home with me and debated whether I should even open it. I wanted to be informed on the subject, but I feared that it might just be temptation from the devil. Reluctantly and with much prayer, I finally decided to see what it had to say and began leafing through its pages. Just as I had expected, it was wholly unconvincing. The writing was poor and unprofessional. The biblical arguments it made for accepting gay couples were flimsy. The book did nothing to convince me that gay couples were okay with God. On the contrary, it convinced me even more that I needed to become straight.

In the meantime, I gradually realized, I couldn't keep dating a girl I had no attraction to, when I didn't even know how long it would take me to become attracted to women. She deserved better. She deserved to have someone long for her the way other guys longed for their girlfriends. For now, I couldn't give her that.

She also deserved to have me tell her the truth about my feelings. I'm sorry to say, though, that I took the coward's way out, letting our relationship gradually fade away as I prepared to move away to college. I can only imagine how difficult it must have been for her. All I could think about was how scared I was—of what I had discovered about myself and of what she would say if she knew that I had never truly been attracted to her in all the months we had been dating.

If I could live that time in my life over again, I would be up front with her from the beginning about my feelings, confessing that I'd realized I was gay, not bi, and opening up about all I was going through. In reality, I was too ashamed to tell her the truth. Our relationship fizzled out, no doubt leaving her wondering what exactly had happened and leaving me feeling more alone than ever. All over one little word I couldn't bring myself to even speak aloud.

PASTOR RICK AND THE SECRET SOCIETY

I wasn't going to let that word define me. I couldn't. Instead, I continued to focus on my one primary goal: becoming straight. Whatever might have caused my attractions to guys, I was sure being gay wasn't what God wanted for me. It definitely wasn't what I wanted for myself.

For one thing, I wanted to have a family someday. I had imagined it many times: wife, kids, and a house in the suburbs. I couldn't have that if I was gay. I wasn't willing to marry a woman for whom I had no attraction, and I wasn't willing to enter into a sinful relationship with a guy. The way I saw it, the only thing standing between me and my perfect future was my complete lack of attraction to women.

There was also another matter: As simplistic as it sounds, I wanted to fit in. I didn't mind distinguishing myself by being at the top of my class or standing up for what I believed in as a Christian; I was happy to be known for those things. Those were good things. But I was the good kid, not the rebel. I was "God Boy." And in my book, being gay was a bad thing. Everyone I looked up to viewed homosexuality as a sin and gay people as sinners. Never in a million years would I want to be known for something sinful.

Ultimately, it came down to one thing. My life had a single purpose: to serve God. I wasn't going to jeopardize that for anything. If God had created people male and female, designed for each other, and if the Bible condemned homosexuality, as I was pretty sure it did, then God clearly did not intend for me to be gay. Whatever might have gone wrong to make this happen, I knew God had the power to fix it. To fix *me*. I just needed willingness and faith.

I was willing. I had faith. Now what was I supposed to do? Was it just a matter of praying and trusting God, or was there more to the equation?

Once again, the internet was my resource. I began searching for information on orientation change, going from gay to straight. This time, I found exactly what I was looking for: groups known as "ex-gay ministries," Christian organizations that offered to help gay people become straight. I eagerly began reading everything I could about these groups. On their websites, they promised "freedom from homosexuality" for all who wanted it. One site had stories of people who had lived gay lives in the past but who had overcome their homosexuality through Jesus. Now they were heterosexually married, and many of them had kids.

That could be me!, I thought.

I stayed up late that night, reading story after story. This was exactly what I had hoped to find. This proved that I could be straight. Most of the men in these stories had lived sexually promiscuous lives with other men before turning their lives around. If even they could become straight, then surely I could! All I had were feelings; I hadn't acted on those feelings at all. That had to be a point in my favor. There was hope for me. I could be normal.

Eager for support, I nervously confided my struggle in my Sunday school teacher, a man I strongly admired. He put me in touch with Rick, an assistant pastor at my church who, he said, had experience working with the issue. That summer, following my high school graduation, Rick and I had conversations about my situation. He didn't seem surprised by my story, and he told me there were many others like me, committed Christians who had same-sex attractions through no fault or choice of their own. He assured me that it was often possible to undo the damage of whatever might have flipped this switch in my brain. In his opinion, I could ultimately be rid of this burden and married to a woman.

"I'd like to introduce you to some people," he said. He explained that there was already a secret group at my church for "men struggling with unwanted same-sex attractions." It was called Homosexuals Anonymous.

Although a number of other support groups in the church met openly with posted schedules, the very existence of this group was kept hidden from almost everyone in the congregation. As Pastor Rick explained the need for secrecy around the group and its members, my already profound sense of shame grew even deeper. The secrecy wasn't only to honor our privacy. It was to protect us from the judgment of others in the congregation. Even though we as Christians knew that everyone was sinful, issues like mine were still viewed and treated differently. Being attracted to the same sex was just too shameful. Other Christians wouldn't know how to handle someone like me.

Following Rick's instructions, I drove around to the back of the church at the appointed day and time for our super-secret meeting of anonymous homosexuals.

I didn't like the word "homosexual." Something about it felt dirty. It made me sound like I was more sexual than everybody else, and in some weird way. I wasn't any more sexual than any of my friends were; it's just that, for some reason, my attractions went in the opposite direction, and I didn't know why.

Rick escorted me into a room where several tired-looking middle-aged men smiled up at me from around a table. These were the anonymous homosexuals of our church. And no one knew they existed. Well, almost no one.

I sat down in a chair a short distance away from everyone else. I felt awkward and uncomfortable. Did these men represent who I was to become? I wondered about their stories and how long they had struggled with the feelings I also had.

I observed silently for most of the meeting. The men talked a bit about the program and how happy they were to be part of it. They explained to me their theories about why they had gay feelings, mostly connected to faulty upbringings and other childhood traumas I couldn't relate to. And they shared their latest progress in trying to become straight.

At one point in the meeting, a tired-looking man with a wedding ring on his finger said that he had some exciting news to share. Everyone leaned forward.

"This weekend," he said, "my wife and kids and I took a trip to the beach. While we were there, a woman walked by in a small bikini. And I *noticed* her."

He sat back with a satisfied smile. The small group erupted in cheers and congratulations. Clearly, for him this was a milestone achievement—noticing a woman on a beach.

I sat transfixed and horrified. Was this to be my destiny? Was I going to end up someday in a room like this one, middle-aged, married to a woman I wasn't attracted to, trying to act the part as well as possible for my wife and kids, and getting excited because after years of therapy, one day I noticed *one* woman walking by me in a bikini on a beach, for a few seconds?

What kind of future was that? What kind of life would that be?

And what did it mean to "notice" a woman on the beach? Even a straight woman might notice another woman walking by with large breasts and a small bikini. She might envy her figure, or simply notice her lack of covering. We all tend to notice other people of either sex who are wearing very little, but that doesn't mean we're sexually attracted to them. Sometimes we wish they would cover up more!

I wanted more than that for my life. If I was going to marry a woman someday, I wanted to be able to do more than just notice one woman once in a blue moon, an event so out of the ordinary that I would go back to my support group and tell them all about it. I wanted to feel the way straight guys felt: attracted to women, desiring women, looking at my girlfriend or my wife and wanting her, wanting her body. I wanted to have to struggle to avoid lusting after women, the way my straight friends did. It shouldn't have to be an effort to see my wife as pretty. I should desire her in the innermost depths of my being.

I left the meeting feeling confused and discouraged. These weren't the "success stories" I had hoped for. Yes, these men were married to women, but they were struggling every day to try to feel some level of sexual attraction to their wives, or to any woman. Meanwhile, their passions, like mine, continued to be oriented toward men, something they fought against on a daily basis.

Though the people who knew them would have considered them heterosexual, these were clearly not straight men. A straight man doesn't have to fight to try to find women attractive; nor does he have to fight to keep from lusting after other men. These men were living in constant turmoil. They were trying their best to live as they believed God wanted them to, but they weren't happy.

This wasn't the kind of future I wanted. I wanted to *change* my feelings, not just get married in spite of them. I wasn't going to be like these guys. I was going to be completely straight.

Right?

For the first time, I began to feel a twinge of doubt.

GOD BOY SNEAKS OUT

I didn't go back to Rick's ex-gay group. I still wanted to change, but those men weren't experiencing the kind of change I wanted. I was going to have to look elsewhere for answers.

In the meantime, I told him, I had one more thing I needed to do. I was about to leave for college, and my parents still didn't know what I was going through. I didn't want to keep this a secret from them, but I was scared to tell them. Would he help me tell them the truth before I left home? He said he would.

Together, Pastor Rick and I formulated a plan. He would call my parents and set up a meeting in his office at church. Both of them were very active in the congregation, so they wouldn't think anything of it. When they arrived at the appointed day and time, I'd already be there, and, together, he and I would tell them the secret I had been keeping for so long.

Plotting something like this felt weird to me. I'd never gone behind my parents' backs before. But I was too nervous to try to tell them my secret alone, and if they knew what the meeting was about in advance, they'd either ask me about it or be worrying about it, so this seemed like the best way to do it. At least this way I was the only one worrying.

Pastor Rick called my parents and set up the meeting for an afternoon only a week before I would leave home to start college. As predicted, they assumed it was just about routine church business and put it on the calendar without worrying about it.

The day of the meeting, I could hardly focus on anything. I tried to keep myself busy around the house to take my mind off of the inevitable, but it was of only limited use. All I could think about was what I would say to my parents, and what they would think when they learned the truth about their firstborn son.

Afternoon came, and the time of the meeting approached. Then something happened I hadn't planned on. My dad stopped by my room, mentioned that he and my mom were leaving for a meeting soon, and asked me to get some chores done while he was gone. Had I been faster on my feet, I could have thought up some excuse for needing to leave the house instead of doing chores at that moment. But I was caught off guard, and I didn't want to lie to my dad. So, like a fool, I just stood there and said, "Sure."

My dad left my room, and I glanced at the clock. I was going to have to leave soon if I wanted to get to the church before my parents. That meant I'd have to sneak out of the house.

Sneak out of the house? I had never sneaked out of the house before, and now I was about to do it for the first time in my life—so I could secretly meet with a pastor. Even then it struck me as funny. Only God Boy would sneak out of the house to go to church. I tried to laugh, but the laughter stuck in my throat.

As soon as the coast was clear, I crept downstairs and made it out the front door without being seen. I was halfway to my car when my dad spotted me. He was outside, walking the dog.

Oops.

I didn't have time to stop and explain, and I was too nervous anyway. I quickened my pace, making a beeline for my car.

"Hey," my dad called, "I thought—"

"I have to, um...I'll be back soon!" I yelled over my shoulder as I jumped into the car, turned the ignition key, and sped out of the driveway, leaving my dad standing in the yard blinking.

I was finally away. My heart was racing. I wondered what Dad was thinking. He was probably perplexed; rushing off with no explanation was very unlike me. I hated leaving things that way. I wanted to go back and explain, but I couldn't. Soon, of course, he would understand.

The drive to the church was a blur, and suddenly I was there. I met Pastor Rick in the lobby, and he escorted me up to his office.

"Your parents should be here in a few minutes," he said. "You can sit here while I wait for them downstairs. Then when I bring them up and they see that you're here, I'll let them know that you have something to tell them. At that point it's up to you to actually tell them, but I'll be here to support you and answer their questions. Okay?"

"Okay," I said, trying unsuccessfully to sound okay.

"Okay, I'll go wait for them in the lobby, then," he said.

"Okay," I repeated.

And with that, I was alone in his office. The room was painfully quiet. I thought about what my parents would say when they saw me sitting there. Would they be surprised? Would he have given them a clue before they made it upstairs? I imagined their faces, and I tried to remember exactly how I'd planned to tell them my secret. I couldn't put the words together in my head. My whole body was trembling. I twisted my hands around each other, trying to focus. I felt queasy.

Telling my parents had been on my mind since I had first realized I was gay. It was the only major secret I had ever kept from them. But it was *because* I was so close to them that telling them the truth was so frightening. If anyone else reacted badly or their opinion of me changed, I could handle it. But my parents were the most important people in my life; if this news changed my relationship with them, my world would never be the same.

I wasn't afraid of my parents' wrath; I knew they would love me no matter what happened. I was just afraid of disappointing them. I had always been their pride and joy, and now I was about to shatter their image of me. I was ashamed too. Having to discuss my sexuality with my parents was embarrassing enough, but having to admit to them that I had sexual thoughts about other boys? It was shameful and humiliating.

As the minutes dragged by, I wondered what my parents would say when they knew. How would they feel? Shocked? Angry? Ashamed? Confused? Hurt? Would they blame me for these feelings, or would they understand that I hadn't chosen them? Would we argue? Or would they just be sad and disappointed? I tried to predict their reaction, but I couldn't. I didn't know how they would feel. I didn't know how I would have felt.

With every noise in the hallway, I started, thinking it was them. I took deep breaths to try to calm myself down. I just wanted this to be over. Soon it would be. And their impression of me would be forever changed. That wasn't a comforting thought.

Then I heard their voices in the hallway. I straightened up and tried my best not to look nervous. They sounded like they were having a pleasant conversation, just chatting and laughing like normal.

They came around the door frame, and everyone looked at me. "Oh! Well, hello," my mom said. I couldn't quite read the expression on her face. She was surprised to see me, of course, but was there anything else? Did she know that this would be bad news? Could she tell how nervous I was? My dad looked slightly confused, but not upset.

Rick motioned for them to take a seat, and they did. "I invited you here today," he said, "because Justin has something he'd like to share with you. Justin?"

This was it. I had to speak. I had hoped his introduction would be longer. I cleared my throat and tried to find the words. He looked at me. They looked at me. I didn't know what to say. I wasn't ready. I needed more time. I stammered out a few words of apology for the way I had rushed off earlier.

"Don't worry about it," my dad said.

Then we were silent again.

I started talking about Liz. My parents knew her; we'd been dating for quite some time, and they loved her. I rambled on for a minute before finally getting to the point. "We...we broke up," I said slowly. I swallowed. "We broke up because..." My voice was failing me. The knot in my stomach felt immense. "We broke up because..." I looked at their faces. For a moment I wondered if they knew what I was about to say. I looked down at my shoes for courage. "...because...I'm"—I couldn't say the "g" word—"not attracted to...to girls."

The words were out. I stared at my feet, a million thoughts running through my head. I wanted to stop, but I knew I needed to say one more thing just to make it clear.

"I'm attracted to...to..."

Come on, Justin, say it.

"...to...guys."

And that was it. That was as much as I could say.

Silence engulfed the room. I kept staring at my feet.

My mom, who was sitting next to me, reached over and put her hand on mine.

Her voice was surprised and confused. She sounded like she was about to cry. But she said the words I needed to hear. "We'll always love you," she said. "No matter what."

My dad nodded his assent. His face was grim. He looked like he didn't know what to say.

Pastor Rick began filling in the details, explaining how I'd come to him and asked him to hold the meeting. He used the "g" word for the first time—"gay"—and told my parents that there was hope for change, but that nothing was a sure thing. My parents listened intently, asking him a lot of questions: Why did this happen? Was it their fault? Was there anything they could do?

My mom eventually did start crying. This wasn't the life she had envisioned for her son. Even so, she and my dad continued to affirm their love for me and their desire to help me live the way God wanted. In all of our minds, of course, that meant I needed to become straight.

The conversation continued into the night. All I could do was sit there, silent.

My parents knew. My deepest secret had been exposed. And like Adam and Eve in the Garden, I felt naked and ashamed.

THINGS PARENTS SAY

I was very fortunate in the way my parents responded. Neither of them had much knowledge about gay people, and both of them had always believed that being gay was a sinful choice. They never suspected that I was gay, and they certainly didn't want me to be. But they loved me, and they recognized that this was difficult for me to talk about. Rather than berating or disowning me, they listened and tried to understand. And they reminded me constantly that they loved me and always would, even if I made decisions they disapproved of.

Not everyone is as lucky as I was. Even my parents and I had many difficult, heated arguments over the years on the subject, and I know many other kids who had it much worse. Some parents have kicked their kids out, disowned them, and written them out of their wills. Some have even told their kids they wished they were dead. Imagine hearing that from your own mother or father! Such responses are by no means limited to Christian parents, but it makes me especially sad to hear Christian parents say things like this. I don't believe that Christ would ever approve of parents treating their children that way.

In one of Jesus' best-known parables, a son demands his inheritance early, leaves home, and wastes all he has on a foolish, extravagant lifestyle. Finally, with nothing left and nowhere to turn, he comes home with his tail between his legs, only to find his father running toward him with arms open wide, ready to embrace him and welcome him home with a celebration.[1]

Jesus uses the story as an illustration of God's unending love for us even when we make countless mistakes (and a reminder to us not to feel bitter or jealous when God shows that grace to others who have made more mistakes than we have). But there's surely an important message here for parents too. Even in the midst of his son's most heinous mistakes, the father never disowns his son or makes him feel unwelcome at home. When the son hits rock bottom, the father doesn't say, "I told you so." Instead, he simply demonstrates to his son that he will always love him, no matter what, even when the rest of the world has no more use for him.

I pray that Christian parents will heed the message of this parable and treat their children with that kind of love, even when they disagree on issues like homosexuality. If we can't get this right within our own families, how are we supposed to get it right on a larger scale? A loving response must start at home.

Most Christians I know would never dream of disowning their gay kids. Still, they may struggle with how to balance a desire to love and support their kids with a responsibility to raise their kids to live moral lives. If their gay son or daughter is going down a path that they believe to be sinful and destructive, how can they lovingly respond without appearing to condone something they believe to be wrong?

Here are some things I often hear parents say, and why they don't work:

"Don't tell anyone."

My parents said this, and so have many other Christian parents I know. My parents were focused (as I was) on finding a way to help me become straight, and they were worried that if people found out in the meantime that I was gay, it would destroy my future chances of being a leader in the church. With that in mind, they asked me not to tell anyone I was gay.

As well intentioned as this advice is, it places a terrible burden on the child. Keeping a secret this big carries with it a tremendous amount of shame and guilt, especially for kids from Christian families. Gay kids are already at increased risk for depression and suicide, and adding to their feelings of isolation by asking them not to talk about what they're going through only makes matters worse.

Moreover, while people in past generations may have been content to "leave well enough alone" and not comment on others' sexual orientation, in today's culture, people will come right out and ask whether someone is gay or straight—especially young people. Asking children to keep such a thing a secret isn't just asking them not to reveal information; it is often asking them to lie deliberately or otherwise deceive people in order to prevent the truth from being uncovered. That kind of behavior tends to wear at one's moral fiber over time.

Understandably, parents worry that if their kids confide in others or come out publicly, they'll end up spending time around other gay people and ultimately making decisions their parents don't approve of. In fact, every parent worries about their kids' decisions, especially romantic and sexual ones, whether the kids are gay or straight. But the way to combat bad decisions isn't by asking kids to keep secrets. The Bible reminds us that sin thrives in darkness.[2] Instead, the best way to cultivate healthy and responsible attitudes is by encouraging open communication—with parents, peers, and Christian leaders. A healthy level of openness can enable a child to develop his or her own identity and make wise choices rather than living under a burden of secret shame and guilt.

"YOU'RE NOT LIKE THOSE PEOPLE."

Before he found out about me, my dad's only impression of gay people was negative. (Actually, so was mine!) He told me several

stories of gay men he had encountered who were doing grossly inappropriate things, including one man caught spying on men using
the urinals, and another man making inappropriate advances toward
teenage boys. These were the representations of gay men in my dad's
mind, so when I told him I was gay, it disgusted him to think of his
own son in that light. "You're not like them," he told me.

He was right; I'm not like the men in the stories he shared, and
neither are most gay people. Christian speaker Peggy Campolo, the
soft-spoken wife of Baptist minister Tony Campolo, often points out
that she and pop star Madonna are both straight women, but they
live very different lifestyles. In the same way, I know gay people
who are as different from one another as can be imagined. Some are
as God-fearing as any straight person I know. Others are far from
it. And, yes, there are gay sex offenders out there just as there are
straight sex offenders. They don't represent everyone.

When parents tell their kids that they must not be gay because
they're not like the negative images in the parents' heads, it doesn't
change their kids' understanding of themselves as gay. Instead, it
convinces the kids that their parents now associate those negative
images with *them*, and that the only way they can avoid that associ-
ation is to pretend not to feel what they feel.

"How could you hurt us like this?"

I'm very happy to say that my parents never said this, or anything
like it, to me. Unfortunately, I know many parents who have.

If you are the parent of a gay child, it's important to remember
that your child was likely struggling with these issues for a very long
time before you became aware of it. He or she did not choose to be
gay and was probably very worried about disappointing or upsetting
you. When gay children don't tell their parents what they are going
through, it is often because they are hoping to figure things out on

their own and avoid hurting their parents. When they do make the decision to tell them, it is a sign of trust and a desire for honesty and a closer relationship. Regardless, this can be a difficult and emotional journey for both parent and child.

The most important thing parents can do is to listen to their children and seek to understand their experiences so far. If the child wants to talk about it, that's a good sign; parents should embrace the opportunity to find out what they've been missing in their child's life. Even if your child makes significant mistakes, this is still your child, whom you love and who is opening up to you about what may be the hardest thing to tell you, something at the core depths of his or her being. Resist the temptation to make it about you. Focus on being there for your child.

"WHAT DID WE DO WRONG?"

While some parents blame their child, other parents blame themselves. Many Christian parents have heard that homosexuality is caused by poor parent-child relationships, so it's especially common for them to wonder if they did something wrong to cause their child to be gay.

In the next chapter, I'll review some of the theories about why people are gay, but in general, I don't believe there's anything parents can do to prevent their children from being gay. I had strong, warm relationships with both of my parents, felt fully and completely loved, was given healthy amounts of discipline and independence, and everything else I've heard recommended to parents. If I turned out gay, any kid can turn out gay. Meanwhile, my three siblings turned out straight, and we were all raised by the same parents.

Having a gay child doesn't necessarily mean parents did anything "wrong." Instead of blaming themselves, parents should focus on showing their child all the love they can and keeping their relationship strong as the family works together through the moral and theological questions they face.

"THIS IS THE DEVIL'S WAY OF TRYING TO STOP YOU FROM DOING WHAT GOD WANTS."

This is another common response from Christian parents. They worry that their children's orientation will prevent them from living up to the full potential of what God has given them.

My parents knew I wanted to do some kind of ministry work in the future, and they worried that this gay thing was going to prevent me from doing that. Instead, these experiences ended up giving me a unique understanding of an important issue for the church, resulting in the book you are holding in your hands today. The very thing my parents were so worried might destroy my future turned out to be something God used in my life to reach a lot of hurting people.

In the Bible, the obstacles that seem the most daunting often turn out to be things God uses for an unexpected purpose. When Joseph's brothers sell him into slavery (Genesis 37), none of them knows this act will ultimately enable him to save many lives. Likewise, the crucifixion of Jesus must have felt to his followers like the worst possible act of the devil, yet Christians today celebrate it as the most powerful evidence of God's love. I encourage Christian parents not to jump to any conclusions about how God will use a situation like this in their child's life. Denying it won't make it go away, but if we respond as Christians, with open hearts to what God will do, we can be surprised at what happens.

When I first told my parents, one of the questions they had for Pastor Rick was what might cause something like this. I had the same question, and he didn't have an answer. In the next chapter, we'll look at the evidence.

CHAPTER 5

WHY ARE PEOPLE GAY?

Over the years, I've shared my journey with many kinds of people in many different circumstances. Their responses depend a lot on their own experiences with the issue.

I've had hundreds of Christians tell me that my story reads like a page out of the book of their own life story. For some, hearing my story marked the first time they knew they weren't alone, just like Brian's story did for me. I've had people break down in tears while trying to tell me what it meant to them to hear about another Christian who went through the same things. No one else seemed to understand them.

Others tell me how puzzling my story is to them, because they grew up in homes where being gay was, or would have been, perfectly acceptable. It's hard for them to fathom what would make a teenage boy so afraid to embrace what, in their mind, would be his obviously natural sexuality.

On many occasions, I've had the privilege of sharing my story with straight Christians who don't know many gay people and who have never really considered what it would be like. Some of them were taught, as I was, that gay people *choose* to be that way, so hearing about the struggles I went through raises all sorts of new questions for them. That's why so many people stop me at some point in the story to ask for my opinion on one of the oldest questions about homosexuality: *Why are some people gay?*

First, let's define what we mean by "gay."

It amazes me how long people can argue about a question like "Is being gay a choice?" without ever stopping to define what they mean by "gay." If one person believes that "gay" means "someone who is *attracted* to the same sex" and another person believes that "gay" means "someone who *has sex with* members of the same sex," then it shouldn't surprise us when they come to two very different conclusions!

In this book, I am using the word "gay" the way it is usually used in our culture: to refer to people's *attractions,* not necessarily to their *behaviors.* Typically, when we say someone is "gay," we mean that he or she is *attracted to the same sex.* By contrast, someone who is "straight" is attracted to the *opposite* sex, and someone who is "bisexual" is attracted to *both* sexes. These words don't tell us anything about the person's behaviors, beliefs, or plans for the future; they only tell us to whom the person is generally attracted. A teenage girl might be "straight" (attracted to boys), but that doesn't mean she's ever had sex with a boy, kissed a boy, or been on a date with a boy. Even if she committed her entire life to celibacy, we would still say that she's "straight," because she's attracted to the opposite sex.

Similarly, when I called myself "gay," I wasn't referring to any kind of behavior in my life. I had never had any kind of sexual or romantic relationship with a guy, and I didn't ever plan to. But even if I never acted on my feelings and never allowed my mind to turn to lust, there was no denying that I was different from other guys in one major way: Where they were attracted to and tempted by girls, I was attracted to and tempted by guys. I was *gay*. They were *straight*.

Some people don't believe we should use the words "gay" and "straight"—or any labels at all—to describe people's attractions. For me, though, having a word to describe my situation was helpful, and I think it's important for everyone to be clear about what these words mean. Throughout this book, when I say "gay," you can mentally replace that with "generally attracted to members of the same sex, not members of the opposite sex."[1]

So when we ask, "Why are people gay?" what we're really asking is, "Why are some people attracted to their own sex?" Let's examine a few of the more popular theories out there.

THEORY 1: PEOPLE CHOOSE TO BE GAY

Growing up, I firmly believed that gay people chose to be gay, but I learned by experience that this isn't the case. I most certainly did *not* want to be attracted to my own sex, and I would have done just about anything not to be. As a conservative Southern Baptist kid, I would never have chosen to be gay. Not in a million years.

Usually, when someone says that being gay is a choice, it's because they're defining "gay" to mean something other than "attracted to the same sex." This is why definitions are so important. Most people can agree, though, that while we do choose our *behaviors*, we don't get to choose to whom we're *attracted*. In case you have doubts about that, let's briefly consider what it would mean if people could choose their attractions.

Whichever sex you're attracted to, you're not attracted to *all* people of that sex, are you? Some of them you find attractive, and others you don't. You don't get to choose which ones your brain sees as attractive.

If we could, we might all like to turn those attractions off sometimes! If you're married, for instance, you might choose to be attracted only to your spouse, and never attracted to anyone else. It would make married life a lot easier, wouldn't it? Unfortunately, you don't get to choose that. Those attractions come whether you like them or not, and then it's up to you how you'll respond to them.

Likewise, if you're single, there may be times when it would be nice to be able to turn *on* attractions to someone you just don't feel anything for, like that really nice person who likes you but whom you just don't find attractive. Unfortunately, while your attraction to someone might shift as you get to know them, it also might not. You can't make it happen by sheer force of will.

None of us can choose to whom we feel attracted. We just are.

Most people discover when they're young that they are involuntarily attracted to people of the other sex. A minority of people, however, discover instead that they are involuntarily attracted to the same sex, and an even smaller minority discover that they're involuntarily attracted to both sexes. None of these people *choose* their attractions; they can only choose how they will respond to them.

I know a lot of kids who were horrified when they realized they were gay, either because of their moral beliefs or because of prejudice against gay people among their family and friends. Like me, they would never have chosen to be gay, but they were anyway.

So, no, it's not something people choose.

THEORY 2: PEOPLE ARE SEDUCED OR TRICKED INTO IDENTIFYING AS GAY

Okay, so maybe people don't intentionally choose to be gay, but is it something they're tricked into? Is it possible they're convinced that they're gay by teasing in the schoolyard or are seduced by an older gay crowd that shows them attention?

I can only speak for myself here, but I certainly was never seduced by anyone. At the time I realized I was attracted to other guys, I didn't even know any other gay people. And while I *was* occasionally teased at school (and really, who *wasn't* teased at some point in grade school?), I didn't ever think I was gay because of teasing; I just thought the kids doing the teasing were bullies. The first time I ever considered that I might be gay was, as I described, because of years of same-sex attraction, not a result of anything I heard at school.

In a similar vein, I'm sometimes asked whether gay people have same-sex attractions due to sexual abuse in their past. My short answer to this is that I wasn't sexually abused, and studies show that the majority of gay people weren't either.

In situations where people were sexually abused and later discover that they are gay, either they or their loved ones may wonder whether the abuse altered their developing sexuality in some way. The impact of childhood abuse on an adult's relationship with his or her sexuality is complex, and because of the extremely sensitive nature of the subject and the uniqueness of each individual's experience, that question ultimately lies outside of the scope of this book. In my case, though, it was an easy question to answer: I'd never experienced any kind of abuse, sexual or otherwise, so abuse couldn't have made me gay.

THEORY 3: PEOPLE ARE GAY BECAUSE OF THEIR PARENTS

One popular theory says that people are gay as a result of problems in their relationship with their parents. This is sometimes called the "reparative drive" model, for reasons I'll explain in a moment. The idea was first popularized in the early 1960s by a psychologist named Irving Bieber. Decades earlier, Sigmund Freud had suggested that children's sexual development depends on their relationship with their parents; he believed, for instance, that a normal heterosexual boy subconsciously wants to kill his father and marry his mother. Bieber—who focused exclusively on men—also believed this was true, and proposed that gay men were gay because poor parenting caused this process to fail.

Bieber argued that gay men came from families "characterized by disturbed and psychopathic interactions" and that gay men's parents "had severe emotional problems." Gay men's fathers, he said, were usually "explicitly detached and hostile," while their mothers tended to be possessive, overprotective, and even "seductive" toward their sons. According to Bieber, male homosexuality was *always* the result of poor parenting. He blamed both mothers and fathers, but in his view, fathers got the lion's share of the blame. Every gay man, Bieber said, had a poor father, because "a constructive, supportive, warmly related father *precludes* the possibility of a homosexual son."[2]

Bieber's theories were extremely influential at a time when very little was known about the subject. Not surprisingly, they resonated especially well with gay men who'd had poor relationships with their fathers. However, there were a number of problems with his research from the beginning.

Bieber's theory was based on questioning gay men in the 1950s about their parents and then comparing their answers to those of straight men, but the men he interviewed were not at all representative of the general population. The interviewees were all already in therapy, many for psychological troubles unrelated to their sexuality. The straight "comparison" group was not a random sample, but was hand-picked by the researchers, who had already decided the basics of their theory before doing the research. Not only that, but as many as a fourth of the supposedly "heterosexual" interviewees were identified by Bieber as having "evidence of severe homosexual problems" (that is, being attracted to other men). In spite of that, they were counted as *heterosexual* for the study because they hadn't acted on their feelings.

As it turns out, there are a number of people—both gay and straight—who grew up with detached, hostile fathers and/or possessive, overprotective mothers. There are also many people—both gay *and* straight—who didn't experience that dynamic at all. According to Bieber, it's impossible for a boy to turn out gay if he has a warm, loving relationship with his father. Yet that's exactly what many gay men had and continue to have to this day.

The psychological community eventually abandoned this approach, deciding that it didn't fit the evidence. However, Bieber's model remained popular in some Christian circles and still is taught today, largely due to the influence of Elizabeth Moberly, a Christian theologian and psychologist.

In the early 1980s, at a time when many Christians were condemning gays as intentionally wicked and sinful, Moberly pushed for understanding. She argued that gays hadn't *chosen* to be this way, but that something had *happened* to them in childhood and they needed the church's compassion. In her book *Homosexuality: A New Christian Ethic,* Moberly outlined her theory of what made people gay. Picking up where Bieber left off, she agreed that parental relationships were the cause, but she altered the theory to include both men and women and added her own ideas about how it might work, focusing on an idea sometimes called the "reparative drive."

Moberly theorized that if a child had a distant same-sex parent, he or she was left with an emotional deficit. The child needed same-sex bonding that was never met by the parent, and so as he or she grew, a subconscious drive would kick in to try to repair that hole. This reparative drive, Moberly thought, was the underlying cause of homosexual attractions. According to her theory, a man was attracted to other men because his father never met his emotional needs, and a woman was attracted to other women because her mother didn't meet her emotional needs. If those needs could be met in healthy (non-sexual) ways, Moberly believed, then those same-sex attractions would go away and opposite-sex attractions would develop.

Dr. Moberly's book didn't offer any compelling new research or evidence for this theory. Nevertheless, her theory was a huge hit with gay Christians who didn't want to be gay. Those who had had poor relationships with their parents saw themselves right away in her theory. Those who hadn't had poor parental relationships simply assumed that it must have all happened on a subconscious level. For both groups, the appeal was easy to see. It gave them a *reason* for their feelings, and it offered a simple *solution*. The answer to their gay dilemma, it said, was to meet their need for same-sex bonding through therapy and strong friendships with other Christians of the same sex. The theory was also a hit with compassionate straight Christians. It said that the church needed to embrace and love gay people, because forming those connections with them was the key to healing them from their homosexuality.

The theory probably would have been a hit with me, too, except for one thing. My upbringing was nothing like what Moberly or Bieber described.

For starters, I grew up in a loving, two-parent, Christian home. I had the sort of family you might see on the cover of a Christian parenting magazine as part of a feature story on "How to Raise a Christian Family."

My dad wasn't absent, distant, or abusive. Far from it. I was his firstborn son, the "miracle baby" born after years of fertility doctors telling my parents they would never have any kids. Realizing he'd been given an extraordinary gift, my dad was determined to be the best possible father to me. From the moment he got home from work each evening, he always made time for me, no matter how exhausted he might have been. I can't think of any time in my childhood that my dad ever turned me down when I asked for his time. Whether it was helping me with homework, playing a game together, or just listening to me talk about my day, he was always there. Only many years later did I realize how truly unique that experience was.

Dad was a stockbroker who was passionate about the need for integrity in his line of work. From the time I was very young, he taught me the importance of Christian moral living. "Justin," he said once, in the midst of a difficult moral quandary of his own, "sometimes you'll be in a situation where everyone else is doing the wrong thing, and you have to stand up for what's right. It's not always easy, but it's important. You never know who might be watching, and God is watching even if no one else is." Those lessons, and his reminders that my name meant "full of justice," had a profound influence on my developing sense of self. I wanted to be like my dad, someone who did the right thing even when it was difficult. I wanted to serve God.

My mom was also nothing like the overbearing "smother mother" Bieber described. A brilliant, effervescent woman, she had been a teacher and an assistant principal before leaving the workforce to become a stay-at-home mom when I was born. She never had a dull moment; after me, there were three more miracle babies, and she somehow managed to juggle all four of us, keep an impeccably clean house, and have a well-balanced, home-cooked meal for six on the table every night. Donna Reed's 1950s sitcom character couldn't have done it better.

As with my dad, what made Mom so special was her integrity. I don't think I've ever met anyone as profoundly admired by those around them as she was. She was deeply religious, but not in the annoying self-righteous way that so many people unfortunately associate with American Christianity. Her faith was the rock she built her life on, not a show to impress others. She had a real love for people and genuinely cared about how others were doing, and that shone brightly through everything she did. She was outgoing, friendly, and always willing to lend a hand. And yet, despite her seemingly impossible schedule, she always found time to retreat to her room each day for quiet Bible study and prayer.

Mom taught a hugely popular Christian parenting class at the large Southern Baptist church my family attended each Sunday, where Dad served as a deacon. Young parents throughout the church flocked to her class week after week, eager for her advice. Not only was she a mom to four children; she also truly understood the delicate balance between providing discipline and guidance on the one hand, and allowing kids the freedom to grow on the other. Ten years of childless marriage had given her and my dad a chance to mature into the right kind of parents, and that was what made her advice so sought-after.

So, yes, there were times when my childhood felt like some kind of cross between *Little House on the Prairie* and *Leave It to Beaver*, only with more modern furnishings. I don't mean to suggest that every day was scripted and flawless, but my parents raised me well, they gave me plenty of love, and I was a happy kid.

Were my parents perfect? Of course not. No parents are. Did we sometimes argue? Yes. But never—never for a moment—did I doubt my parents' love for me. Never did I wish for different parents. Even at the height of my own teenage angst and all the feelings of being misunderstood that come with that time in life, I felt loved and supported by my parents. They never smothered me and never felt distant. My relationship with my parents may be one in a million, but there it is.

As you can imagine, then, from the first time I heard about this "bad parenting" theory, I knew it couldn't be the whole story. It definitely wasn't *my* story. My dad had always been someone I could talk to about my problems, and my mom had always kept a healthy balance of being an involved mom without being overinvolved. Meanwhile, among my straight friends, I knew that one was terrified of his alcoholic father, another was raised by an overprotective single mom, and another had a family that seemed great from the outside but had always left him feeling misunderstood. I didn't have any of those problems, but I was gay and they were straight.

Over the years, I've met many other gay people. Some of them had terrible childhoods. Some of them had wonderful childhoods. In that respect, they're no different from the many straight people I know.

To this day, many Christian counselors still teach a modified version of Bieber's 1962 theory alongside Moberly's "reparative drive" language. Since Bieber's depiction of a "hostile" father and "seductive" mother with "severe emotional problems" sounds so harsh, its proponents today describe the theory with softer terms like "distant or absent father" and "overbearing or overprotective mother" instead. Distant fathers and overprotective mothers are extremely common in American society, so this allows a larger percentage of gay people to say, "Hey, that sounds like me!" But these same dynamics are very widespread among straight Americans as well, and they are not at all present for many gay Americans. If distant fathers and overbearing mothers made people gay, there should be far more gay people in American society than there are. Meanwhile, I should have been the straightest guy in the world.

Elizabeth Moberly gradually withdrew from the public spotlight to study cancer instead, but today a psychotherapist named Joseph Nicolosi has picked up her torch. Rather than modifying the theory to account for the many stories that don't fit, however, Nicolosi has taken the theory to an even greater extreme, speaking frequently in blanket generalizations that gloss over the real complexities of the issue and the experiences of many. "You will hear a shallowness in the voice of any homosexual who claims to love and respect his father," Nicolosi told a reporter in 1996. "On the other hand, when the straight man talks lovingly about his father, you will hear a richness in his voice."[3]

But Nicolosi's assertions are simply not accurate. I know many gay men who truly love and respect their fathers, and many straight men who don't. Meanwhile, scientific research does not support Nicolosi's claim that the fathers of gay sons are typically "immature," "narcissistic," or "inadequate."[4] In reality, both good and bad fathers have gay sons, and both good and bad fathers have straight sons. Despite Nicolosi's claims, there is no credible evidence that parents determine their children's sexual orientation.

THEORY 4: PEOPLE ARE GAY BECAUSE OF THEIR BIOLOGY

Ask gay people why they think they're gay, and a lot of them will respond that they feel like they were *born* gay—that for some reason, their brains are wired differently from straight people's and have been since birth.

Historically, a number of Christians have objected to this idea. They've argued that if gay sex is a sin, then God wouldn't allow people to be born with a biological attraction to the same sex. But that doesn't seem like a very good argument to me. Just because an attraction or drive is biological doesn't mean it's okay to act on, so whether behavior is sinful or not doesn't tell us anything about whether the related attraction has biological roots.

For example, suppose a man is just "wired" to be attracted to women. His hormones and brain structures work together to give him feelings of attraction when a pretty woman walks by, and that doesn't stop just because he gets married. Does that make it okay for him to cheat on his wife? Of course not. His attractions may be rooted in his biology, but acting on them is still sinful.

We all have inborn tendencies to sin in any number of ways. If gay people's same-sex attractions were inborn, that wouldn't necessarily mean it's okay to act on them, and if we all agreed that gay sex is sinful, that wouldn't necessarily mean that same-sex attractions aren't inborn. "Is it a sin?" and "Does it have biological roots?" are two completely separate questions.

But *is* biology involved or not? For an answer to that question, we have to look at scientific research.

It's amazing how much research has been done on this topic. Scientists have examined genes, hormones, and brain structures. They've studied humans, rats, monkeys, rams, and fruit flies. They've explored everything from fingerprint patterns to family birth order. And the results they've found are as complex as they are fascinating. At the risk of oversimplifying the issue, here are a few of the things researchers have discovered.

Physical brain differences

Men's and women's brains are different in a number of measurable ways. Several studies have shown that certain structures in gay people's brains more closely resemble the corresponding structures in the average brains of the opposite sex than the corresponding structures in the average brains of the same sex. In other words, some parts of gay men's brains look more like those parts look in straight women than in straight men; and in lesbian women, those brain regions look more like those of straight men than like those of straight women. This doesn't mean that gay men have women's brains or that lesbian women have men's brains; it means that *specific structures* in their brains seem to have developed in ways that are more typical for the opposite sex. This may be due to differing hormone levels in the womb.

Our brains continue to change while we're alive, so it's possible these differences could be the *result* of being gay rather than the *cause*, but most scientists think that's unlikely. Many researchers now believe that these different brain structures help explain why some people are attracted to the same sex instead of the opposite sex—their brains may truly be different from birth.

Body differences

Men's and women's bodies are different, too, and not just in the obvious ways. Subtle differences like finger length, eye-blink response, and likelihood of left-handedness tend to exist between men and women, and some of these are thought to be due to the different hormones they are exposed to during pregnancy. Research has shown differences between gay people and straight people regarding these kinds of measurements as well, suggesting again that gay people might have been exposed to different hormone levels than their straight counterparts at a critical period of development in the womb.

Other differences

Differences between men and women show up in non-physical ways as well. Women, for instance, tend to perform better on tasks requiring verbal skills, and men tend to perform better on tasks requiring spatial skills. Once again, in these and other cases, gay people, on the average, perform more like the opposite sex. Gay men average better than straight men on verbal skills and worse than straight men on spatial skills. Lesbians average better than straight women on spatial skills but worse than straight women (closer to straight men) on verbal skills. This adds to the evidence that gay people's brains are built differently than straight people's of the same sex.

Studies on animals

Scientists have also found similar brain differences in animals that help confirm the human results. For instance, 6 to 10 percent of rams mate only with other males, and their brains show the same kind of structural differences that have been found in gay humans. Meanwhile, researchers have been able to change which sex rats try to mate with by changing the hormones the rat is exposed to in the womb. Rats, rams, and other animals are not humans, but experiments have conclusively proven that at least some animals' "sexual orientation" can be determined by hormones during their fetal development.

THE OLDER BROTHER EFFECT

Studies have also shown that gay men, on the average, have more older brothers than straight men. Of course, having older brothers by itself doesn't make people gay; plenty of gay men have no older brothers, and plenty of straight men have lots of older brothers. Statistically, though, gay men are more likely to have more older brothers. Is this due to social reasons (like being picked on in childhood) or biological reasons (like being exposed to different hormones in the womb)? Well, according to recent research, the older brother effect only works if the brothers are biologically related through the same mother, not if they were half-brothers with the same father or adoptive brothers raised in the same home. Interestingly, the effect still shows up when men have older brothers who were born to the same mother but not raised in the same home with them, so if further research continues to find that trend, it can't be due to social factors. This strongly suggests that something biological is involved.

Based on these and other studies, many scientists now believe that sexual orientation is related to the hormone levels a baby experiences during its development in the womb. According to the theory, these hormones help distinguish boys' brains from girls' brains, but if the hormone levels are different from the usual amount at a certain time in fetal development, parts of the baby's brain (including parts responsible for sexuality) develop closer to what is typical for the other gender.

In his 2011 book *Gay, Straight, and the Reason Why*, esteemed researcher Simon LeVay reviews the many different theories and studies on the subject, concluding that:

> Sexual orientation is an aspect of gender that emerges from the prenatal sexual differentiation of the brain. Whether a person ends up gay or straight depends in large part on how this process of biological differentiation goes forward, with the lead actors being genes, sex hormones, and the brain systems that are influenced by them.
>
> The biological perspective on sexual orientation stands in marked contrast to traditional beliefs, which have remained largely silent on the origin of heterosexuality while ascribing homosexuality to family dynamics, learning, early sexual experiences, or free choice....[T]here is no actual evidence to support any of those ideas, although we cannot completely rule out that they play some role. In my view, differences of opinion on this score often result from differences in what we mean by sexual orientation. Biological factors give us a sexual orientation in the sense of a disposition or capacity to experience sexual attraction to one sex or the other, or to both. Other factors influence what we do with those feelings.[5]

If this is true, it would explain why some people feel like their brains are "wired" to respond to the same sex instead of the opposite sex. It may be that that part of their brain really is wired as if it were the brain of the opposite sex. It would also explain why some gay people seem to have interests, speech patterns, skills, and even mannerisms that are more like straight people of the opposite sex—the hormone levels they received could have determined the development of multiple parts of their brains, not just the ones responsible for sexual and romantic attraction. In other gay people, different parts of the brain could have been affected, which would explain why some gay men seem more feminine and some lesbians seem more masculine while others don't. There could be a number of reasons for the differing hormone levels, and the tendency of women's bodies to respond differently to a baby after several male pregnancies might be one of them.

Despite the amount of evidence, there are still many unanswered questions. Researchers haven't definitively *proven* that hormones are the cause, and if they are, a lot is still unknown about why. Some scientists have searched for a single gene or set of genes that might cause this to happen, but the results have been inconsistent, and no "gay gene" has yet been found. Sometimes studies have shown evidence that seemed to contradict the latest theories, so scientists had to do more research to determine whether those studies had flaws or whether the theories needed to be changed.

At this point, the evidence makes it look very likely that biology has something to do with sexual orientation, but scientists are still learning, and nothing is set in stone. It's not only that we don't know what causes people to be gay; we don't know what causes people to be straight, either! Some research suggests that men's and women's sexuality may be influenced by different factors, and bisexual attraction (which is barely explored in the research) is much more common among women than among men. Twenty years from now, the theories might look very different from the theories we have today, or we might have more concrete information to confirm the theories of today. For now, we can only make educated guesses and realize that there's still a lot we don't know.

CONCLUSION: WE DON'T KNOW!

So what's the answer? Why are some people attracted to the same sex? The truth is, we don't know for sure. The biological theories have the most evidence to support them right now, but even they have lots of questions, and at this point, we can't "prove" anything. We can only make educated guesses.

In light of all the unknowns, it can be very tempting just to choose a theory that "feels right," regardless of the evidence. For a gay person who had a troubled childhood, a history of sexual abuse, or poor parental relationships, it can feel "obvious" that these things caused him or her to be gay, even if it's actually coincidental. For others, it can feel just as obvious that they were "born that way," making genetic or other biological theories more appealing.

It's especially tempting to choose a theory that we think will fit better with our political or theological worldview. If you believe that gay relationships are sinful, for instance, it's more appealing to assume that gay feelings result from childhood trauma—because if people are born with them, that leads to the uncomfortable thought that God might have *created* people with a deep longing for intimacy and no legitimate means to fill it. Conversely, if you are an advocate for gay rights, it might be much more appealing to assume that sexual orientation is inborn; research shows that people are more likely to be sympathetic to gay rights measures if they believe people are born gay or straight.

For these reasons and many more, the question of orientation origin has become a battleground for gays and Christians on all sides of the issue. In actuality, these arguments are built on nothing. Gay sex could still be sinful even if same-sex attractions are inborn; we humans are born with all kinds of sinful temptations. Likewise, civil rights shouldn't depend on whether something is biological; fair is fair either way.

I believe our goal should be truth, not ideology, and that we must have the humility to admit that we still don't have all the answers. The current research gives us promising leads, and based on what I've seen and experienced, my own personal guess is that biology plays at least a significant role in all this. It doesn't really matter, though.

In the future, we may have definitive evidence to tell us what causes differences in sexual orientation. For now, the important thing is to keep an open mind and listen compassionately to people's stories.

CHAPTER 6

JUSTIN IN EXGAYLAND

As a teenager, I didn't know anything about what caused me to be gay. Sure, I was curious about it, but what I cared about more was finding a way to be rid of it and become straight. In the meantime, I had college to deal with.

I moved into a university dorm, where I went back to hiding in the closet. It was nerve-racking and lonely. Once more, I was on my own with my secret, now even without the few friends I had confided in. Here I had a whole new set of friends, and none of them knew I was gay.

My college roommate was a nice guy, also from the South. Unlike me, he wasn't from a conservative evangelical background, so I hoped he wouldn't judge me if I came out to him.

I tried broaching the topic, searching for a way to casually ask how he might react to meeting gay people on campus. "I don't know," he admitted. "I've never met any."

That wasn't exactly confidence inspiring. I decided not to tell him right away.

I poured myself into making new friends and taking hard classes. Even so, I was continually haunted by questions about my faith, my sexuality, and my future. I prayed for guidance, but I still had far more questions than answers. I looked for Christians who could help me, but I was far too scared to come out to anyone on campus. I talked to my parents about it by phone, but it was tough and the conversations were stressful; I felt ashamed of my sexuality, and they were still grappling with what it all meant.

The ex-gay path still seemed like the most logical way forward. The men at Homosexuals Anonymous hadn't been the success stories I had been hoping for, but, I reminded myself, they were still in therapy. They weren't done yet. Perhaps the real success stories were the ones I had heard about on Christian radio and read about in Christian magazines, the ones who were now leading ex-gay groups instead of attending them. I had to find out.

I discovered another local ex-gay ministry and gave them a call. A kind-sounding man on the other end of the phone listened to my story before apologetically informing me that no, there wasn't anything they could do for a nineteen-year-old with no sexual experience. Everyone in their group was much older and struggling with a lifetime of sexual addiction. Their focus was on changing those behaviors. They didn't have any resources for a teenage virgin who just didn't want to be gay.

Undeterred, I continued to research ex-gays through the internet and in books. My parents, too, were willing to do whatever it took to get me answers to my questions. They made phone calls, wrote letters, and read even more books. They helped set up opportunities for me to meet with high-profile leaders in the ex-gay movement, and they offered to spare no expense to send me to any ex-gay conference I wanted to go to. One way or another, we were going to get this fixed and put it behind us.

Or so we thought.

MEET THE PARENTS

My parents went with me to my first ex-gay conference.

I was anxious. Spending a weekend discussing sexuality—particularly *my* sexuality—with my parents was not my idea of a good time! Even so, I knew it was important for me to go.

This particular conference was advertised for ex-gays and their parents. As it turned out, most of the attendees I met there were parents whose children were living openly gay lives. Their children hadn't come with them, but the parents were there to learn what they could do to help bring their children back to the Lord.

The conference opened with a praise and worship session. Here, in the midst of so many Christians singing their songs of praise to God together, I felt much more at ease. This—*this*—was what it was to be a Christian: broken, hurting, imperfect people, united in love and gratitude to God. I could have worshiped forever in that room. I felt peace.

Alas, it was not to last. The keynote address was more about controversial political issues of the day than about how to support Christians wrestling with their sexuality. The speaker charged his audience to fight against the "gay agenda," painting the world in simplistic "us vs. them" terms: *We* were the Christians. *They* were the gays. *They* must be stopped at all costs.

"I think," he said with a broad grin, "that ultimately *our* values are going to prevail."

His mostly straight audience cheered. I felt uneasy. More and more, I felt like the gay people out there maybe weren't so different from me. I was still a Christian, and I still stood for Christian values, but I was gay too. This polarizing language didn't sit well with me. It didn't seem very much like Jesus.

"Ultimately *our* values are going to prevail." I thought about that. I imagined a gay conference meeting at the same time, with a speaker saying those exact same words. If this was to be a battle of Gays vs. Christians, where did I fit in?

Other speakers followed, many of them self-professed ex-gays. The ex-gays spoke often about the childhood traumas they believed had caused them to become gay—nearly always sexual abuse, poor parenting, or some combination of both. Being gay, they insisted, was not something you were born with; it was something that happened to you as a child.

This theme permeated the conference. After one of the sessions, I picked up one of the ministry's brochures. Inside was a question-and-answer section. Among the questions, I saw this:

> Q: Is homosexuality preventable in my child?
>   A: Absolutely. Show unconditional love for your child and
>   ensure that he or she has positive and healthy doses of love
>   from both parents.

In other words, if your child is gay, then you must not have done your job right as a parent.

I wondered if that was really a healthy message to be sending at a conference full of parents who were already worried about their gay kids. I wasn't sexually abused. I didn't have any trauma. I had wonderful parents. What would these people say if they heard *my* story?

When the time came for breakout sessions, my parents chose one geared toward parents, while I went to the intriguingly titled session "The Root Causes of Male Homosexuality." This session was being taught by two friendly, clean-cut young gentlemen. As the session started, one of them held up two books. In one hand, he held a Bible; in the other, he held Elizabeth Moberly's *Homosexuality: A New Christian Ethic.* "Everything we're going to tell you this afternoon is based on these two books," he said.

I hadn't yet read Moberly's book, but I had read about it on the internet, and I knew it didn't fit me. It made me uneasy that the speaker came across as equating that one unproven theory with the *Bible.*

Each of the men told his story. Both had distant fathers. Both had overbearing mothers. For forty-five minutes, they explained the classic reparative drive theory in great detail, insisting that this distant father/overbearing mother paradigm explained every gay man in the world.

I squirmed in my seat, annoyed at the misinformation. I didn't have a distant father or an overbearing mother. I had wonderful, loving parents. How could they make claims about *everyone* based on their own limited experiences?

"Homosexuality," one of them said, "is an inability to relate to the same sex." He explained that gay men are gay because they're unable to properly relate to other men, leading them to "sexualize their emotional needs for male companionship."

Unable to properly relate to other men? I had always had plenty of close, healthy male friendships. I had more male friends than female friends, though I had plenty of each. I always had close guy friends. I'd never felt unable to relate to them. Nothing about this sounded like me at all.

The fact that their theory didn't fit me was one thing, but what really bothered me was watching how this talk was affecting the parents in the room. A large percentage of the attendees were straight parents of gay sons, and according to these guys, it was *their* fault that their sons were gay. Judging from their faces, many of them were taking it pretty hard. As I looked around, the parents' expressions seemed to be registering a mixture of hope and concern. On one hand, these men were offering them hope that their gay sons could still become straight with the right therapy. On the other hand, they were hearing that it was their own faults—and especially the fault of the fathers—that their sons were gay. One single mom had shared with me earlier that her gay son now had AIDS. I wondered how she was feeling right now, thinking that her only son's untimely death might be her fault for not providing a male role model.

I had to say something. I couldn't watch these parents struggle with needless guilt. If I didn't reassure them, who would?

The presenters opened the floor for questions. I nervously raised my hand, and they called on me. I stood up and introduced myself. "The model you've described doesn't sound like my childhood at all," I said. "I'm attracted to the same sex, and I don't know why. But I do know that I always had a good relationship with both of my parents, and I always felt fully loved and accepted by them. And it just really bothers me to see all of these parents here, feeling guilty and thinking that they didn't show their kids enough love, and that it's their fault that their kids are gay. I mean, what if it's not that? What if it's something else? I don't know what, but something else. I just think we should consider that possibility. I hate for all these parents to blame themselves."

I suddenly realized that I was giving a speech more than asking a question. My face got hot and I sat down. The presenters seemed perturbed, but I had said what I needed to say. They dismissively agreed that parents shouldn't focus on self-blame, then quickly moved to another question.

I wondered if I had done the right thing. I hadn't meant to be confrontational or argumentative.

As if in answer to my silent question, a man in front of me turned around and spoke to me as the session ended. "I'm so glad you said what you did," he said. "If you hadn't, I was going to." He leaned in to tell me his story. "The stuff these guys were talking about, that fits my childhood to a T. My father was cold and distant. He was never there for me. I never felt loved by him. I didn't have a good male role model in my life. My mother was bossy and overprotective. Every little thing those guys talked about sounded exactly like how I grew up."

His eyes lit up as he arrived at the twist in his story. "I'm heterosexual," he said. "Never had a gay thought or feeling in my life. When I got married and had a son, I didn't want him to have the kind of childhood I did, so I made sure I was always there for him. Everything my father wasn't. My son and I have a terrific relationship. He says so, and I know so. A few years ago, I found out that he's gay. According to these guys, I should have been gay, not him!" He chuckled wistfully.

People were getting up to leave the room. A college-aged girl walked over and shook my hand. "Thank you," she said to me. "My brother is gay, and our parents aren't anything like those guys said. It's very good to know that there are other gay people who didn't have that kind of family either. I thought I was crazy, listening to them describe something that sounds nothing at all like my family." She introduced me to her mother, and the three of us had lunch together.

Later that day I ran into Jesse, one of the presenters of the "Root Causes" workshop. He recognized me and walked over, glancing at my name tag.

"Justin," he said, the slight edge to his voice belying his gentle smile, "I know you have your own beliefs, but during this weekend I think it would be helpful if you would just listen to what *we* teach."

His tone caught me off guard. I tried to be conciliatory. "Oh, gosh, I honestly didn't mean to sound confrontational this morning," I said. "I just didn't want all those parents to feel guilty, you know?"

"Well, the people you've been talking to may have told you things that are different from what we teach, but you're only here for three days, and I think it would be most worthwhile to you to just listen for the time you have left here."

The people I'd been talking to? "Wait a second," I said. "I didn't say that stuff because of anyone I've been talking to. This is coming from me. I don't fit the Moberly theory. That's just my life. I didn't have a distant father or any of that stuff."

"I didn't think I did either," he replied coolly, *"until I got into therapy and started looking harder."*

I didn't know what to say to that.

What kind of ministry takes a person who thinks he has a wonderful relationship with his father and convinces him that he actually has a bad one? This was feeling less and less like the work of God to me.

As I met more people at this conference and others, I discovered that I was far from alone. Many people told me similar stories of growing up happily, having healthy relationships with their parents, and then being pressured by ex-gay groups to find fault with their upbringing. But even as the evidence piled up that there were plenty of gay people *without* distant fathers and overbearing mothers, that paradigm remained far and away the most popular explanation these ministries had for our gay feelings. The people I kept meeting who didn't fit that pattern were largely ignored or shoehorned in, forced to revisit their childhood memories over and over until they found some sort of problem to blame everything on. Challenge that, and you just might be labeled a heretic.

As it was, I was losing my faith. Not in God, but in ex-gays.

I had brought a notebook with me to the conference. I jotted down all that had happened and read back over the notes. I sighed. *This could make a good book someday,* I thought.

Ha. Yeah, right.

DOWN THE RABBIT HOLE

In one of my favorite scenes in *Through the Looking-Glass*, the second of Lewis Carroll's two Alice books, Alice meets Humpty Dumpty, who tells her that "un-birthday" presents are better than birthday presents, because there are 364 days for "un-birthday" presents:

"And only one for birthday presents, you know. There's glory for you!"

"I don't know what you mean by 'glory,' " Alice said.

Humpty Dumpty smiled contemptuously. "Of course you don't—till I tell you. I meant 'there's a nice knock-down argument for you!' "

"But 'glory' doesn't mean 'a nice knock-down argument,' " Alice objected.

"When I use a word," Humpty Dumpty said, in rather a scornful tone, "it means just what I choose it to mean—neither more nor less."

"The question is," said Alice, "whether you can make words mean so many different things."

"The question is," said Humpty Dumpty, "which is to be master—that's all."

Alice was too much puzzled to say anything; so after a minute Humpty Dumpty began again. "They've a temper, some of them—particularly verbs: they're the proudest—adjectives you can do anything with, but not verbs—however, I can manage the whole lot of them! Impenetrability! That's what I say!"

"Would you tell me please," said Alice, "what that means?"

"Now you talk like a reasonable child," said Humpty Dumpty, looking very much pleased. "I meant by 'impenetrability' that we've had enough of that subject, and it would be just as well if you'd mention what you mean to do next, as I suppose you don't mean to stop here all the rest of your life."

"That's a great deal to make one word mean," Alice said in a thoughtful tone.

"When I make a word do a lot of work like that," said Humpty Dumpty, "I always pay it extra."

In Wonderland, words mean whatever the characters choose for them to mean, resulting in much confusion for poor Alice, who has no way of seeing into their heads. In the real world, communication depends on a *shared understanding* of what a word means.

Word meanings do change over time as our culture changes, but these are gradual shifts. Any meaning of a word must be widely understood before we can safely use that word to communicate. If I suddenly start using a word to mean something different from what most people mean by that word, I'll only confuse people at best. At worst, by choosing a definition that's more convenient for me, I could deliberately mislead them.

The word "gay" in our culture usually means "attracted to the same sex." In movies and on television, when characters say they're gay, we understand that that means they're attracted to their own sex. If a teenage boy says, "Mom, Dad, I think I'm gay," he's saying that he's attracted to his own sex.

So when I first heard the testimonies of people who said they "used to be gay" but weren't anymore, I interpreted that to mean that they used to be attracted to the same sex, and now they weren't. I thought that "ex-gays" were people who used to be gay but now were straight—attracted to the opposite sex.

That turned out not to be true.

Online and at ex-gay conferences, I did hear a number of testimonies of people who said they had been healed of their homosexuality—the "success stories" of the movement. I listened to them carefully, asking lots of questions when possible. But what I heard wasn't what I had expected.

Most of the men's stories followed a predictable pattern. Like me, they had developed attractions to other guys at puberty, but unlike me, nearly all of them had decided to act on those feelings at some point. Many had sordid stories of promiscuous, anonymous sex and/or drug and alcohol abuse. In their minds, these addictive and risky behaviors represented what it meant to be gay, and they had found that lifestyle to be woefully unfulfilling. Somewhere along the way, they had become Christians or reignited their faith, prompting them to feel convicted that the lives they were leading were sinful. With the help of ex-gay groups, therapy, and prayer, they had walked away from their past behaviors.

The testimonies were powerful reminders of how God changes lives. It was largely faith in God that enabled them to overcome a history of sexual addiction and substance abuse. Their behaviors had completely changed, and they were happier for it.

But there was one thing missing in all of their testimonies. None of them seemed to be becoming straight. They had changed their behaviors, sometimes in dramatic ways. Some had not had any sexual contact in years. Others had gone so far as to date and marry a member of the opposite sex. But almost universally, when I asked, they confessed that they still had the same kind of same-sex attractions I did.

In ex-gay circles, I learned, the word "gay" didn't mean "attracted to the same sex." At ex-gay conferences, I often ran into ex-gay leaders who publicly testified that they were "no longer gay" even while privately confessing that they still had same-sex attractions. How was this possible? Were they just lying to everyone? No, not exactly. But like Humpty Dumpty, they had redefined their terms without explaining what they meant.

Instead of using "gay" to mean "attracted to the same sex," they redefined it to refer to sexual *behaviors* they were no longer engaging in or a loosely defined cultural "identity" they didn't accept. According to their new definitions, anyone who attended an ex-gay group could call themselves "no longer gay" without ever experiencing any change in their attractions. Even the ex-gays who sometimes slipped up and gave in to their temptations through occasional sexual trysts still considered themselves "not gay" because they didn't "identify that way."

I could understand that they didn't want to identify with their former way of life. In their minds, "gay" encompassed a whole sinful and self-destructive lifestyle. But by giving public testimony that they weren't "gay" anymore, they were leading millions of Christians to believe that they had become straight, when that wasn't true. And those misleading testimonies were getting a lot of attention on Christian radio, in Christian magazines, and in churches around the world.

Part of the problem was that neither these leaders, nor their audiences, were careful to distinguish between sexual *behaviors* and sexual *attractions*. When people like me said we were gay, it was because of our *attractions*. When the ex-gay leaders said they *weren't* gay, it was because of their *behaviors*.

When other Christians heard these testimonies of men who used to live promiscuous gay lives but had experienced "healing" and were now married to women, they naturally assumed that the men's *attractions* had changed as well and that they were now straight. That wasn't true, but no one seemed particularly interested in correcting the misconception.

The ex-gays knew, of course, that they were still attracted to the same sex, but many of them dismissed this as "residual temptations" resulting from a lifetime of behaving badly. "Those years of gay life will always have some effect on me," one ex-gay leader explained to me. "I will never be as if I didn't have that in my past." Another leader insisted that same-sex-attracted Christians like me who *hadn't* acted on their feelings would have a relatively easy time ridding themselves of those feelings and becoming completely straight. He didn't actually know anyone who had done it, but still…

Other ex-gays explained their continuing attractions as part of a "process" or "journey." Although they hadn't fully changed their attractions *yet*, they were sure that they were in the *process* of changing and that these attractions didn't have quite as much of a hold on them as they had in the past.

In one sense, I have no doubt this was true. In the past, many of them had experienced their attractions as something like an addiction or compulsion. With therapy and prayer, they had broken the stranglehold their sex drives had once had on their behavior. *They* were in control now, not their sex drives, and that was a freeing and healthy experience. In addition, many of these men were getting older, and their libidos no longer felt as urgent as they had in their teenage years. But if a heterosexual woman overcomes a life of sexual addiction, that doesn't mean she is becoming less heterosexual, and if a heterosexual man finds that the urgency of his sex drive toward women isn't as strong at age sixty-eight as it was at eighteen, that doesn't mean his *orientation* has changed. It's just a natural part of life.

For all the ex-gay talk of this journey toward becoming straight, no one ever seemed to actually get there.

That wasn't the message the Christians back home heard, though. They heard that thousands upon thousands of people were "leaving homosexuality," and that those ex-gays' lives provided proof that there was hope for their gay loved ones to become straight too.

Christians really are a compassionate bunch, even though the cultural reputation we have right now doesn't reflect that. Because so many Christians—especially evangelical Christians like me—believed that gay relationships were sinful, they also wanted to believe that there was some way that gay people could become straight so that they could legitimately enjoy all the benefits of romance and marriage. The ex-gays, too, wanted to believe this and to provide hope to others. Unfortunately, sometimes that desire for hope got in the way of being completely honest.

I wasn't immune to this. In 1996, shortly after realizing I was gay, I read a column by advice columnist Ann Landers in which parents of a gay son asked about counseling to help him become straight. "A 20-year-old male who has romantic fantasies about other males is unquestionably homosexual," Landers wrote in response. "Counseling will not 'straighten him around.' Nor is there any medication that will perform that magic."

At the time, I was convinced Landers was wrong. I worried about all the struggling teens out there like me, and I knew I needed to set the record straight (so to speak) and tell them that change *was* possible. I wrote a letter identifying myself as a gay teen who was becoming straight, urging others to trust God and have hope that they, too, could become straight like me. My life was proof.

The letter sat on my desk for days. I couldn't quite bring myself to mail it. At the time, I believed with all my heart that I was going to become straight and that I was in the process already. But in the letter I had exaggerated the amount of "change" I was actually experiencing. I hadn't lied, but I hadn't been completely honest, either. The trouble was, if I was honest about the lack of attraction change I had experienced so far, I knew no one would take my story seriously. They would write me off as deceiving myself. If I waited until after my feelings had changed before writing, I'd be too late to respond to this column. I had to respond right away, and I was so certain that I was in the process of becoming straight that it didn't feel like a lie to *lead people to believe* that I was further along in the process than was actually true.

In the end, I couldn't send the letter. It felt too much like deception, and as a Christian I believed it was wrong to lie, even for what I was sure was a good cause.

I thought back to that letter when I later noticed the differences between some ex-gay men's public testimonies and the real-life struggles they shared in private. I'm convinced that many of them, like me, didn't really want to be deceptive; they just wanted to provide hope, and sometimes that meant not quite telling people *everything*. They'd minimize the amount of same-sex attraction they still felt, for instance, and focus on their commitment to their wives without mentioning their lack of sexual attraction to the female form or the related impact on their marriages. It seemed justified; who would expect them to reveal such intimate struggles? And yet the end result was that the picture they painted of gay-to-straight change wasn't quite the reality.

I'm sure their intentions were good. But the deception, even if unintentional, had disastrous consequences.

TERRY'S STORY

As I wrestled with what I was learning about the ex-gay movement, I had no idea that someone I knew was wrestling with these very same questions.

Terry was a family friend. He and his wife knew my parents and went to our church. I didn't know him well, but he struck me as a nice guy in a happy marriage.

I didn't know Terry was gay. His wife was his best friend, and he had married her as a "step of faith" toward becoming straight. They had adopted children, and he did his best to love his wife in every way he could, but the truth was that he had never been physically attracted to her, and marriage hadn't changed that. What they had was a friendship, not a romance.

Terry agonized over the situation. He was trying to follow God by being a faithful husband and good father, but a friendship is not a substitute for a marriage, and after years of trying, nothing had made him straight.

When Terry's wife was killed in a tragic car accident, he was devastated. He had lost his best friend, and it only made his loneliness feel all the more unbearable. His wife was dead, and he had never been able to see her the way a straight man would have. The grief tore him apart.

As time passed and Terry's life returned to normal, he had to think about what to do next. He had married once thinking that he would become straight. Now he knew better, and he could avoid making the same mistake again. Still, the pressure of being single and having to hide his same-sex attractions made him lonelier than ever. Seeking advice, he confided his story in a Christian counselor referred by the church.

The counselor encouraged Terry not to give up on his quest to become straight. He urged Terry to get to know women in the church and allow them to provide the solace he was craving. He warned Terry not to let his doubts get in the way of doing what God obviously wanted him to do: find the right woman and get re-married.

Trusting the guidance of his spiritual adviser and confidant, Terry did just that.

But this marriage didn't work either. On the outside, Terry con-tinued to pretend everything was going well. In truth, as it became more apparent that he was gay and wasn't going to become straight, his marriage was crumbling. Eventually, everything fell apart, re-sulting in tremendous anger and pain on all sides. Everyone was devastated: Terry, Terry's wife, and Terry's kids.

I didn't know about any of this until I ran into Terry a few years ago and he told me the story. Today he is bitter and angry at the church. He feels lied to, cheated out of years of happiness by a promise of change that never materialized. There is tremendous pain in his eyes whenever he talks about his experiences. When I asked for his permission to tell his story, he quickly agreed.

"I just don't want anyone else to go through what I've been through," he said.

Terry's is one of so many stories I could tell you of people who gave their whole hearts to trying to change their orientation, only to have everything come crashing down around them. The experi-ence has left many people feeling broken and betrayed, some feeling so wounded by the church that they can't bring themselves to set foot inside a worship service anymore.

These were some of the most dedicated and devout Christians you could ever meet. They were willing to sacrifice everything to please God. But years upon years of trying to change and being told it would happen didn't do anything to make them straight. Instead, it only damaged their faith and their feelings of self-worth. When they finally came to the point of telling the truth about what they were feeling, their ex-gay mentors accused them of "backsliding," and the churches they had so loved seemed to have no place for them.

In a Gays-vs.-Christians world, admitting you're gay makes you the enemy of Christians. After hearing some of these people's horror stories, I'm amazed that any of them have any faith left at all.

RED FLAGS

The Christians who continue to recommend ex-gay ministries to people do so with the best of intentions. They've heard testimonies by ex-gay leaders or seen ads promising "hope for change," and they've believed it.

Every time I see one of those ads, I think of the companies who market diet "miracle pills" promising to melt away the unwanted pounds. Less reputable companies have been known to pay fit models to temporarily gain weight for a "before" picture, then return to their normal exercise and eating habits, leaving them looking muscular and trim for an "after" picture that in reality has little if anything to do with the drug. The ad crows about how many pounds they lost in only a few weeks, while fine print at the bottom warns: "Results not typical."

If they were being completely honest, ex-gay organizations would put "results not typical" at the bottom of their published testimonies as well. Like the diet ads, those testimonies often don't tell the whole story, and even if they did, they don't represent what happens to most people who go through these ministries. If Christians were truly aware of what does happen, they'd never recommend these ministries again.

Christians need to be aware. Sadly, the warning signs date back to the very beginning of the ex-gay movement.

Homosexuals Anonymous began its life as a part of Quest Learning Center, an institution founded by Colin Cook promising "freedom from homosexuality." Cook, a married-with-children ex-gay "success story" who developed the Homosexuals Anonymous program, wrote in 1982 that "a change in orientation is [not] a requirement for acceptance with God or entrance into the fellowship in the church," but that "the orientation may be healed," that "freedom from homosexual drive…is a real possibility," and that "all who desire it may realize their inborn…heterosexuality."[1]

Four years later, Cook was forced to resign when a number of his male clients came forward to charge that Cook had been sexually molesting them in the course of therapy, telling them it was to help desensitize them to male stimuli. Cook finally confessed to inappropriate behavior, but told a reporter the next year that he had managed to overcome that impulse, and that "99.9%" of his same-sex fantasies were now gone.[2]

Eight years later, *The Denver Post* reported that Cook was still engaging in sexual contact and phone sex with his male counselees.[3] Cook's theories on orientation change continue to influence ex-gay groups today.

Michael Bussee and Gary Cooper were two of the original cofounders of Exodus International, an ex-gay referral organization that today is the largest ex-gay ministry in the world. Both were married with kids. Early on in the ex-gay movement, Bussee helped coin the term "ex-gay," and he and Cooper gained a reputation as two of the movement's most famous success stories. Together, they traveled across the country, speaking to excited Christian audiences and telling them that, yes, it was possible for gay people to become straight.

In 1978, when psychological researchers contacted their ministry for an opportunity to interview some ex-gays and see whether orientation change was really possible, Bussee and Cooper combed through the files of about 300 members, narrowing the list to 30 who, in their opinion, had changed. Of those 30, the researchers found 11 who agreed to talk to them and whom they identified as having successfully "changed to heterosexuality" based on their self-descriptions. Only 5 of the 11 claimed to have gone from exclusively homosexual to exclusively heterosexual, however; the others all admitted to continuing homosexuality in some form.[4] Michael Bussee and Gary Cooper were two of the five successes.

It was shortly after that study, on a plane on the way to another speaking engagement, that Bussee and Cooper broke down and confessed to each other that they were both still gay and had fallen in love with each other. Not surprisingly, their marriages did not survive. The movement they'd helped to start, however, did.

Twenty years later, I was dipping my toe into the ex-gay waters for the first time, knowing nothing of Colin Cook or Michael Bussee. By then, the most famous ex-gay testimony in the world was that of John Paulk, the chairman of the board of Exodus International and the head of the Homosexuality and Gender department of Focus on the Family, an influential Christian nonprofit. When I shared with friends and family that I was beginning to doubt that ex-gay therapy worked, many of them pointed to John as the proof that I was wrong.

John had written a book called *Not Afraid to Change: The Remarkable Story of How One Man Overcame Homosexuality.* In it, he told how he had changed from a promiscuous drag queen living a sex-and-party lifestyle to a heterosexual family man with a wife and son. Together with his wife, Anne, he loudly proclaimed that such change was possible for anyone who wanted it, and the two of them appeared on national talk shows as proof. In 1998, John and Anne were on the cover of *Newsweek,* leading even more of my friends to point to him as evidence that I could become straight. John's story was everywhere, and in his role with Focus on the Family, he was largely responsible for ensuring that his "change is possible" message made it into the homes of millions of Christians. He wasn't just a leader in the ex-gay movement; he was the poster boy, living proof that orientation change really could happen.

Like most other ex-gay leaders, John stopped short of explicitly saying that his same-sex attractions were gone, but he strongly implied that they were. He referred to himself as a "heterosexual" who was "formerly gay," someone who had "changed [his] sexual orientation" and "come out of homosexuality."

To most people, that meant he was straight, but I was skeptical. It didn't match what I had seen in other ex-gays. I suspected he was still living with same-sex attractions just like I was, even though he was married to a woman.

When I shared these suspicions with my Christian friends, they accused me of being uncharitable. "John Paulk isn't gay anymore," they'd say. "Just read his testimony. He overcame homosexuality."

It wasn't until a couple of years later that the truth came out. John was on a business trip in Washington, D.C., when a gay activist recognized him at Mr. P's, a local gay bar. Witnesses claim that John lied about his identity and flirtatiously tried to buy a man a drink, leaving hurriedly when another activist arrived with a camera to get his picture. When confronted later about the incident, John claimed he hadn't known it was a gay bar, and that he only went in to use the restroom. He later confessed that that was a lie, but claimed he didn't have any inappropriate motives for going to the bar. After the incident, he was removed from his position at Exodus, but he continued to serve as the homosexuality specialist for Focus on the Family.

Over a year later, Focus on the Family president James Dobson cited John Paulk in his book *Bringing Up Boys* as the best proof that gay people can become straight. "Prevention is effective," wrote Dobson. "Change is possible." Immediately after using John as a shining example of orientation change, Dobson bolstered his argument with a quote from a psychologist about the reality of such change. That psychologist was George Rekers—the same man who would find scandal in 2010 for hiring a male escort as a travel companion.

Stories like these—and there are many of them—make me sad. Each of them encompasses far more pain and tragedy than we can know. When I think about John Paulk, for instance, I think about all the pain in his life that led him to the ex-gay movement, all the years of self-deception as he tried to play the role of the straight husband and father, and all the hurt he, his wife, and his family must have experienced when the truth was revealed. He's not a villain; he's a human being who surely thought he was on the right path despite occasional slipups. I think, too, of all the individuals, families, and churches who heard him speak about the reality of his change, and who made life-altering decisions for themselves and their loved ones based around the belief that if John Paulk had become straight, anyone could become straight. I think about the stories of Christians who killed themselves in despair when they were unable to change and the parents who disowned their children for self-identifying as gay. I think about the damage so many Christian churches have done to so many people because they misunderstood what was really happening and ended up pushing people away from God.

Then again called they the man that was blind, and said unto him, Give God the praise: we know that this man is a sinner.

He answered and said, Whether he be a sinner or no, I know not: one thing I know, that, whereas I was blind, now I see. (John 9:25 KJV)

At the start of my journey, I had been blind to all of the pain and the damage the church was doing. Now my eyes had been opened. I didn't have all the answers, but I couldn't go back. I had seen too much.

TRUTH IN ADVERTISING

To this day, Exodus and other ex-gay organizations continue to promote a mixed message when it comes to orientation change. Some leaders within these ministries have been pushing for years for more openness and honesty about the reality that therapy can't make gay people straight and that what's typically happening is *behavior* change, not *orientation* (that is, *attraction*) change. They've argued for more "truth in advertising," urging their organizations to stop leading people to believe they can become straight and to focus instead on helping people overcome sexual addictions and improve their relationship with God.

Unfortunately, those people have been frequently outnumbered by those who find the "anyone can change" message to be too appealing to resist.

To his credit, Alan Chambers, Exodus's current president, has openly admitted that he continues to be attracted to men even though he's married to a woman.

"Do you still struggle with same-sex attraction?" reporter Lisa Ling asked him in a 2011 interview.

"Sure," he responded. "Do I have to be careful with what I look at on the internet or in movies? Yeah. But I don't know that I'm any different than any other married man who has to be careful with those things."[5]

Of course, as my dad points out, straight married men don't have to struggle to avoid looking at *men* on the internet. By contrast, I'd be willing to bet that Alan doesn't have any struggle to avoid looking at *women* in that way. Alan and the other ex-gays like him haven't actually become straight. They are still attracted to their own sex. By most people's definitions, they'd still be "gay," even though that's not a word they like to use for themselves.

Yet go to Exodus's official website and you'll find these words:

> Are you struggling with unwanted same-sex attractions?...
>
> You have come to the right place! For over thirty years, Exodus International has offered hope and help to people seeking freedom from homosexuality....
>
> The bottom line—*you don't have to be gay!* [6]

I showed this page to my friend Ron, a gay Christian who has committed himself to lifelong celibacy. "Of course you don't have to be gay," he joked drily. "You can be 'SSA' [same-sex attracted] instead. All you have to do is to drop that nasty three-letter word and put a lovely three-letter acronym in its place."

Ron knows, as I do, that "not being gay" in Exodus lingo means changing the word you use for yourself and calling it a change in "identity." It doesn't mean actually becoming straight. Exodus can't promise to help gay people become straight. They can't promise that God will change people's attractions, no matter how much faith they have. But misleading language like this—telling people with "unwanted same-sex attractions" that they "don't have to be gay"—leads a lot of Christians to believe that that's exactly what Exodus and groups like them are offering.

As long as that's the message Christians are hearing, there will continue to be heartbreaking stories like John's and Terry's.

And James's.

James and I met several years after my involvement with the ex-gay ministries. He was about my age, celibate, and a Christian. He confessed to me that he, too, was struggling with his same-sex attractions. We became friends, and although we didn't live near each other, we kept in touch by phone over the years. We both enjoyed intellectual conversations—and sometimes friendly debates—about issues of the day, and we openly shared our struggles as gay Christians in a world where gays and Christians are at war.

But where I had become convinced that ex-gay ministries didn't work, James wasn't so sure. He was deeply uncomfortable with his orientation, and the claim that gays could become straight was very appealing to him.

Eventually his discomfort with his sexuality proved too much for him to bear, and he told me he was going to pursue an ex-gay path. I honestly told him my concerns and my fears for him, but promised that whatever he decided, I would always be his friend.

Time passed, and he told me he felt like he was becoming straight. Then he told me he had met a girl. They had become friends, and it was such a great friendship that he was sure it could turn into something more.

"Be careful," I cautioned. "This isn't just about you anymore. This is about her life as well."

He assured me that he knew what he was doing.

They started dating, and James enthusiastically talked about the relationship and his new girlfriend every time we spoke. I had grown to know James pretty well by this point, and I could tell by the way he talked about her that his feelings for her weren't the same kind of passionate feelings a straight guy would have for a girl, or that James still had for guys. He was, I thought, blinded by love—not romantic love for his girlfriend, but love for the idea of being in love—or, perhaps more accurately, love for the idea of being straight. I realized that it wasn't this girl he was so passionate about; it was the simple fact that she was a girl. She was a friend, but she had come to represent something much more important to him, and the thing she represented—the promise of heterosexuality—had become far more important than the actual human relationship they had.

James began talking about asking his girlfriend to marry him.

"Does she know about your attractions?" I asked him. "I mean, does she know that you're still attracted to guys?"

"She knows some of it," he said. "I didn't tell her everything because I didn't want her to worry too much."

"What did you tell her?" I asked.

"I told her that I used to have attractions to guys," he said.

"But you *still* have attractions to guys," I said.

"They're going away!" he said. "Anyway, it's in my past."

"Did you tell her you're also not attracted to girls?" I said.

"I'm attracted to *her*," he said defensively.

"You told me that you didn't feel the same things for her that you do for other guys," I reminded him.

"It's getting better," he said unconvincingly.

"Please be careful, James," I urged. "She deserves to know the truth."

He assured me again that he knew what he was doing.

James proposed, and soon the two were married. After the wedding, James told me how sure he was that he had made the right decision—how happy he was to finally be married. Also, he mentioned impishly, it was nice to finally be able to have sex.

Sex had been one of James's primary concerns. He had a reasonably strong sex drive, but he believed it would be wrong for him to be in a relationship with a guy, so getting married to a woman had felt like his only option to tame his feelings.

Thanks to that pent-up sexual frustration, James had no trouble performing sexually with his wife. But rather than tame his sex drive, the sexual contact seemed only to ignite it.

James began calling me more frequently now, and I noticed that he often tried to steer our conversations around to sex. He delighted in sharing graphic details of his and his wife's sex life. He confessed that he was still as attracted to guys as ever. He confessed that his fantasies were all still about men, not women. And he told me what I had suspected but didn't want to ask: that his wife's body didn't really turn him on sexually, but that he was able to perform with her by fantasizing about men.

And then he said something that knocked the wind out of me.

"Sometimes," he said, lowering his voice to a seductive whisper, "*I think about you.*"

"Dude! That's not okay," I hissed back into the phone. "You're married! You can't say things like that."

I realized what was going on. James had feelings for me. He was trying to meet needs through our friendship that his wife couldn't meet because she was a woman. Telling me about his sex life had been his way of vicariously having a sexual connection with another guy without admitting to himself that that was what he was doing. It was, perhaps, the same thing that made ex-gay support groups so appealing to married men struggling with same-sex attractions.

Even though I thought it had been a mistake for James to get married, now that he was married, there was no way I could participate in undermining the vows he had made to his wife. Perhaps he wasn't being physically unfaithful, but he was being emotionally unfaithful, and I couldn't be part of it.

I stopped talking to James on the phone, though he still sent me occasional updates through email. James ended up making "friends" with a local guy, and in one of his emails, he confessed to me that the two of them had had sexual contact. I was horrified and wrote back to remind him that he was cheating on his wife.

He told me not to worry, that it was only "fooling around" and not full-blown sex.

From the outside, James's marriage looks happy. His wife still doesn't know the full extent of his same-sex attractions. She doesn't know that he knows me or that he tried to flirt with me while they were married. She doesn't know about his local friend, who has been putting increasing pressure on James to take their relationship in a more sexual direction—pressure James has so far resisted, but not entirely spurned. Deep down, though, I'm sure she must suspect that something isn't quite right in their marriage.

Those who know James would consider him an ex-gay success story. On the basis of his testimony, they would encourage their gay friends and family members and acquaintances to follow in his footsteps.

I hope and pray that no one does.

CHAPTER 7

THAT THE MAN SHOULD BE ALONE

When television host Piers Morgan asked Donald Trump whether he would hypothetically accept ten billion dollars in exchange for not having any sex for the next ten years, with his wife or anyone else, Trump replied, "No, I'd absolutely take my wife."

"Really?" Morgan asked incredulously.

"Well, I have to say that," Trump joked. "I've got to go home."[1]

That's easy for Trump to say; he already has plenty of money. I'm sure there are many Americans—especially those living in poverty—who would gladly accept even a fraction of that amount to go without sex, and many of us go without sex every day because we are single and believe that God has called us to wait.

But Trump's answer raises an important point. Not only is sex a significant part of the human experience and something few of us would want to go without; it also represents something much deeper: love.

After creating Adam in the Garden of Eden and observing that

"It is not good that the man should be alone," God gave him Eve, a partner and life companion; not simply a good friend but a sexually attractive lover. For the vast majority of us, that relationship represents the single most important factor in our lives after God. A spouse provides companionship, comfort, support, love, and so much more. Those who are single search eagerly for someone to date and ultimately to marry; those who are married rely on their spouse far more than even they realize. The apostle Paul saw marriage as a concession, not the ideal, but even he recognized that it is a concession many of us would be deeply unhappy without.

And if we believe that God created sex as a bonding agent to bring couples together, then we must agree with Paul that sex is an important part of the marriage relationship. So a question like "Would you be willing to go without sex?" isn't just a question about forgoing physical pleasure; it's really asking, "Would you be willing to give up the special relationship you have with your spouse?" For any happily married person, that relationship is something money just can't buy.

If you asked me whether I'd rather have ten billion dollars or the opportunity to fall in love and have another human being face this life alongside me, I have no doubt what I'd say. I could buy a lot of gadgets and gizmos with ten billion dollars, but not one of them could hold my hand at the end of a difficult day or look into my eyes and make me feel at peace with my lot in life.

Keep your money. I just don't want to be alone.

I've met people who seem to have what some Christians would call "the gift of celibacy." Whatever challenges they may find in singleness, it also seems to be the situation in which they most thrive. They don't particularly mind being alone; they may even prefer it. Ask them if they would like to have a significant other someday, and they have no hesitation in shaking their heads and saying, "Why? I'm perfectly content the way I am." They seem to be wired that way.

But the rest of us aren't wired that way. We struggle with our singlehood, and though we may surround ourselves with friends and things to do and never complain about being alone, being single remains a burden rather than a blessing for us. It is a burden we bear because it's been given to us, but it is not one we would have chosen for ourselves. We long for God to say to us, too, that it is not good for us to be alone, and to fashion someone out of the earth to be our companion.

Roger Ebert understands the importance of that companionship. Thyroid cancer robbed him of his TV career, his ability to speak, and portions of his face, leaving him severely deformed. Through it all, his wife, Chaz, gave him strength and support. In a 2010 entry in his blog, Ebert writes about the importance of such connections:

> What do lonely people desire? Companionship. Love. Recognition. Entertainment. Camaraderie. Distraction.
>
> Encouragement. Change. Feedback. Someone once said the fundamental reason we get married is because we have a universal human need for a *witness*. All of these are possibilities. But what all lonely people share is a desire not to be—or at least not to feel—alone....
>
> Why do people marry with no prospects of children? Babies are not the only thing two people can create together. They can create a safe private world. They can create a reality that affirms their values. They can stand for something. They can find someone to laugh with, and confide in. Someone to hold them when they need to be held. A danger of the internet would be if we begin to meet those needs without feeling there has to be another person in the room....
>
> A few weeks ago, something happened. Chaz needed emergency surgery. There were two nights when I was alone and she was in the hospital, just as there were months when she was alone and I was in the hospital. And in the middle of the night a great fear enveloped me. If "anything happened"

(as they say), I would be so terribly, terribly alone, and sad. I
would miss her so much. This feeling came over me in a wave.
I pulled the covers tighter around me. Then I would know
what loneliness was.[2]

There are, of course, many single people in the world, and I'm not
suggesting that one needs a spouse in order to have a happy, fulfilling life. But for those who have a spouse or don't particularly
feel the need for one, it can be far too easy to offer trite platitudes
about how God is sufficient, ignoring the realities of loneliness that
so many single people face. After all, seeing that Adam was alone,
God did not simply say, "I am sufficient for you"; nor did God expect Adam to meet those needs with a *friend*.

As I contemplated my future, I found myself experiencing the
kind of loneliness Ebert describes. Was I destined to be alone? What
sort of future did I have?

Growing up thinking I was straight, I had always assumed I knew
what my future would look like. I would date girls until I found the
right one, and then we'd fall in love, get engaged, get married, and
have kids. I would work in a job where I could serve God with my
talents, and I'd be a loving husband and devoted father, just as my
father had been. That was what I wanted, and what I had been sure
my future was supposed to be.

Even after realizing I was gay, I'd thought I was still on that path,
that with prayer, faith, time, and therapy, I could become straight
and still live out my dream future. I'd been confident that that was
God's plan for my life.

Now, realizing that I might always be attracted to guys instead of
girls, I had to face some harsh truths. I had to face the fact that I
might never again be the "golden boy," so respected in my church
and Christian community, and that the stigma of being gay could
follow me my entire life. And I had to face the realization that my
future wasn't going to be what I had always assumed it would be.

But what would it be? If I couldn't become straight, I had basically three options.

One option was to hide the extent of my same-sex attractions, pretend to be straight, and marry a woman in spite of my lack of attraction for her. This would allow me to have all the perks of marriage, raise a family, and be respectable in the eyes of others, even though I wasn't really straight.

I only briefly considered that option before dismissing it outright. I not only lacked sexual attractions to women; I lacked any kind of romantic feelings for them. I knew that without romantic or sexual attractions, such a marriage would be a sham at its core and would be completely unfair to my wife. She would deserve a relationship with someone who felt things for her that I could never feel. Beyond that, I knew I would never feel comfortable in my own home trying to "play marriage" with someone I felt nothing for.

A second option was to have a relationship with someone I *could* fall in love with: another guy. The romantic feelings I lacked for girls, I had for guys instead. When I became close friends with a guy I really cared about, I felt all kinds of happy, intoxicating, silly, tender, exciting feelings bubbling to the surface, feelings I had to suppress because I knew he could never return them. I was beginning to realize that these were the feelings that straight people felt in the presence of the opposite sex, the reason they went to such great lengths to impress one another and the reason they wanted to be in each other's presence whenever they could. It wasn't just about sex; it was about human connection and love.

Around the right guy, I felt like I was walking through the clouds and radiating sunlight from within. I wouldn't mind making a fool of myself or reading sappy love poems or standing out in the rain with a boom box over my head like John Cusack in *Say Anything*, if it would get his attention and please him. But when I met guys who made me feel this way, I always fought to keep any evidence of those feelings locked away inside. It was hopeless to feel that way for someone who isn't attracted to your gender.

But what if I met someone who made me feel that way *and* who had the same feelings for me? The possibility seemed almost unimaginable. I'd spent so many years suppressing my feelings that I had never considered that someone might someday return them. Just considering this possibility made my heart leap for joy like almost nothing I had ever experienced. I began imagining what it might be like to fall in love with someone who loved me back. For a moment, I felt amazing, like nothing in the world could touch me.

The feeling was fleeting, as harsh reality crashed back in. Even if I did meet someone like that, could God approve of such a relationship? If I committed to abstain from sex entirely, could I at least have a sex-free romance? Or was it the very idea of romance between two men that God abhorred?

I looked to the Bible for guidance on this question, but the things I found didn't help. In Genesis, I read the story of Sodom, a city destroyed by God after a threat of male-male gang rape. In Leviticus, male-male sex was called an abomination, punishable by death. In Romans, homosexuality was linked with idol worship and rebellion against God. In 1 Corinthians, "homosexual offenders" were one of the sinful groups Paul said wouldn't inherit the kingdom of God. Taken together, it seemed clear that God condemned gay sex, but none of these passages were any help to me in figuring out how a gay *person* should live and whether there might be a place for a nonsexual romantic relationship—whether I might still be able to fall in love as long as I maintained boundaries about sex.

As beautiful as the idea of falling in love seemed, I couldn't help but worry that it was splitting hairs. Would God really approve of romance in a situation where He condemned sex? If male-male sex was so offensive to God, I imagined that male-male romance would be as well, even if it wasn't explicitly mentioned. I was committed to God first and foremost, so if God didn't approve it, I couldn't have it.

The third option, of course, was lifelong celibacy. No relationship, no sex, no romance. I didn't like the sound of that at all. Still, I knew that if I wanted to serve Christ with my life, and if He was calling me to celibacy, then I would have to be celibate.

I considered what this would mean. Obviously, it would mean no sex. Ever.

Imagine telling any teenage boy that he can never have sex, that he must go his entire life without being able to experience it even once. I imagine his response would be less than enthusiastic. Mine was likewise. As a teenager, abstaining from sex is difficult enough when you know you're waiting for the right time. It's far more difficult when you know there will never be a right time, even if you find the right person.

It wasn't just the physical pleasure I wanted; I craved the intimacy of sex. I craved that experience of total vulnerability with another human being.

And yet, as difficult as I knew it would be to go without sex for the rest of my life, I felt I could handle that. It wasn't what I wanted, but if that was where God ultimately called me, I would do it, and I'd be fine.

Other parts of lifelong celibacy were harder for me to handle. To go without sex was one thing, but to go without romance and companionship was quite another. People don't marry for the right to have sex; they marry for love and the opportunity to build a life together with another human being. They marry because when everything goes wrong and life is at its most challenging, it's comforting to have a hand to hold. Because in the darkness of the night, a bed feels a lot less empty when you are lying next to someone who loves you.

I imagined what kind of future I would have as a celibate gay man. I thought of my grandfather, who developed Parkinson's disease and was cared for in his later years by his loving wife and children. When I got older, who would care for me if I couldn't care for myself? I would have no spouse to support me and no children to look after my well-being. When I got old, would anyone care? If I suffered from Alzheimer's or dementia as so many in my family had, who would notice and get me the help I needed? Who would make sure I wasn't taken advantage of or mistreated? Was I doomed to die alone and unwanted?

I thought about all the years leading up to that. I imagined coming home from work to an empty house, day after day. I would never have someone to cuddle with on the couch, never watch my child take his or her first steps, never love someone as my parents loved each other, and never have that special person I could lean on and serve Christ together with. I had dreamed about these things for years, but now they seemed impossible.

That future looked bleak indeed. Was that really what God wanted for me? More importantly, if that *was* what God wanted for me, was I willing to accept it?

I don't have the words to convey how much this question weighed on me. I knew I couldn't continue calling myself a Christian unless I was willing to accept whatever God had planned for me, even if it was a life of loneliness. I also knew I couldn't just lie to God, pretend I'd be okay with it, and then try to find some other solution. God knows your heart. You can't lie to God.

After agonizing over the decision I knew I had to make, I finally reached the inescapable conclusion: I had to follow God, whatever that might mean. I knelt down in my bedroom and I made a promise to God.

It sounds ridiculously melodramatic to tell the story now, and I hesitated to put it in print. But that prayer was a turning point in my life, and that night still stands out to me as one of the most important nights of my life.

Dear God, I prayed, *I don't want to be celibate. I don't want to be alone. I want to fall in love with someone and spend my life with that person. But even more than that, I want to serve You. And if Your will is for me to be celibate my entire life, I will do it. Please show me what You want for my life, and help me to do Your will, whatever it is.*

I prayed and prayed that night. And God heard me.

It would be wonderful to say that God spoke to me in an audible voice that night and gave me a direct revelation about what to do. It would make a terrific story. However, that's not what happened. Instead, I felt a wave of peace rush over me. For the first time since beginning my journey, I knew things were going to be okay. Deep down in my spirit, something told me that I wasn't going to get the answers I wanted right away, but that they would come in time, as long as I kept trusting the Holy Spirit.

Whatever the future might hold, I was committed to endure whatever God called me to. And God was going to be with me.

The church, however, was another matter.

CHAPTER 8

SOUTH PARK CHRISTIANS

In an episode from the first season of the controversial animated series *South Park*, young Stan discovers that his dog Sparky is gay and decides he just needs good training.

"Sit, Sparky," he commands. The dog sits.

"Good boy. Now shake." The dog lifts his paw, and Stan shakes it.

"Good boy. Now...don't be gay! Don't be gay, Spark; don't be gay!"

Sparky only cocks his head, confused.

"Did it work?" Stan's friend Kyle asks.

The punch line goes to wisecracking Cartman: "He still looks pretty gay to me."

As I opened up about my struggles to the Christians in my life, I started feeling a lot like Sparky. When many Christians found out I was gay, their only response was to shout uselessly, "Don't be gay! Don't be gay, Justin; don't be gay!"

Yes, but I am gay. So what do I do now?

"Don't be gay!"

But how? What if those programs don't work? What if God doesn't change me? What if I'm like this for a really long time, or forever? How do I live my life today, *as a gay Christian who wants to follow Jesus?*

"Don't be gay!"

Sure, the ex-gay world was like a bizarre Wonderland, but at least people there understood that I hadn't *chosen* to be attracted to guys. They knew what it was like, because they had the same attractions I did, and they didn't blame me for what I felt. My experiences with the rest of the Christian world were very different. The Christians I knew typically assumed it was all a matter of choice, so admitting the truth about my feelings only subjected me to ostracism, misunderstandings, and the brand of "unrepentant sinner." And that was even while I was trying to become straight. I dared not admit to most Christians that I was thinking of giving up on ex-gay therapy.

I tried to break the news as gently as possible to my parents. They still had their hearts set on seeing me become straight. They were convinced that this "gay" thing was an obstacle that would keep me from ever having a normal, happy life, not to mention fulfilling my dream of doing Christian ministry work. They knew a lot of people wouldn't understand, especially in the church. And they were afraid for me.

When I told them I wasn't going to actively pursue an ex-gay path anymore, their concern for me morphed into a series of arguments about my future. They were afraid I was throwing away my life. I said I didn't *want* the life I saw in those groups. They said I was giving up on God, and that I needed to hold out hope. I countered that I was still open to what God wanted to do in my life, but that I wasn't going to spend my whole life waiting for something that might not even be God's plan for me.

For years I had been praying for God to change my feelings and make me straight. Now I had started praying for God's will to be done, whatever that was. Ever since, I had been feeling more and more strongly that the "ex-gay" thing just wasn't it. God had something else in mind for me.

Now if I could just convince anyone else that I hadn't suddenly become a heretic. Until then, I was back to feeling all alone, misunderstood by the very church I loved so much.

"Don't be gay, Justin! Don't be gay!"

Eager for the advice of a mature Christian leader, I set up a meeting with one of the pastors of my Southern Baptist church back home. This particular pastor was a longtime family friend and someone I deeply respected. If anyone would hear my story, I knew he would.

On the day of our meeting, he brought me into his office and listened intently as I poured out my frustrations. I told him how my self-discovery had rocked my world. I told him how I had tried for years to rid myself of these feelings, and that they weren't going away. I told him that I felt the word "gay" best described my situation, but that I was still celibate and seeking God's guidance on what to do next. I told him that the "ex-gay" thing didn't seem to work.

When I was done talking, he looked thoughtful. I asked him what advice he could offer me. He had been to seminary and counseled many people through difficult times in their lives. What should I do?

"Well, Justin," he responded, sitting back in his chair, "I want you to know that as long as you stay celibate and don't enter into a sexual relationship with another man, you are welcome to continue worshiping here as part of the congregation. So I don't want you to worry about that."

I looked back at him, stunned. It had never even crossed my mind to worry about that.

"Of course," he added, almost as an afterthought, "if you did enter a relationship, we'd have to ask you to leave. But that's the same way we would respond to, say, a heterosexual man in an adulterous relationship."

He said more things after that, but I didn't hear them. Suddenly, all I could think about was whether I might someday be kicked out of the church that had been my spiritual home for almost my entire life. Until that moment, I'd never thought of that. Why would I? I wasn't an unrepentant sinner. I was trying my best to live the way God wanted me to, and to be honest about feelings I didn't want or ask for.

In my pastor's defense, he was surely trying to be compassionate. He wasn't trying to threaten me; he was trying to explain church policy. His church, like many others, taught that people living in sexual sin should be asked to leave the church as a form of discipline. (More on this in Chapter 15, "The Way Forward.") I'm sure his intent was to reassure me that he didn't view my feelings themselves as a sexual sin and that he thought I was doing the right thing by staying celibate.

But I hadn't come to him with concerns about being kicked out of the congregation. I had come to him for understanding, compassion, and advice about what to do. I was scared about the future, not knowing if this meant I'd have to be alone for the rest of my life, and I was worried about what my fellow Christians would think of me. And in that frame of mind, all I heard from him was, "We'll allow you to stay...for now. Just make sure you don't do anything that might change that."

That hurt.

Before I left, he encouraged me to reconsider the ex-gay ministries.

Other Christians went further in their attempts to help, but the help they thought they were providing wasn't always the help I needed. One of my friends, after hearing I was gay, told her mom. Her mom contacted Focus on the Family. Focus then sent me a pack of resources promoting the same ex-gay groups I already knew didn't work, featuring testimonies from many of the same people I already knew weren't really straight.

Then there was another very well-intentioned Christian acquaintance of mine. When I told him I was gay, he grew concerned and promised to do all he could to help. Days later, he came to me with a brown paper bag and a serious look on his face.

"Listen," he said, "I would normally really frown on this, but I care about you, and desperate times call for desperate measures."

He handed me the bag, and I opened it up. Inside was a *Playboy* magazine.

"I thought maybe this would help awaken your natural desires," he said.

"It doesn't work like that," I said.

"Just promise me you'll try it," he urged.

Not wanting to argue with him, I relented and said I would. After he was gone, I leafed through the pictures of naked, buxom women. It was my first real exposure to pornography, and it made me feel dirty.

And for the women? Nothing. Not even the slightest bit of arousal or attraction. Only revulsion and self-loathing from the sleaziness of it all. The experience made me feel sick to my stomach.

Not all Christians were so charitable. I tried sharing my story with a handful of close Christian friends, but most of them responded by condemning my feelings as sinful and telling me that if I would only give my life over to Jesus, I wouldn't feel that way anymore.

"But I have given my life to Jesus," I'd say. "And I recommit myself every day."

"If you really had faith and trusted Him," they'd counter, "God wouldn't allow you to be gay."

What could I possibly say to that?

"Don't be gay! Don't be gay, Justin; don't be gay!"

"Did it work?"

"He still looks pretty gay to me."

BANNED

I had only told a few people, but rumors about my sexuality were already spreading through my Christian circles on campus. Out of the blue, friends were asking me if the rumors were true and quoting the same Bible passages to me over and over. I tried to explain that I was celibate and that I wasn't violating the Leviticus prohibition of "lying with a man as with a woman," but it didn't make any difference. In their minds, gay was bad, and that was all there was to it.

Tired of being badgered and afraid that the rumors would follow me through any local Christian community, I turned to online Christian communities for fellowship.

Online, no one had to know I was gay. Sometimes, when I needed to unwind, I would hop on my computer and spend hours chatting away with other young Christians in my favorite Christian chat room. It was nice. In this one space, I could be just me—not the gay guy, or the gay Christian guy; just me, a Christian who loved Jesus.

I made a few friends in the chat room. Occasionally, as I got comfortable enough with someone, I'd reveal a few details about my personal life, but for the most part I enjoyed my anonymity. Everyone there knew me by a screen name, and that was the way I liked it. There was some irony, I thought, in the fact that to be known for myself, I had to hide part of myself and use a pseudonym.

One afternoon we were chatting away about some minor point of theology. I was just getting into the discussion when, without warning, the window closed and a message popped up on my screen:

YOU HAVE BEEN BANNED.

What? Surely that was a mistake. I tried to reenter the chat room but, sure enough, I had been kicked out and banned by one of the room moderators.

I sent a private message to the guy in charge.

"What happened?" I asked. "I just got kicked out, and now I can't get back in."

His response was only three words: "Are you gay?"

I was dumbfounded. How did he know? Who could have told him?

"Who said I was gay?" I asked, not answering the question.

"It doesn't matter. Are you gay?"

I briefly considered lying, telling him that it wasn't true and that someone had given him bad information. It would have been easy, but I couldn't do it. I had to be honest.

"Yes," I typed back, "but I wasn't saying anything about gay stuff in your chat room. I really am a committed Christian, and I'm not sexually active or anything." Maybe he would understand.

"We don't allow gay people in the chat. It's a Christian chat," came the reply.

"I'm a Christian," I said.

"We don't allow gay people in the chat," he repeated. "That's the rule."

I knew he wasn't trying to be mean; he just didn't understand. If I could help him understand, I was sure that would make the difference.

"I know you're really busy," I said, "but can I tell you my story to explain? I think if you knew how I got to this place, it might help."

"Sure," he said. At least he was willing to listen.

I told him my story, typing as quickly as I could and hoping he wouldn't close the chat window before I was done. I explained how I had grown up a committed Christian, how I had struggled for years with my feelings of attraction to other guys, how I had prayed desperately for God to take them away, and how I had kept myself sexually pure, never having been with a guy or a girl. I told him how I would be straight if I could, and how I only admitted to being "gay" because it was the honest truth; I was attracted to the same sex. I explained it all, and he listened to it all, occasionally asking a question or offering a "wow."

Maybe I was getting through.

At the end of my story, I asked him, "So if you were in my shoes, would you have done things differently?"

"I don't know," he said after some thought. "Maybe not."

"Well, now that you know the rest of the story, and know that I'm not trying to 'recruit' anybody or start any debates in the chat room, and that I really am pursuing God with my whole heart, is it okay if I come back in the chat?"

"Sorry," he said. "We don't allow gay people in the chat."

That was the last time I was allowed in my favorite Christian chat room.

JOB DOES THE JOB

I began to take comfort in the book of Job. It's a fascinating book, and it's one of those stories everyone thinks they know, but few know it as well as they think they do.

The story most people know goes something like this: God and Satan have a conversation in which God brags about Job's righteousness. Satan argues that Job wouldn't be so righteous if he had to endure suffering, so God allows Satan to take away Job's wealth, health, and children. As Job suffers from painful sores, having lost everything, his wife encourages him to curse God, but he remains faithful. In the end, God rewards his righteousness by blessing him with even more than he had at the start.

That's the story most people know. But that story takes up only three chapters out of a forty-two-chapter book. The other thirty-nine chapters center on what I think is the most important part of the story: the response of Job's friends.

Job's three friends appear to be good people who care about him. When they hear of his suffering, they come and sit with him for a week without saying a word. Unfortunately, then they open their mouths and screw it all up.

Over the course of thirty-nine chapters, they argue back and forth with Job, telling him that he needs to repent from his sin and turn to God, and that if he'll just do that, God will heal him and stop his suffering. The more Job insists that he *is* trusting God, the more they argue that that *can't* be the case, because God wouldn't let a righteous man suffer the way he's suffering. Clearly, they say, God must be punishing him for something, and it's only his own arrogance that's keeping him from acknowledging it. He insists that they're wrong, and they just use that as more evidence against him.

Some friends!

Obviously, these guys care about Job. They're not bad guys. They want to help. But their theology tells them that if God is just, then suffering must be evidence of God's discipline, because God wouldn't punish a good person for no reason. It seems like a logical argument. It's just that in this case, they happen to be completely wrong.

Job's friends make the mistake of putting their own theology ahead of the testimony of their friend. They get cocky about their religious beliefs (which seem to make perfect sense!) and fail to recognize that they are the ones—not Job—who need a lesson in humility. Instead of telling Job what God would or wouldn't allow to happen, they ought to simply take his word for what he's experiencing and offer him comfort and support, not lectures.

At the end of the story, Job is vindicated, and God rebukes Job's friends. If only things always worked out so neatly! But the story serves as an important reminder to all of us that sometimes, when people are hurting, they don't need our advice and theological theorizing as much as they need our understanding and comfort. As Proverbs 18:13 says, "To answer before listening—that is folly and shame" (TNIV).

When I had read the book of Job before, those thirty-nine chapters of dialogue with his friends had always seemed like a waste of space. Now, they became powerfully relevant. I found myself resonating strongly with Job's lament, "A despairing man should have the devotion of his friends, even though he forsakes the fear of the Almighty. But my brothers are as undependable as intermittent streams....Now you too have proved to be of no help; you see something dreadful and are afraid" (Job 6:14–15, 21).

My Christian friends, too, had proved to be of no help. My homosexuality was "something dreadful" to them, something they were afraid of, and the only way they knew to handle it was to tell me it would go away if I just trusted God. Nothing I said could convince them otherwise.

Bit by bit, I was learning a painful lesson. In this Christians-vs.-Gays culture, Christians weren't such great people to be around if you were gay. They might lecture you, talk down to you, or quote the Bible at you, but they weren't very likely to make you feel loved. Quite the opposite.

But all my close friends were Christians. I didn't have anyone else to talk to.

CAMPUS CHRISTIANS

I don't mean to suggest that every Christian was antagonistic. The trouble was, there were a lot who were, with the result that I always felt like I had to have my guard up in any Christian setting. I never knew when my very presence was going to turn into a controversial issue.

For a while, I was nervous about getting involved in any Christian group on campus for fear of being found out and becoming an object of scorn. Gradually, though, I ventured out, finally getting involved in a Bible study group meeting in my dorm.

The people in the group were nice, and they warmly welcomed me. They weren't connected to my usual social circles, so by the end of my first year in the group they still didn't know I was gay, and I still hadn't told them. Although the members of this group had become my friends, I had held them at arm's length emotionally. They had given me no reason not to trust them, but they were Christians, and unfortunately that was enough.

At the last meeting of the Bible study group, we had a time for sharing what God had been doing in our lives that year. As we went around the circle, I got tenser and tenser. *It's now or never,* I thought. After several silent prayers for courage, I took a deep breath and told them the truth—the real struggles I had been going through.

They all just sort of stared at me like they weren't quite sure what to say. A couple of the girls came over and hugged me, thanking me for sharing. The guys sort of nodded awkward affirmations but didn't say much.

No, it wasn't the enthusiastic support I wanted from the church, but it was something. One of the girls, Ronda, stayed afterward to encourage me. We became fast friends, and her Catholic boyfriend, Marc, ended up being my roommate the next year. They were my reminder that not all Christians were uncomfortable around gay people. Maybe it wasn't so simple as "Christians vs. Gays" after all. I wasn't the only one on the middle ground.

Encouraged by this, the next year I decided to join one of the larger campus-wide Christian groups, a group I'll call Campus Christian Fellowship, or CCF for short.

Being around a large group of Christians still made me nervous, but I wasn't going to let my faith wither. I needed something like this, and the previous year's Bible study had proven to me that it was possible to spend time in a group of serious Christians without ever having to get into a discussion of my sexuality. I just wouldn't say anything, and it was all going to be fine.

I managed to (mostly) calm my nerves enough to make it to their orientation meeting. I did my best to watch myself to make sure I didn't seem too gay; I was starting to realize that some people could tell by things like vocal inflection or careless mannerisms, and that had me paranoid. With my most masculine mannerisms and in my most masculine voice, I introduced myself to some of the many new faces around me. They welcomed me warmly and handed me a copy of the schedule for the year.

I looked over the folded yellow page. The event titles were the sorts of things I expected:

"September 5—Drawing near to God."

"September 26—Spurring one another on in Christ."

And then I saw it. "October 17—Homosexuality: Combining Compassion and Truth."

Oh, great.

Listed under the title was the name of a speaker who was coming from a ministry in another state. I didn't have to read any further to know it was an ex-gay ministry.

I went back to my dorm and looked up the speaker online. His name was Derek; he was apparently what ex-gays sometimes called an "ever-straight"—someone who was involved in ex-gay ministry but had never identified as gay or had any kind of same-sex attractions. In other words, he was just a straight guy who wanted to help gay people become straight like him.

Well, *this* was going to get interesting.

I was curious about Derek and his message. If he was going to come to my campus to talk to Christians about gay people, I wanted to know what he was going to say. Would he really offer them a message of compassion? Or was he just going to make things worse for people like me who wanted to tell the truth?

I sent Derek an email asking for more information on his ministry. Since he was with an ex-gay ministry, I already assumed he believed that gay relationships were sinful and that some kind of change was possible. That much was a given. What I wanted to know was whether he could at least agree that there's a difference between *behavior* and *orientation*, and that I wasn't sinning by simply being *attracted* to guys—something I didn't choose and couldn't control.

I asked him this question point-blank. His response surprised me. In a verbose, unnecessarily convoluted email, he danced all around the subject at hand. "Bottom line," he said, "we'd say the whole behavior/orientation distinction is bogus and in real life actually detrimental to folks who buy into it."

Bogus? In what way? I wrote him back for clarification, explaining more of my situation and why it was so important to me for Christians to understand the difference. Even if they condemned gay sex, I didn't want them to condemn me for attractions I wasn't even acting on. After all, those attractions might be *temptations* to sin, but temptation isn't sin itself.

In his reply, he disagreed. Some kinds of attractions are inherently sinful, he said, even if we didn't choose to experience them and never give in to them. To say otherwise was a "biblically unsubstantiated assumption," he claimed, arguing that the primary reason people care about distinguishing behavior from orientation is for "self-justification." After all, he said, although "you would like to think that your attraction, because you didn't consciously or deliberately choose it…is not something that you have any responsibility for," it was really like a chain smoker: "Would the guy in the iron lung because he spent all his life smoking say he chose his emphysema?"

I was nothing short of astounded by this conversation. He wasn't just saying that I should try to become straight. He was saying it was *my fault* I was attracted to guys; that I had somehow made it happen; that even if I fought those temptations with every ounce of my being, never lusted in my heart, and never had any kind of sexual or romantic relationship for the rest of my life, I was still sinning just by admitting I was gay—something he acknowledged I might never be able to change.

What sort of messed-up theology was that? And if *that* was to be the church's message to gay people—"Hey, we know you didn't choose to feel this way, but since you do, you're now in perpetual sin regardless of how you live or what you do"—where was the motivation even to try to live holy lives at all?

And *this* was the guy who was about to come to campus to tell hundreds of Christians about gay people. This wasn't going to make anything better—not for those Christians, not for me, and not for any other gay people they encountered in their lives. It was only going to make things a whole lot worse.

I considered that the CCF leaders were probably unaware of the details of Derek's theology. I was sure they'd never intentionally invite someone who would condemn people just because of their temptations. Most likely, I thought, they had invited him because he represented an ex-gay ministry, and, like many Christians, they thought ex-gay ministries were the most loving form of ministry Christians could offer to gay people. I disagreed with them about that, but it was an understandable belief.

I envisioned the potential blowup on campus when the gay community found out about this guy coming to speak. I knew it could do permanent damage to any future relationship between gays and Christians on campus, a relationship I was hoping, somehow, someday, to be part of building. I worried, too, about the impact a speaker like this might have on any other closeted gay Christians in CCF. I couldn't be the only one, and if there were others, some of them might be struggling even more than I had been. If they were feeling alone, having someone use the Bible to preach at them and blame them was the last thing they needed.

Maybe if I just talk to the CCF leaders, I thought, *I can help avert disaster.*

◆

The next week, I stayed late after the Campus Christian Fellowship meeting, watching for an opportunity to talk to Warren and Claire, a married couple who served as the paid staff leaders of the group. They seemed friendly, so I decided to take my concerns to them. After the meeting, I spotted Claire with a free moment, so I approached her.

"Hi, Claire!" I said, my hand outstretched. "I'm Justin Lee. I'm new, but I'm really excited to be involved."

"Nice to meet you, Justin," she said with a smile.

"Can we talk?" I asked.

"Sure," she said.

I glanced around at all the people. "Maybe someplace a little more private?" I ventured.

"Of course. How about over here?" She motioned to me, and we stepped into a quieter adjoining room.

I wasn't sure how to start. "Um, so I was looking at the schedule for this year—"

"Uh-huh..."

"And I noticed that there's an event coming up about homosexuality, with a speaker from out of town."

"Right..."

I realized I was sweating. "Well, I guess I should explain. I'm a committed Christian, but I'm also gay." Her brow furrowed at this, but I kept talking. "I'm celibate, but I'm attracted to the same sex. I didn't choose to be. I don't know why I am. But it's true."

She fidgeted uncomfortably but didn't say anything. I continued. "Anyway, I looked up this guy who is supposed to come speak, and I'm concerned about some of the things he says. He seems to believe that just being tempted like I am makes you a sinner, and I'm not sure that's the message you really want to send....Is it?"

She was frowning now. She took a deep breath before responding. "You would have to talk to Mandy about that," she said flatly. "She's the one who recommended him."

"Mandy?" I asked.

Claire explained that Mandy was another leader in the group and a personal friend of Derek's. As she told me how to get in touch with Mandy, I became aware that her manner had changed noticeably. She was frowning at me with her arms folded in front of her. Her voice had become a low monotone. Suddenly it seemed that she had a very pressing need to be somewhere else.

I contacted Mandy after the meeting, but she was out of town. She promised to meet with me at some point before the speaker came.

After Claire's somewhat icy response to my question, I was nervous about going back to CCF the next week, but something pushed me to do it anyway.

It seemed divinely inspired when Warren, Claire's husband and co-leader of CCF, made his way over to me during the meeting and invited me to have lunch with him the next day.

"I'd love a chance to sit down and chat with you," he said. "It would be great to just get to know you and talk a little over lunch."

And so the next day there we were, sitting in a quiet section of one of the campus dining rooms. As I ate, he peppered me with questions. "How's life?" "How are your classes going?" "What else is new?"

It was nice to have a leader of the Campus Christian Fellowship take an interest in me. I was sure his wife had told him by now that I was gay, so that made this the first time a Christian leader, knowing

I was gay, had taken an interest in me for me and not as a pretense for preaching at me about my sexuality. It felt good.

Then, without warning, Warren pulled out a big, thick Bible and dropped it on the table with a thud. "Justin," he said, his tone suddenly serious, "I'd like to hear your thoughts on some Bible passages."

Ah. So this was it.

He had opened the Bible and was thumbing through the pages. "Here," he said, turning the Bible so I could see it. "Leviticus 18:22 says, 'Do not lie with a man as with a woman.' How do you respond to a passage like that?"

I didn't even need to look. By now I knew the passage by heart. "I'm not lying with anybody," I tried to explain. "When I say I'm gay, that's not a statement on my sexual behaviors; it's just being honest about what I feel. And besides—"

But he wasn't listening; he was already thumbing to the next page he had marked.

"First Corinthians 6:9," he said, interrupting. "It says homosexuals won't inherit the Kingdom of God."

"It says 'homosexual *offenders*,'" I pointed out. "Whoever they were, they were at least *doing* something. I'm not doing anything."

He didn't acknowledge the comment. "When God created humanity, he created Adam and Eve," he said, his voice growing in intensity. "The Bible says a man will leave his parents and cleave unto his *wife*. It doesn't say anything about homosexual partners. It's clear God designed men and women for each other. Men and men aren't designed to fit together the same way."

So much for Warren wanting to know my opinions. None of this was about me at all. It was about Warren preaching against the sin of homosexuality. By the end of lunch, I knew exactly where he stood. He still didn't know the first thing about me.

◆

Mandy contacted me shortly thereafter to let me know she was back in town and free to meet about the upcoming event. I shared my story and concerns with her, but while she was warmer than Warren and Claire had been, she ultimately agreed with Derek. She said that being gay was sinful even if I wasn't acting on my feelings, and she pushed me to go back to ex-gay therapy. She also gave me a small booklet about homosexuality. They were going to pass these out at the event when Derek came to speak, she said.

Back in my dorm, I looked over the booklet. It not only argued that gays could become straight; it also perpetuated a number of ugly stereotypes about gay people, suggesting that they were sex fiends and pedophiles, obsessed with kinky sex and virtually incapable of monogamy. This wasn't the kind of message a Christian group should be sending during a talk billed as "combining compassion and truth." Real compassion would mean teaching people how to be more sensitive to the needs of the gay people they encounter and helping them understand our struggles better. This was just the same "Don't be gay!" message I had been hearing all along, supplemented by misleading and unfair characterizations. It was heartbreaking.

I took the booklet to Claire before Derek's talk. In my gentlest, most conciliatory tone, I pointed out my concerns and shared my worries with her about the impact of a Christian group's passing out a booklet like this. "Please," I said, "I'm begging you, don't pass this out. It would only make other people like me feel unwelcome."

She sighed. Reluctantly, she agreed not to pass them out—on one condition.

"Justin," she said, quietly and slowly in that same low monotone, "I don't want you to feel unwelcome here at CCF. We love you and we want you to be able to come and worship with us and explore

God's Word with us. But," she said, placing a hand on my arm, "the one thing I need from you is for you to respect our views about homosexuality, and leave your own agenda at home."

I stared back at her, shocked and unsure what to say in response. She patted my arm, gave a faint smile, and walked away without another word.

Back in my dorm room that night, her comments burned themselves into my brain. My *agenda*? No one had ever accused me of having an "agenda" before. The only "agenda" I knew I had was my day planner, and although I was certainly happy to leave that at home, I was pretty sure that wasn't the one she was talking about.

I tried to make jokes about it to cheer myself up, but I felt only an overwhelming sadness.

It was official. God Boy was now the heretic.

CHAPTER 9

THE POISONED YEAST

It's easy to sit in judgment of Warren and Claire.

Yes, they should have taken more time to listen before talking. But in some respects they and the many others like them are victims too. They are victims of decades of misinformation that has been perpetuated in certain Christian circles.

These Christians are not bad people. I knew from years of growing up in an evangelical church that Christians could be among the most giving, loving, compassionate people in the world. The Christians I knew were generous with their time and their money. They were quick to sacrifice of themselves to help anyone they knew in need. If they found out that a neighbor or friend had experienced a tragedy, they were the first to call and offer to bring food or babysit or simply be a shoulder to cry on. The Christians I knew were flawed, yes, as all of us are; but they truly did live their lives as evidence of their belief in a loving God who wants us all to love each other.

It was hard for me to square my experience of Christians *before* coming out with my experience of Christians *after* coming out. My interactions with Warren, Claire, and those like them felt anything but loving. If this had been my first exposure to Christianity, I would have wanted nothing to do with it.

So why the discrepancy?

Part of it, I believe, is simply that human beings are flawed, Christians included. Warren and Claire were uncomfortable about the subject of homosexuality, and it showed in their interactions with me. But I think the biggest factor is the amount of misinformation about gays that people like Warren and Claire have been exposed to.

Misinformation is a powerful force. In his book *The 7 Habits of Highly Effective People*, Stephen Covey illustrates the concept of paradigm shifts with a story about an experience he had on a New York subway:

> People were sitting quietly—some reading newspapers, some lost in thought, some resting with their eyes closed. It was a calm, peaceful scene.
>
> Then suddenly, a man and his children entered the subway car. The children were so loud and rambunctious that instantly the whole climate changed.
>
> The man sat down next to me and closed his eyes, apparently oblivious to the situation. The children were yelling back and forth, throwing things, even grabbing people's papers. It was very disturbing. And yet, the man sitting next to me did nothing.
>
> It was difficult not to feel irritated. I could not believe that he could be so insensitive as to let his children run wild like that and do nothing about it, taking no responsibility at all. It was easy to see that everyone else on the subway felt irritated, too. So finally, with what I felt was unusual patience and re-

straint, I turned to him and said, "Sir, your children are really disturbing a lot of people. I wonder if you couldn't control them a little more?"

The man lifted his gaze as if to come to a consciousness of the situation for the first time and said softly, "Oh, you're right. I guess I should do something about it. We just came from the hospital where their mother died about an hour ago. I don't know what to think, and I guess they don't know how to handle it either."

Can you imagine what I felt at that moment? My paradigm shifted.[1]

Covey's story is a powerful example of how a little information can alter our entire understanding of a situation. Now imagine things from the other side. Suppose you knew, and assumed that Covey knew, this man's situation already. Wouldn't Covey's irritated request for the man to control his children, however restrained he might have intended to be, come across as incredibly insensitive and rude? I would be tempted to think of him as rather a jerk for saying something like that.

All of us have the potential to be jerks, or worse, if we are operating based on faulty information. If I see a thief getting away and I run out and tackle him, I'm a hero. If he turns out to be just an innocent man going for a jog, I'm not only a jerk; I'm guilty of assault! So it is that actions intended to be loving can be anything but loving if someone is acting on misinformation.

This is especially true in situations where one person sees danger and another person doesn't. Suppose I discover that the building is on fire but you don't believe me when I tell you. If I love you, I'd pull you out of the building kicking and screaming rather than let you burn to death. Sure, you might be ticked at me in the moment, but I'd be saving your life. Once you realized the real danger you had been in, you'd be grateful I ignored your protests, right?

Of course, if I was wrong about the fire, then I've just become the deranged nutcase who forcibly dragged you outside for no reason at all.

Warren and Claire were trying to save me, thinking they knew something I didn't. They thought, as I had thought years before, that they understood this subject and that they had answers I lacked. They had been taught, as my parents had and my Christian friends had, that being gay would only lead to misery and separation from God, and that I could avoid that fate by choosing to become straight.

THE ONLY GAY PERSON IN THE ROOM

Our Campus Christian Fellowship had an affiliation with a larger, national Christian organization that held regional conferences for Christian college students. I had already decided to attend the regional conference with my CCF friends before learning that the theme of this year's conference was sexuality.

Great.

Included in the weekend's events was a class promising the "truth" about homosexuality, taught by an ex-gay leader named Mark.

Speaking to a packed room of mostly straight evangelical Christian college students, Mark explained to us all that "there's hope for the homosexual." However, he warned, some homosexuals would claim that they couldn't change. "They'll tell you that they're 'born this way,' that it's biological," he said. "But that has never been proven."

Mark spent most of his workshop time trying to disprove any biological link to sexual orientation. He listed several famous studies that had suggested such a link, such as an early study that had shown brain differences between gay and straight men, and another that had suggested a possible genetic influence. He then picked each study apart for the audience, showing how each left unanswered questions.

By now, I had already read all of these studies and many others, and I knew he was right on most of his facts. But I also knew that in many cases, the study authors themselves had raised the questions that he was now using to discredit them, and that none of these researchers had claimed their studies proved anything about the cause of homosexuality, only that they provided more data to help other researchers get closer to the answer. A few times, Mark got something wrong or left out an important detail and I wanted to say something, but I held my tongue. This was his show, not mine.

Mark concluded his presentation with a brief explanation of the father/mother theory I had heard so many times by now. This, he insisted, was the true origin of homosexual feelings.

When Mark opened the floor for Q&A, I already knew what I wanted to ask.

"I have two questions," I said, when he called on me.

"Sure, go right ahead," he said.

"Well, you said in your presentation that we should reject the biological theories, because there's no conclusive proof that there's a biological link."

"That's right."

"But then you told us that it's really because of distant fathers and overbearing mothers. Is there any conclusive proof of that?"

He looked at me like a deer caught in headlights. I suddenly felt bad for asking the question. He looked genuinely shocked, like no one had ever asked him that before.

"No," he said simply.

I swallowed. I hadn't meant to embarrass him. I wanted to make a point, but I hadn't really expected him to concede it. I realized I'd caught him off guard, and I really didn't want to be a jerk. I just wanted the truth to come out. That was all.

I softened my tone as I asked my next question.

"Well, my other question was, Is there any other possible expla-nation for why someone might be gay? Because—" Suddenly I was nervous. The room was full of conservative Christians, and every eye in the room was on me. I was about to come out to all of them. "Because I'm gay," I continued. "I didn't want to be, and I didn't choose to be, but my whole life I've only been attracted to guys, not girls. And I didn't have a distant father or an overbearing mother."

"Oh yes, there can be other reasons!" he exclaimed, seemingly happy for the question. Where other ex-gays had insisted on Bieber's theory as the only explanation, Mark didn't mind theoriz-ing about other causes at all…as long as they weren't biological.

"Sometimes," he said pointedly, "it's a matter of sexual abuse, for instance."

"Well, I wasn't abused," I replied.

"Sometimes it's something else," he said, unfazed. "Like maybe you were separated from your parents as a child?" He looked at me expectantly.

"No, I'm pretty sure that never happened."

"Maybe you were on an incubator as a baby."

I shook my head.

"Or you could have been adopted."

I shook my head again.

He continued to rattle off suggestions until I stopped him.

"Here's what bothers me," I said. "I'm willing to bet that if we took a poll of this room right now, and asked anyone to raise their hand if they had a distant father, or an absent father, or an overpro-tective mother, or were adopted, or sexually abused, or were on an incubator, or any of these other things, almost every hand in here would be up for at least one of those—except mine! None of them applied to me, and as far as I know, *I'm the only gay person in the room!* At some point, it seems like you're just throwing everything at the wall to see what sticks, and you're not really explaining anything at all, because this stuff could apply to anyone."

Mark didn't seem to get my point. "Well, if I could sit down with you and talk to you for long enough, I could figure out what caused it for you!" he said.

"If you really want to, I'd be happy to," I replied, curious to see where this would go.

"Meet me after this session and I'll figure it out," he shot back. I had become his new challenge.

After the session was lunch. Mark invited me to sit at a private table with him. As we ate, he grilled me on every aspect of my childhood. Every detail was a potential cause of my gay feelings. At one point, he asked which denomination I'd grown up in.

"Southern Baptist," I told him.

"Well that could be it, then," he said, "because a Baptist church probably didn't give you opportunities for artistic expression, and if you were an artistic child, that might have created a form of defensive detachment."

I tried not to laugh. I thought about how my Southern Baptist friends would respond to the suggestion that their entire denomination was making people gay. Even Mark didn't seem to buy that one, in spite of the fact that he had come up with it.

He was most interested, though, in trying to find something that had made my childhood imperfect. I was a rarity, a happy kid raised in a two-parent Christian home by his biological mother and father, with no divorce, adoption, abuse, or trauma, having plenty of one-on-one time with his father, bonding well with both parents—I was a minority within a minority, growing up in the kind of environment few children are privileged enough to experience. And that was driving him crazy.

Finally, after his long series of questions had failed to turn up anything he could blame, he asked in exasperation, "Wasn't there *anything* unusual in your childhood? Anything at all?"

I racked my brain to think of what might have been unusual. In many ways, the most unusual thing about my upbringing had been how wonderfully absent of dysfunctional elements it had been.

There was one thing that was out of the ordinary. I have a hereditary condition called alopecia areata, which causes unpredictable hair loss. Although many people have never heard of it, it's a surprisingly common disorder, affecting over 4 million people in the United States alone, most often developing in childhood. As a kid, I lost my hair a few times, though it always grew back. Today, I just keep my head shaved.

I mentioned this to Mark as the only unusual thing I could think of.

"Aha!" he shouted, pointing an accusing finger. "You lied to me!"

I was perplexed. "Lied to you?"

"Yes, you told me that you had an idyllic childhood. And losing your hair was clearly a traumatic experience."

"Whoa. First of all," I corrected, "I never said my childhood was 'idyllic.' I said it was happy, and it was. I was happy. I'm sure my childhood wasn't perfect; nobody's childhood is perfect. But if we have to live perfect childhoods in order to come out straight, then how is anybody straight? The truth is, I was very happy. And, secondly, as obvious as it might seem to you that losing my hair must have been traumatic, it honestly wasn't."

That was true. I was only four when I lost my hair, too young to care about what my hair looked like. Have you ever seen a four-year-old boy look in the mirror and worry about his hair?

My parents had learned everything they could about alopecia before I even knew I was different from anybody, and they always had the right attitude about it. My dad used to say, "Everybody's got problems. Some kids lose their hair due to chemotherapy. Aren't you glad the worst thing in your life is that you've just lost your hair? And hey, you don't have to wash it, or comb it, or blow it dry..."

As a kid, I learned all about the condition, and was happy to in-form any curious classmates. It was never an issue for my friends. And, sure, I got teased sometimes. So did the kids with glasses or freckles, and the ones who were too tall, or too thin, or too fat, or too short.

Alopecia is traumatic for many children, especially for girls. But it was never a big deal to me. And of all the people I've met over the years who have the same condition that I do, I know only one who's gay.

I told Mark all of this, but he wouldn't listen.

"You're being defensive," he told me. "You're not willing to admit it, but this was the traumatic event that sent you down the path of homosexuality."

"But it really wasn't traumatic!" I protested. "I think I would know."

"You're just not willing to face how traumatic it really was," he insisted.

What was I supposed to say to that?

"Justin," he said, leaning across the table, "if you want me to, I can help you. I've found freedom, and you can find it too. But you have to stop being so defensive."

I wondered what he considered "freedom." He had shared earlier that his continuing temptations were so strong, he couldn't trust himself to have the internet or cable TV in his home, for fear of "surfing for naked bodies." But I wasn't surfing for porn, and I wasn't sexually active. What exactly did he think I was going to gain by becoming more like him?

It didn't really matter to me what Mark thought of me. I would likely never see him again, and I was getting used to the realization that there would always be people looking down on me.

It was Mark's influence that bothered me. No matter what I said, Mark was going to keep going to groups like this one and telling thousands upon thousands of Christians that being gay was caused by faulty parenting, that it only led to misery, and that anyone who wanted to become straight could. They would believe him, because he said he'd been there. And they would pass those beliefs on to their children and other Christians, who would act upon that misinformation whenever they encountered gay people.

Jesus understood that one of the biggest threats to the church was the potential for this new movement he was starting to be derailed by false teachings and misinformation that could infect the church like a cancer.

"Be on your guard against the yeast of the Pharisees and Sadducees," he said (Matthew 16:6), referring to religious teachers of the day who claimed to serve God but whose legalism and false teachings had the potential to distort the good work God's people were doing.

Yeast is a common biblical symbol for an idea that permeates an entity or group and alters it, for good or for evil. As the apostle Paul points out, "A little yeast works through the whole batch of dough" (Galatians 5:9).

A little bit of misinformation, like yeast or poison, can work its way through the entire church, contaminating an important force for good in the world and turning it into something doing damage. With the church contaminated by misinformation, people feel that they have two choices: either accept the church and the misinformation along with it, or reject the whole thing.

The third option? Fight the misinformation.

In the words of author Bruce Bawer: "They [some gay people] think that their enemy is conscious oppression and that their salvation lies in the amassing of power, when in fact their enemy is ignorance and their salvation lies in increased understanding."[2]

Christianity isn't the problem. The problem is the yeast.

CHAPTER 10

❖

FAITH ASSASSINS

In the second *X-Men* film, the evil William Stryker plots to kill all the mutants of the world. Realizing he's no match for their superpowers, he finds a way instead to poison and control their minds, causing them to use their powers to fight *for* him instead of against him.

It's a popular strategy for fictional villains. Nearly every cartoon I watched as a kid had at least one episode in which the heroes were somehow hypnotized or brainwashed into doing their enemies' bidding. Often, this comes in the form of something that removes the heroes' free will—*The Manchurian Candidate*'s subconsciously conditioned sleeper agent who doesn't know he's an assassin, for instance, or *Star Trek*'s Captain Picard being turned into a robotic Borg drone.

Other times, the plot is craftier. In one action thriller, the hero races across town, dodging roadblocks and breaking laws, all in pursuit of a van he believes is carrying a bomb. Only after arriving at his destination does he realize in horror that he's been tricked. In the film's shocking conclusion, we learn that the van he was following was clean; the bomb was in *his* car, and he's just brought it to the very destination the villains wanted.

A good twist ending, like a good magic trick, depends on misdirection. While you're watching one hand, the magician is doing something with the other hand. While you're focused on the van, the villains are planting the bomb in the car. And while so many of us in the church have been focused on the "threat" to our culture posed by homosexuality, we've missed the realization that the church in our culture is under attack—not by gays, but by Christians.

We Christians are the sleeper agents. The bomb is in *our* car. *We* have become the unwitting assassins of people's faith.

The Christians are killing Christianity.

A popular bumper sticker reads, "Lord, save us from your followers." People laugh at it because they know exactly what it means without having to ask. The reputation of Christianity in our society is poor because the reputation of Christians in our society is poor.

This is especially—but not only—true of those of us called *evangelical* Christians, a term (from the Greek for "good news") for a subset of the church that emphasizes the idea of a personal relationship with Jesus and salvation through his death and resurrection. Evangelical Christian author Philip Yancey writes:

> Recently I have been asking a question of strangers—for example, seatmates on an airplane—when I strike up a conversation. "When I say the words 'evangelical Christian' what comes to mind?" In reply, mostly I hear political descriptions: of strident pro-life activists, or gay-rights opponents, or proposals for censoring the Internet. I hear references to the Moral

Majority, an organization disbanded years ago. Not once—*not once*—have I heard a description redolent of grace. Apparently that is not the aroma Christians give off in the world.[1]

Political issues matter, from war to abortion to poverty to same-sex marriage. As Christians, we ought to care about these issues, because they affect people's lives. But Jesus was known for his compassion, not for his politics. The messiah people were expecting was a political leader; the Messiah they got was a suffering servant. If his followers are now known more for our politics than for our grace, something is wrong.

Sadly, that's not the only thing wrong. Our bad reputation extends far beyond our political views.

As a young man, I took a job waiting tables at a local chain restaurant. I soon discovered something very curious: *No one* wanted to wait tables on Sundays, even though most of the staff wasn't religious and I was one of the few who went to church.

"Sundays are the worst," one of the servers explained to me. "That's when the church crowd goes out to eat."

"What's wrong with the church crowd?" I asked.

"Oh, honey," she said. "They're usually the most demanding, and they're always the worst tippers. I guarantee you, if you see your table praying before the meal, you can mentally subtract a third from your tip."

Standing nearby, the manager cracked a smile. "They already gave at church," he said. "They don't have any money left."

In North Carolina, as in most states, servers work almost exclusively for tips. We were paid just over two dollars an hour, including time we spent setting up before the diners arrived and cleaning up after our shifts had ended. Waiting on tables where people sat for a long time and didn't leave much of a tip could mean that you didn't have enough money to pay your bills at the end of the week.

As much as I hated to admit it, it was true that the obviously

Christian tables—the ones where people prayed before the meal or where church or God seemed to be a big part of the discussion—were often the stingiest with their tips. Even worse, some of them would leave fake "money" as part of their tip—pieces of paper designed to look like high-value bills until you picked them up and realized they were tracts telling you about giving your life to Jesus. Why would anyone think that tricking and disappointing a broke food-service employee would be a good way of spreading the Christian good news? Not surprisingly, behavior like this only served to further convince my co-workers that they wanted nothing to do with Christianity. The devil himself couldn't have planned it any better.

Don't misunderstand me. I know that Christianity isn't about us at all. It's about Jesus. Our human failure to live up to what we believe doesn't make the gospel any less true. But as the old saying goes, we are the only "Jesus" most people will ever see. People inside *and* outside of the church judge Christianity by what they see in its practitioners.

I don't know why the Sunday morning churchgoers who ate at my restaurant were such poor tippers. There could be many reasons. People having drinks with friends on Friday or Saturday night were often the best tippers, and I'm sure alcohol played some part in loosening up their wallets. Statistics show that Christians as a group are actually incredibly generous with their money. But my restaurant co-workers weren't looking at statistics. They were looking at the people sitting in front of them, people who had no idea they were representing God in that moment, for better or worse. Experiences like these shape how Christianity is viewed by our culture far more than we realize. And if our reputation can be damaged by poor tipping, how much more can it be hurt by the perception that we are actively *hostile* to an entire group of people!

OUR OWN WORST ENEMY

Everyone makes mistakes, and there will always be times when Christians don't represent the faith well. That has been true throughout history. But it only takes one key ingredient to completely ruin the church's reputation: bad yeast.

As the yeast of misinformation about gay people has spread through the church, it has turned the church not only into the perceived enemy of gays, but into its own worst enemy as well.

Well-intentioned Christians, believing that being gay is a sinful choice or can be easily changed, speak and act accordingly, recommending ex-gay ministries and fighting against cultural acceptance of homosexuality. To those who know better, this comes across as hurtful and unkind. As the Christians fight harder for what they believe is the truth, following the van they mistakenly believe is a threat to us all, they honestly don't realize that *they're* the ones creating the conflict, dealing death blows to the church's image. From an outside perspective, our reputation just gets worse. Instead of Christians sometimes looking like jerks in spite of our faith, it now looks like we're jerks *because* of our faith. In the eyes of gay people and those who love them, Christianity itself has just become the threat.

Throughout history, one of the most compelling arguments for the truth of Christianity has always been the evidence of changed lives. We can't put God in a test tube. We don't hear a booming voice from the sky when we pray. We see God at work in the hearts and minds of believers whose lives have been changed by their encounter with Jesus Christ. That is what draws people to the church.

"A new command I give you," Jesus said to his followers. "Love one another. As I have loved you, so you must love one another. By this everyone will know that you are my disciples, if you love one another" (John 13:34–35 TNIV).

Sadly, that's no longer what we're known for. In a world where Christians are known as the biggest jerks, the "changed lives" argument no longer holds any sway. As science continues to explain previously unexplainable natural phenomena, our behavior is taking away one of the strongest reasons people have to believe.

We Christians can say Jesus changed our hearts, but if our reputation is that of uncompassionate culture warriors, why should they believe us? We can say that God is loving and merciful, but if the church isn't loving and merciful, why would we be in any sort of position to know that God is?

At its best, the church is something amazing and beautiful, caring for our neighbors with no regard for ourselves, serving the poor and disenfranchised, offering hope and comfort in times of tragedy. We are a family to those who have none and an arrow pointing to the One who loves us unconditionally and who forgives us over and over. When the early Christians talked about being "not of this world" (John 15:19; Romans 12:2), it was because they knew how hard it was to love their enemies and continue being generous in the midst of oppression and persecution. Who could say that about the American church today?

In some ways, I think, Christendom is better off when it must function as an oppressed minority. Christians who live under the threat of persecution have to put their lives on the line for their faith, and it strengthens them. The early Christians suffered and died to share the gospel. They gave all they had. They didn't have time to get comfortable and stingy and self-involved. In today's America, Christians are ostensibly the majority. Three quarters of Americans self-identify as Christians. Without that oppression, it's much easier for a sort of "cultural Christianity" to develop—one where people call themselves Christians, use Christian language, and so forth, but without really internalizing the gospel or actually having to put their lives on the line for what they say they believe. We as a church have become spiritually lazy, substituting aggressive culture-war tactics for the generous, self-sacrificing humility Jesus taught and modeled.

Cultural aggression is easier, and it allows us to think we're still "not of this world," even as we use worldly strategies to get our way.

As Jesus was being arrested, Peter drew his sword and cut off the high priest's servant's ear in an attempt to defend him. Jesus immediately rebuked him, saying, "Put your sword back in its place, for all who draw the sword will die by the sword" (Matthew 26:52). Jesus' way was never the way of aggression or the culture war, but sometimes we forget that, and the swords come out. We think we're defending the gospel. We don't realize we're actually attacking it.

A RECIPE FOR KILLING THE CHURCH

Our failure to live out the gospel doesn't only affect Christianity's reputation outside the church; the poisonous yeast is killing the church from within as well.

In the classical Greek myth of Jason and Medea, Jason is faced with the task of defeating an army of warriors much too strong for him. His clever strategy, suggested by Medea, is to throw a stone into the midst of the warriors without being seen. Not realizing that the stone came from outside their camp, the warriors angrily turn on each other, defeating themselves with minimal work on Jason's part.

It's a famous story with an important lesson. If you want to destroy a movement, sometimes the most effective way is by turning it against itself. Here's a simple recipe:

1. Pick two different but both critically important elements of the movement.
2. Convince members of the movement that these two elements are actually in opposition to one another.
3. Watch as people pick sides and destroy each other.
4. Finally, watch as the movement's reputation goes down the drain as a result.

Nowhere is this strategy proving as effective as in the modern American church.

So far, I've been speaking about the church as if it were nearly unified in its approach to homosexuality. In fact, that is not the case. Many Christians have been working for a more welcoming and compassionate church for years. Unfortunately, what has resulted is a major schism—a rift through the church dividing one denomination from another, splitting churches within the same denomination from each other, and even tearing apart individual congregations.

It often seems that there are two distinct groups calling themselves Christians. Each group looks at the other and sees its flaws, and in an effort to avoid making the same mistakes, it moves farther in the opposite direction. As a result, instead of learning from one another, the two groups just keep getting more and more polarized.

On one side are churches like the one I grew up in. They care deeply about following the Bible and teaching proper Christian doctrine. They emphasize the reality of their faith: For them, the Christian faith isn't just a set of moral ideas; it's a set of core teachings about Absolute Truth. It isn't just one of many paths to truth or peace; it *is* Truth. They emphasize that Jesus wasn't just a great moral teacher but was in fact the real, unique Son of God—the Creator of the universe in human form. For them, therefore, it matters what we believe about God, about Jesus, about heaven, about sin, about the Bible, and about every other major doctrinal point of the faith. Unfortunately, in their zeal for correct doctrine, many Christians on this side come across as preachy and condescending, putting legalistic adherence to certain Bible passages over listening to and loving people.

Only Christians on this side, for instance, would come up with a video game like Spiritual Warfare.

Spiritual Warfare was a video game I played as a kid. It was designed by a Christian video game company and was widely viewed as a rip-off of The Legend of Zelda, a popular game by

Nintendo. The look and feel of the games were virtually identical, but Spiritual Warfare had Christian themes in place of its predecessor's fantasy themes. In The Legend of Zelda, you're on a quest to save a princess; along the way, you collect various weapons and battle monsters. In Spiritual Warfare, your quest is against the powers of darkness. Rather than weapons, you collect the fruits of the Spirit—only they're actual fruits: bananas, apples, pomegranates, and the like. (Yes, really.)

It gets worse. Rather than monsters, your enemies are *the unsaved*. When you encounter them, you *throw the fruits of the Spirit at them*—or blow them up with "vials of God's wrath." Then they convert, dropping to their knees and vanishing instantly.

I could write a book about all the things wrong with that game. As hilarious as it is, it's also tragically reflective of the worst elements of many churches, treating non-Christians as obstacles or enemies, throwing the fruit of the Spirit *at* them and expecting them to repent, convert, and disappear.

That's not the gospel. It never has been.

It is the horror at this extreme that sends so many people—Christian and non-Christian alike—heading as fast as they can in the opposite direction. But in so doing, some of them have thrown the baby out with the bathwater, abandoning the idea that the Bible is in any way trustworthy, or that the core elements of Christianity—a personal God, the supernatural miracles of Jesus, the reality of an afterlife—are anything other than superstition. As these basic Christian concepts become linked in the popular mindset to ignorance and homophobia, even many churches are turning away from them, keeping the rituals of the faith but without any real belief that Jesus actually rose from the dead or that there's anything more for us after we die.

A few years ago, I was visiting a new church and heard a sermon about the feeding of the five thousand, the Bible story in which Jesus feeds over five thousand people with only a handful of loaves and fish. It is one of the most famous miracles of Jesus, used by the gospel writers as evidence that Jesus wasn't just a great teacher, but was indeed the supernatural Son of God.

The preacher read the passage and then, acknowledging that supernatural miracles are hard for modern Americans to swallow, suggested that the passage didn't have to refer to anything supernatural at all. Perhaps, he said, these five thousand people who claimed to have no food were actually hiding bits of food under their cloaks, afraid to bring it out in the midst of a hungry crowd. When Jesus began passing out the little bits of food he had, everyone else began bringing their food out too, so that there was enough for everyone with plenty left over. The real miracle, the pastor suggested, was that Jesus taught people to *share*.

But this is not at all what the gospel writers suggest. The texts make it clear that the incident was viewed as a supernatural event, not merely a lesson in generosity. If Jesus was able to rise from the dead, why would it be difficult for us to believe that he could multiply food? And if he was not able to rise from the dead—if that is simply a metaphor of some kind and not a real event—then what exactly is Christianity about, anyway?

The idea of Christianity without the supernatural—without the Resurrection—is not new. It was one of the earliest heresies of the church. In his letter to the Corinthians, the apostle Paul says:

> But if it is preached that Christ has been raised from the dead, how can some of you say that there is no resurrection of the dead? If there is no resurrection of the dead, then not even Christ has been raised. And if Christ has not been raised, our preaching is useless and so is your faith. More than that, we are then found to be false witnesses about God, for we have testified about God that he raised Christ from the dead. But he did not raise him if in fact the dead are not raised. For if the dead are not raised, then Christ has not been raised either. And if

Christ has not been raised, your faith is futile; you are still in your sins. Then those also who have fallen asleep in Christ are lost. If only for this life we have hope in Christ, we are to be pitied more than all others. (1 Corinthians 15:12–19 TNIV)

From the beginning, Christianity has made certain claims about Truth—about the nature of God and the universe, about life after death, about sin and repentance and grace. Unfortunately, some churches are now so worried about being arrogant and unbending like certain *other* Christians that they fail to stand for anything at all. They hang question marks over all the major doctrines of the faith or throw them out entirely. Bit by bit, they lose the things that set them apart as Christians.

The Canadian comedy troupe The Frantics has an old sketch about a church called Worshippers 'R' Us. The sketch opens with an energetic preacher who says:

Welcome, brothers and sisters, to Worshippers 'R' Us, the first church of *all* denominations! Please open your generic prayer books and pray along with me as you stand, sit, kneel, face Mecca, or dance.

The congregation dutifully chants along:

O large Person or Persons of whatever gender or branch of the animal kingdom, who did something great and is now some-place where we aren't, please forgive us for whatever You deem bad, and help us to do whatever strikes You as good, whether that be to work hard, eat no pork, or wage a holy war. Grant us whatever You tend to grant, unless You don't interfere with earthly concerns. Watch over us, or save us from evil, or let us find out for ourselves, or damn us randomly. Amen. Praise Al-lah. Have a nice day.

It's a comic exaggeration, but I've been to churches that felt not so different from this fictitious one. Fear of ever alienating anybody has nearly turned "doctrine" into a bad word for them. They put little to no faith in the Bible as a guide, implicitly conceding that it probably is a homophobic book after all. Meanwhile, their departure from mainstream Christianity in so many ways only further convinces other Christians and non-Christians that "real" Christians are anti-gay.

TASTES GREAT...LESS FILLING

In an old series of Miller Lite beer commercials, two beer drinkers (both Miller Lite fans, naturally) would break out into an argument or even a fistfight over whether the beer was preferred because it "tastes great" or is "less filling."

"Tastes great!" one would shout.

"Less filling!" the other would argue with equal enthusiasm.

The joke, of course, was that (according to Miller, at least) both of these things were true, and they didn't have to be at odds with each other at all. The comedy was all in the absurdity of watching two people on the *same team,* both preferring the same brand, fight it out for reasons that made no sense.

Sometimes, when I look at the church today, I feel like I'm living in that commercial.

"God's Truth!" one side shouts.

"More loving!" comes the response.

"God's Truth!"

"More loving!"

"God's Truth!"

"More loving!"

But there shouldn't be a clash between "God's Truth" and "more loving." In the Bible, Truth and Love are two sides of the same coin.

You can't have one without the other. God's Truth is all about God's Love for us and the Love we ought to have for one another. We are being untrue to that Truth if we treat people unlovingly. And we are missing out on the full extent of that Love if we try to divorce it from Ultimate Truth.

We Christians must work to repair this schism in the church. If the church is to survive much longer in our culture, it must teach and model the Christianity of Jesus—a faith that combines Truth and Love in the person of Jesus Christ, revealed to us in the Bible and lived out in the everyday lives of his followers.

That is what we say we believe. It's time we start acting like it.

CHAPTER 11

THE OTHER SIDE

You might think that the negative messages I heard from Christians would drive me away from Christianity. Indeed, many people I know walked away from the faith for that very reason. I couldn't do that. I had known God's presence in my life from a young age, and I couldn't turn my back on that.

Nor did those negative messages make me straight. I don't believe they've ever made anyone straight; all they've done is give people a reason to lie in order to fit in. I refused to lie.

What the messages did do was make me hate myself.

I had grown up in a sort of insulated bubble, with no exposure to openly gay people at all. In today's world, with admired, openly gay celebrities like Ellen DeGeneres and Neil Patrick Harris and popular TV shows like *Will & Grace* and *Glee,* it seems bizarre to imagine a world before "gay" was such a mainstream part of our culture. As a young person in the late 1990s, however, I had no concept of a happy, successful gay person. I had no gay role models. I didn't know anything about gay life.

The people I looked up to were my parents and various leaders in the church. Theirs was the life I wanted to imitate. Yet all of them were straight, and all of them looked down on homosexuality. It was hard for me to see my sexuality as anything other than an obstacle keeping me from getting where I wanted to go.

In his book *A Place at the Table*, gay author Bruce Bawer writes about being in a store and noticing a fifteen-year-old boy trying to work up the courage to reach for a gay newspaper:

> Standing there, he reached down to the foot-high counter, slipped out from under some other periodical a copy of a gay weekly called *New York Native*, and, trying to appear casual, opened it to the first inside page....
>
> As I stood there behind him, I looked over his shoulder at the pages of the *Native*. I don't remember the specific contents: there were, I suppose, the usual articles about AIDS research, gay bashings, and recent gay-rights advances and setbacks....What leapt out at me, and stayed in my mind for some time afterward, were other things: a photograph, probably accompanying a review of some cabaret act, of a man in drag; photographs of black-clad men in bondage, presumably in advertisements for leather bars and S&M equipment; and photographs of hunky, bare-chested young men, no doubt promoting "massages" and "escort services" and X-rated videotapes.
>
> These pictures irked me. The narrow, sex-obsessed image of gay life that they presented bore little resemblance to my life or to the lives of my gay friends—or, for that matter, to the lives of the vast majority of gay Americans. Yet this was the image proffered by the *Native* and other such magazines....That image had provided ammunition to gay-bashers, had helped to bolster the widely held view of gays as a mysteriously threatening Other, and had exacerbated the confusion of generations of

young men who, attempting to come to terms with their homosexuality, had stared bemusedly at the pictures in magazines
like the *Native* and said to themselves: "But this isn't *me*."[1]

I first read those words while sitting in my college library, trying to
find something to help me make sense of who I was. I felt like that
kid, looking at the only images I'd seen of gay life, and saying over
and over, "But this isn't *me!*"

I'd tried looking for gay people on the internet, but most of
what I'd come across was gay men looking for sex. I'd tried leafing
through gay magazines, but they seemed full of the same-sex equivalent of the sleazy, near-pornographic imagery I had always diligen-
tly avoided in the straight world. As a Christian, I wanted to live
a life focused on serving God and others, not egocentric carnality.
The images I was seeing of gay people weren't me. And if that was
what "gay" was, I didn't want to be it.

The trouble was, I already knew I was gay. This is what left me
feeling so torn. In rejecting those images of gay life, I thought I
had to become straight, driving me toward the ex-gay ministries.
But the ex-gay ministries clearly didn't work, so my honesty drove
me back toward admitting I was gay. This is why, even while admitting I was gay, I felt the need to constantly apologize or explain
myself; I didn't want to be associated with the kind of hedonistic,
sex-obsessed lifestyle that was my only image of gay people. I didn't
know where to find any other image.

Today, of course, there are plenty of other images of gay people,
and as more people come out, that will continue to change. Does
this mean, then, that stories like mine are a thing of the past, at least
in America? Not at all. In fact, it means that kids today are going
through this process much younger than I did. I've met many kids
from Christian backgrounds like mine who have realized they're gay
by twelve or thirteen years old. These kids have advantages I didn't,
but they also have frightening new challenges. By the time I was

asking the tough questions, I was in college and on my own. Gay kids today are going through the same struggles at an age when they are much more vulnerable to predators and bullies. They're also still completely dependent on their parents, some of whom may react very badly to learning the truth about their child. For the sake of these young people, it's vital that the church get a better understanding of this issue.

When Bawer's book came out, asserting that sex-laden images and stereotypes of gay culture were unfair and harmful to the millions of gay Americans who didn't fit the stereotypes, some took issue with his approach, arguing that he had gone to the opposite extreme and was demeaning gay people whose lives didn't fit within "mainstream society." Whatever the case, his words were exactly what I needed at that point in my life. Thanks to books like *A Place at the Table* and Mel White's *Stranger at the Gate: To Be Gay and Christian in America*, I realized that there was more to being gay than the images I had seen.

Bolstered by the knowledge that I wasn't alone, I set out to find other gay people I could relate to. I searched the internet for gay Christians, and after several fruitless attempts, I finally stumbled upon a gay Christian chat room. To my amazement, there were people in it. Real, live gay Christians.

Everyone in the chat room was significantly older than I was, but I didn't care. I nervously introduced myself, and a chorus of screen names happily welcomed me to the chat room. They seemed nice! Maybe they would have some answers for me.

I told these anonymous gay Christians my story, and they sympathized. Many of them had been rejected by their churches too. But here I discovered a major difference between them and me. While I was still wrestling with what my future would look like, they had already found their answer. They were all either in, or seeking, relationships with someone of the same sex.

This surprised and intrigued me. Everything I'd read in the Bible seemed to condemn homosexual relationships, so I was curious to know how this group of Christians had managed to reconcile their behavior with the Bible. If they had a good answer, it could change everything.

Unfortunately, they didn't have a good answer. They hardly had any answer at all. Years later, I would discover that there *were* gay Christians in relationships who had done a lot of deep thinking and study about what the Bible had to say and had thought-provoking biblical arguments to back up their conclusions. These, however, were not those Christians. When I asked them about the Bible passages that dealt with homosexuality, they largely dismissed my questions without real answers. Some of them chided me for even asking them, and a few of them accused me of being an ex-gay plant trying to disrupt their community. This environment felt just as anti-intellectual as the ex-gays, but on the other side.

I left the room feeling more discouraged and alone than ever. I had thought that if I could only meet other gay Christians, then we would have a lot in common and I would get the answers I so craved. As it turned out, it was going to take a lot more than that.

GAYS WHO COULDN'T SPELL

It didn't matter. I wanted more than internet support anyway. More and more, I found myself craving a real-world connection with others who knew what it was like to feel all of this. Chat rooms could be nice, but they were just words on a screen. I wanted to have friends in the flesh.

The campus directory listed a student group called GALBA. According to its official charter, GALBA stood for Gay, Lesbian, and

Bisexual Issues Awareness Group. I tried without success to figure out how to make the acronym fit. Apparently these gays couldn't spell.

GALBA didn't seem to do much, from what I could tell. They had no website, and I'd never seen a meeting advertised. But at least they existed! After some hesitation, I decided to look up the student president of the group and see if he had any answers for me. I sent him an email, and he agreed to meet with me at lunch in the campus cafeteria the next day. His name was Jules.

Jules could hardly have been more different from me. He was loud, boisterous, and self-assured. Everyone knew he was gay, and he was just fine with that. If an attractive guy walked by, he would turn his head to look—and if they caught him, so what? He didn't care. Jules's philosophy was that he was going to be himself, and if anyone had a problem with it, that was their problem.

Not me. I was a people-pleaser. I was shy. I was uncomfortable with my sexuality. And I was terrified to be seen sitting at the same table as the president of the campus gay student group. Not all of my friends knew I was gay yet, and I wasn't ready to tell them.

I furtively glanced over my shoulder as Jules happily chatted away about his plans for GALBA. Occasionally he would raise his voice enthusiastically or break into a good-natured guffaw, his laughter seeming to echo loudly off the walls and draw all eyes directly to our table. Over and over, I had to stifle the urge to beg him to quiet down.

Jules explained that the group had dwindled to almost nothing in recent years, and that at the moment, *he* was pretty much the entire group. He wanted to rebuild it, and he wanted my help in doing so. I wasn't sure I was ready for all that attention, but I told myself I couldn't be scared for the rest of my life. This was my chance to meet other gay kids on campus, and I intended to take it. I agreed to help—as long as I didn't have to be too publicly visible. He laughed.

The first GALBA meeting I attended consisted of only four people: Jules, a graduate student, the club's faculty adviser, and me. Even I knew we couldn't possibly be the only four gay people on the entire university campus. So where was everyone?

I asked Jules about this and he explained that although there were many other gay students on campus, a lot of them lived in the metaphorical closet. The environment on campus was overwhelmingly conservative and overwhelmingly Christian, with strong Baptist roots. Not surprisingly, many students opted to keep quiet rather than risk ostracism. Jules told me stories of students he knew in secret same-sex relationships, publicly pretending to be just friends or roommates while privately carrying on a romance. He told me, too, about methods some were using to arrange sexual trysts with strangers—from internet postings to messages scribbled in bathroom stalls. They'd meet for a secret sexual encounter, then return to their normal lives to pretend that they were straight.

This repulsed me. I couldn't imagine meeting anyone for a sexual encounter in a bathroom, and I was firmly against one-night stands. Once more I felt the cold stab of revulsion in the pit of my stomach. Was that all gay people were about? *But that isn't me!*

I had to remind myself that there were thousands of students on this campus. There had to be at least hundreds who were gay. Of those, Jules knew a few who were out and a few more who were secretly hooking up. So where was everyone else? At least a few of them, I thought, must be like me. If only they knew there was a place for them, whether for support or friendship or just solidarity.

"We've got to publicize this thing," I told Jules.

He agreed. Over the months that followed, Jules and I worked together to publicize GALBA. We put up signs, followed leads, and privately met with some of the low-profile gay students on campus.

"You know," Jules said to me one day as we discussed plans for the group, "next year I'm going to be a fifth-year senior, and I'm going to need help running the group. Would you like to be the vice president?"

I blinked at him for a moment. Vice president of the gay student group? But I was God Boy! What would people say? Even so, I knew he was right. If I wanted to see a support group for gay people, I was going to have to help build it myself. Right here, right now.

"Yes," I said. "Let's do it."

We did do it, and GALBA grew by leaps and bounds. With the help of other new members, we turned GALBA into a support group, force for change, and social outlet all rolled into one. People turned out for meetings, and I met many of the gay, lesbian, and bisexual students on campus.

I began to feel like I had two separate and incompatible identities: Christian Justin was a grown-up God Boy, active in CCF, well versed in Scripture, perhaps a future minister. Gay Justin was a leader in GALBA, working to change the campus environment, but *persona non grata* in the eyes of the church. As Christian Justin, I had my Christian friends, and as Gay Justin, I had my gay friends. I was the physical embodiment of the Gays-vs.-Christians culture war—yet somehow I felt oddly out of place in both communities.

I had imagined that once GALBA had more members, I would meet others with stories like mine, gay Christians struggling to reconcile their faith and sexuality, eager to work with me to help groups like CCF understand us. Instead, I discovered I had very little in common with the other GALBA members. As a group, they weren't particularly religious, and they didn't seem to have much interest in what CCF or any other Christian group on campus thought of them. Some had grown up in Christian homes, but most had either dropped Christianity altogether or relegated it to a relatively minor part of their lives.

At first, this puzzled me. We were in the Bible Belt, and a large percentage of the student body was Christian. My experiences with ex-gay groups had already taught me that Christians were just as likely as any other group of people to discover themselves to be gay, so statistically, there should have been many gay Christians on campus—and at least a decent percentage of them should have been committed evangelicals like me, including quite a few members of CCF. So why weren't there more Christians at GALBA?

Whenever the topic of religion came up around my new gay friends, I listened carefully to what they had to say about it. Gradually, the sad truth dawned on me.

It was all about the culture war.

The one big thing the gays and the Christians had in common was that they both believed in a Gays-vs.-Christians cultural dynamic. They might not all phrase it that way, and some might limit their antipathy to a particular subset of the other group—evangelicals, say, instead of all Christians—but at the end of the day, belief in this dichotomy was so strong on both sides that even those of us who should have known better, the gay Christians, had bought into it.

Yes, there were gay Christians on campus. They were all over. But they had grown up, like me, seeing "Gays vs. Christians" as the only option. You had to pick one or the other, and whichever one you didn't pick had to be squelched or hidden or forgotten.

What a horrible choice: Would you be a good person, or be an honest person? Deny what you believe about God, or deny what you know about yourself? Condemn yourself to a lifetime of faking it, or condemn yourself to an eternity in hell?

Given the choice, some people chose to serve God, living every day with their own private pain. They were the ones smiling and singing in CCF meetings as they secretly tried to change their feelings, desperately hoping no one would find out. Some of them were in ex-gay ministries, yearning for a day that would never come, a day they'd be straight. Some wouldn't even be able to admit the truth to themselves, much less anyone else. They might marry someday and have families, and their spouses would always feel that something was wrong but never know exactly what it was.

Others would make the opposite choice, deciding to be honest about their feelings and live their lives in the here and now, casting aside the theology of their youth, something they would come to view as dangerous and harmful. Having seen how Christianity turned their families and other people against them, many of them would blame God, or organized religion, or Christianity, or certain brands of Christianity, for years of guilt and pain and abuse hurled at them and their gay friends. Whatever joy or peace they might have taken from their faith as children would be gone; they would come to view Christians with suspicion, and if they did manage to hold on to some aspect of Christianity, it wasn't likely to be a major focus of their lives anymore. "Spiritual, but not religious," some of them might say to describe themselves, if they were even spiritual at all. And while some of them might not view the loss of their childhood faith as a tragedy, for many there would be an undeniable hole left behind, something that "spiritual but not religious" couldn't quite fill—nor could parties or drinking or sex or romance or money or any of the other ways they might try.

It wasn't that there weren't any gay Christians to begin with. It was that in a Gays-vs.-Christians culture, everyone had to pick a side. One side would never set foot at a GALBA meeting. The other would never set foot at CCF.

The effect of all this was to create a self-perpetuating cycle. A significant percentage of GALBA members were not only not Christian; they were actively antagonistic toward Christianity. CCF's history of bringing ex-gay speakers like Derek to campus only made things worse.

When I casually suggested that GALBA should reach out to CCF to offer to open a dialogue between the two groups and, I hoped, educate CCF members about gay issues, I already knew I'd encounter resistance from CCF. What I *didn't* expect was the strength of hostility to the idea from within GALBA. Though a few members thought it would be a nice step, others were angry at the suggestion. "Why should we try to reach out to them when they've already made it perfectly clear how they feel about us?" was the general sentiment. "We don't need their approval."

And so, in this microcosm of society, as the Christians judged the gays and the gays shunned the Christians, the misunderstanding and resentment fed into itself, giving all the more reason for people to feel a need to pick a side.

I felt compelled to break the cycle. If I could help build a bridge between these two groups on a college campus, maybe I could do it in the real world too.

All this time, I had been thinking that if I could just help the Christians understand, then the gay community would eagerly embrace an attempt to reach out. Not so.

Yes, I was gay. But I couldn't have been more out of touch with the other gay people I knew.

THE OUTSIDER

The bigger GALBA got, the less connected I felt. It was an odd pattern. I would meet a closeted gay guy on campus, often from a background similar to mine, and introduce him to the people at GALBA—only to watch him come out, gain confidence, and then effortlessly fit into a gay world that still felt incredibly foreign to me.

What was keeping me from fitting in? Was it some kind of internalized homophobia from years of feeling inferior because of my sexuality? Was it the fact that I insisted on keeping one foot in the CCF world, a world that so many GALBA-ites had branded the enemy? Was it my Southern Baptist upbringing and my "goody two-shoes" persona?

One of my friends called me "the straightest gay guy I've ever met." One of the guys from GALBA said to me, "Justin, you've got a lot to learn about gay culture."

It was true. In spite of now being one of the most visible gay guys on campus, I didn't know very much about gay culture at all. What I knew was Christian culture—specifically, evangelical Christian culture in America. That was my world, and it always had been.

Part of me resented the implication that I had to change. Why should my sexual orientation force me to change my tastes in music, clothes, recreation, and so on? Why should I have to change my sexual ethics, such as the belief I had been raised with that you were supposed to wait for marriage before having sex? Why should I have to abandon my evangelical faith? Couldn't gay people be just as diverse as straight people? Not all straight people listen to the same music or believe the same things or go to the same places to hang out. Why couldn't I just be me? Did I really have to change everything that made me unique in order to fit in?

No, I didn't have to, and I wasn't going to. I was going to be myself, and I was going to keep standing up for the diversity of the gay community—diverse in religion, interests, tastes, backgrounds, body types, and every other way. I made up my mind never to abandon myself in the name of "fitting in."

Still, if I was going to stand up for the gay community and try to build bridges on its behalf, I needed to break out of my childhood bubble.

I didn't really hang out with the other GALBA leaders socially. They rarely invited me to go along when they did things, even though I counted several of them as friends.

I privately asked one of them about it. Did the others not like me for some reason?

"Honestly?" he said.

I nodded.

"Well, you've gotten the reputation of being antisocial."

"Antisocial? Why?" I asked.

"Because you never go out to the club with us. If you always say no, then people don't have a reason to keep asking."

The club in question was a local gay bar, the favorite hangout spot for my gay friends and many of the other GALBA members.

"Yeah, but bars and clubs really aren't my scene," I said.

"You've never been. How do you know it's not your scene?"

"I just know."

The truth was that I was intimidated. Southern Baptists frown on alcohol, even in moderation. My parents had both been raised as teetotalers, and they raised me as one. My grandfather, a man whose memory I felt a strong emotional connection to, had refused to sell alcohol in his grocery store as a matter of moral conscience. When I was very young, he had been killed while working in the store—shot in the stomach by a would-be robber who was heavily intoxicated at the time. As a kid, I blamed alcohol for my grandfather's death, and all my life, I had never seen any positive, moderate use of alcohol to counteract that image. Yes, Jesus drank wine, but that was 2,000 years ago. In my church we drank grape juice, and my mom didn't even have a bottle of wine in the kitchen for cooking. The images of alcohol use I saw at college—loud frat boys binge drinking at parties and the like—certainly weren't helpful in changing my negative perception.

With all the emotional baggage I had regarding alcohol, the idea of going to a bar was intimidating enough. Add to that the fact that this was a *gay* bar. The only image I had of gay bars came from a scene in the British film *Beautiful Thing* in which two teenage boys venture to a seedy little gay bar. Inside, they find gay couples talking and making out all around them as a drag queen hits on them both. It makes me laugh now, but for a kid with no knowledge of the gay world, it was an unsettling depiction of gay life.

Karen and Erika were the ones who finally convinced me.

Karen and Erika were two of my straight female friends. They had gotten to know some of the guys from GALBA, and when they found out the guys were going out to the gay club one weekend, they decided to join them and ask me to come along.

"No thanks," I said, as I always did.

"Oh come on!" they insisted. "We'll stay with you, and if you don't have fun, we can come home."

I was hesitant. Me? At a club? I gave them every reason I could think of why I shouldn't go, and they gave me every reason they could think of why I should.

"Okay," I said reluctantly.

The club was in an old, unattractive building. As a good Christian kid from the suburbs, I knew I was out of my element before we even stepped inside. We paid our entrance fees at the door and I followed my friends in.

A low bass line and pulsing beat filled the room. A couple dozen men, ranging from my age to middle age, were moving about on the dance floor while dozens more men stood nearby, sipping their drinks and watching. A crowd of others milled about the room, going to and from the bar, talking and laughing loudly.

I stood just inside the doorway to take it all in.

"I like the music," I said, looking toward the dance floor. "But does it have to be so loud? That can't be good for your hearing."

"Quit being such an old man," one of my friends teased.

"What?" I shouted back.

They dragged me toward the dance floor. "Come on, dance with us!"

"I don't know how to dance," I protested.

"Just move to the music. That's all anyone does."

For the next half hour, I stood with my friends on the dance floor, self-consciously trying to "move to the music." The lights and beat were intoxicating in a way; it was easy to see how this could be a welcome place of relaxation and escape. But I was still too uptight and nervous to have any fun.

It wasn't the dancing per se that bothered me. Although many Southern Baptists in the past had frowned upon dancing and some still did, my church had never had a problem with it. In another context, I likely would have gotten over my initial fears and discovered how much fun it can be. But at this time, in this context, I couldn't get myself to relax. It was hot, my ears were buzzing, and I couldn't shake the feeling that my parents would disapprove.

"I'm going to take a break!" I shouted to Karen, who was dancing next to me.

"Do you want me to come with you?" she shouted back.

"No, I'm okay. I'll be back!"

I left the dance floor, pushed my way through the crowd, and began to explore the room. The club actually consisted of several rooms, I discovered, and as I got farther from the loud techno dance floor, the relative silence was welcoming.

There were men—and a smaller number of women—everywhere, of all ages, shapes, and sizes. Some were deeply engaged in conversation with each other; others were quietly surveying the room. Most, though, seemed to be just enjoying themselves without much notice of anyone else.

I had imagined that my first trip to a gay bar would involve being leered at and hit on by sleazy-looking older gay men. Much to my surprise, no one even seemed to notice I was there. At first I was relieved to be able to pass by unnoticed. But then I started to wonder: Was there some reason no one paid attention to me? Was I unattractive? I had to laugh at myself. The stress of this whole gay Christian thing was starting to make me neurotic! Deep down,

I realized, in the midst of my loneliness and depression, I was secretly wanting someone to notice me just so I could turn them down!

God, I've discovered, has a sense of humor. As I was thinking about being ignored, a young woman near my age approached me. She was pretty obviously drunk.

"Hi," she said with a smile.

"Um, hi," I stammered back, not having *actually* expected anyone to talk to me.

"You here with someone?" she asked.

"Just my friends. They're back there." I pointed toward the dance floor.

"You have a boyfriend?"

I silently shook my head.

"You have a girlfriend?"

I shook my head again, laughing to myself. Had she expected to find a straight man in here?

"Wanna dance?" she asked.

"Oh, I, uh, um, no…thank you," I said. And then, by way of explanation, I added, "I just needed a break from the music."

"Oh, okay," she said, and walked away.

I felt bad. I hadn't meant to make her feel rejected, but I really didn't want to dance with anyone. For the moment, I just wanted to be alone with my thoughts.

The more I walked around the club, the more I didn't like it. Everything about it felt sleazy, and away from the dance floor, the air was thick with cigarette smoke—another vice my Southern Baptist parents would have been upset about. Even though there weren't any sleazy men hitting on *me,* there was definitely a vibe of lust in the place, and it made me uncomfortable. Years later, my gay friends would tell me that I had picked a really bad club to be my first experience, but at the time it was all I knew. To me, this club represented all gay clubs, and it wasn't where I wanted to be.

As I made my way through the crowd, looking for an escape from the smoke and noise, I saw someone go through a door a few yards ahead of me, and I thought I felt a breeze. Was that a door to the outside? I walked over to it, but it was shut now and I hesitated to open it without knowing where it led.

A tall man was standing next to the door, chatting with some others. "Um, excuse me," I said, "but where does this door go?"

He grinned down at me. "You've got to pay to go through there," he said with a wink.

I looked back at him, confused. Was he kidding? Was this a doorway to some kind of seedy back room? If so, I wanted no part of it. Or was he just trying to take advantage of my naiveté? I waited a moment, hoping he would explain further or give me some clue that he was joking, but he looked serious. My face was hot, so I turned around and walked away, feeling like a fool.

It was, I later discovered, the door to the patio. No admission fee required.

THINGS FALL APART

I had hoped that the outing to the club would help me feel connected to the other gay guys. But instead, it had the opposite effect. I felt more alienated than ever. It seemed like everyone in the gay world spoke the same language, and no one had ever taught me. Worse, their language felt fundamentally at odds with everything I had been taught in the church, everything that made me God Boy, everything that made me *me*. I wasn't like the other gay people I had met. I wasn't having sex. I didn't want a hookup. I didn't drink. I didn't smoke. I didn't like to dance. I was just a sheltered Southern Baptist boy who wanted to serve God and couldn't help being attracted to other guys.

I was a freak.

Back at the Christian fellowship, rumors were circulating that I was gay, and people were beginning to treat me differently. I kept having to defend myself over and over from well-meaning Christians who'd begin with the words, "I think you should see this Bible passage…" and I was getting tired of having to explain how I could be gay and Christian.

For a while I stopped taking calls from my parents, because I was tired of arguing with them about it all. My dad wrote a letter expressing his deep disappointment and begging me not to let Satan keep me from doing God's work—which is what would happen, he said, if I accepted myself as gay. I read and reread the Bible passages on homosexuality, trying to make sense of them and figure out what to do. My choices, it seemed, were to be branded a sinner and live my life alone; to abandon my faith, the one thing I held most dear in the entire world; or to lie to everyone, pretend I was straight, and forget about it all.

I prayed more fervently than ever for God's help. And I fell into a deep depression.

I had originally been admitted to the university on a prestigious, full-tuition, merit-based scholarship. In order to please the scholarship committee, I was taking a challenging course load, trying to validate their faith in me. But now, the added stress of that course load was more than I could bear. I couldn't focus, and my grades were slipping.

At night, I couldn't sleep. I wandered around campus in the dark, begging God for answers, wanting to know why I was this way and what I was supposed to do about it.

During the day, I daydreamed about ways to kill myself. I didn't really want to die, but I couldn't see any future in this world where I could possibly be happy. I felt like I was staying alive out of obligation to God, not because I had anything at all to live for.

The suicidal daydreams got more regular and more vivid. I started skipping class for the first time in my life. Sometimes I would sit in the floor of my room and just cry. Other times I just felt numb. I'd sit in the hallways late at night, wishing silently that someone would come by and see my pain and find some way to help me. No one ever did. Even if they had, it probably wouldn't have mattered.

Something inside me prompted me to confess to my parents that I was depressed and needed help. They immediately offered to pay for whatever therapy I needed, and suggested that I find a good psychiatrist to talk to about my depression. I agreed, and made an appointment with a local psychiatrist who came with a good recommendation. He was also a Christian, which I hoped would help him understand my dilemma.

My first meeting with the psychiatrist was mostly informational. He asked me some basic questions and then encouraged me to explain my problem in my own words.

I told him that I was depressed and suicidal, and that I felt like my depression stemmed primarily from feeling torn between being gay and being Christian. I told him how important my faith was to me, and that discovering I was gay had turned my life upside down. Now I felt alone and no one seemed to understand.

He nodded his head slowly. "Well, I can see where that would be a dilemma." He paused. "You know, Justin, the Bible does make it quite clear that God condemns homosexuality, and that being gay is a sin. For example, in First Corinthians, chapter 6…"

I didn't return for a second visit.

A second psychiatrist handled the revelation of my dilemma better than the first one, but he still didn't know how to help me. He prescribed antidepressants, but they were only a stopgap measure; they didn't do anything to help the underlying cause.

My depression wasn't about a chemical imbalance. It wasn't even really about my loneliness. Without realizing it, I had internalized the culture war, and it was tearing me apart inside. I couldn't deny my faith, I couldn't deny the truth about myself, and I couldn't keep living two separate lives.

I made up my mind: Something had to change. It was time for me to stop being afraid and stop letting the culture war define me. With God's help, I was going to find my path in life, regardless of what others might think.

CHAPTER 12

BACK TO THE BIBLE

From the moment I knew I was gay, one question had hung over me like a storm cloud: How did God want me to live? I still didn't feel like I had gotten any definite answers. I had promised God I would stay celibate if that's what I was called to, but I had never felt any confirmation in my spirit as to whether or not that *was* what God was calling me to. My future options were uncertain.

By now I knew that there were many Christians, gay and straight, who believed that the Bible could be reconciled with same-sex relationships and that the traditional view of them as sinful was based on a misinterpretation of Scripture. They argued that none of the Bible passages apparently condemning homosexuality applied to modern-day monogamous, Christ-centered gay relationships. So far, none of their arguments had convinced me. I suspected this was a case of people trying to justify their own sin, but I wasn't sure.

Conversely, my church taught that gay relationships were always sinful and outside of God's will for humanity, and most of my

Christian friends agreed. But these were the same Christians who believed I had chosen to be gay and that I could simply choose not to be—something I already knew wasn't true. How could they base their arguments on a careful and prayerful exploration of the complexities of the issue if they had gotten such basic facts wrong?

If God was calling me to celibacy, I would be celibate, but I needed to be sure. To settle this issue once and for all in my own mind, I had to ignore the half-baked ideas on both sides and go straight to the source—not just a quick perusal of what the Bible had to say, but an honest, prayerful, in-depth study.

THE SODOM STORY

The obvious place to start was with the story of Sodom and Gomorrah.

One of my favorite Christian musical artists at the time was a clever satirist named Steve Taylor. One of his older songs, "Whatever Happened to Sin?," lamented the tendency of some churches to overlook the importance of moral living in their quest to love everyone. I didn't want to be one of those Christians. I wanted very badly to live a moral life in accordance with God's will. Out of the whole song, one verse in particular stuck out for me. In it, Taylor's narrator takes on a gay-affirming pastor, responding to him with the line, "If the Lord don't care and he chooses to ignore-ah, tell it to the people of Sodom and Gomorrah!"

It was from Taylor's early work—not necessarily indicative of his later views and perhaps not the best rhyme of his career—but the message came through loud and clear: God had destroyed two whole cities because of homosexuality. If that was true, could God's view on the subject have been any clearer?

As I soon discovered, it wasn't quite that clear at all. The only mention of homosexuality in connection with either of these cities was in the story of Sodom in Genesis 19. (There's no mention in the Bible of homosexuality in Gomorrah at all.)

In Genesis 19, we're told that God has already decided to destroy the wicked city of Sodom. At this point, the Scriptures don't specify what's so wicked about it, only that it's a city so wicked that it deserves annihilation. But there is one righteous man, Lot, who lives in Sodom with his family. So God sends two angels to Lot to warn him of the impending destruction.

The angels arrive and decide to spend the night in the city square. Lot warns them that this is not safe and ushers them into his own house. It is there that these mysterious travelers reveal to Lot their true identities and intentions. And then something strange happens.

We're told that *every man in the entire city* surrounds the house and threatens these angels with gang rape. Ultimately, the angels blind the crowd and escape.

If the angels had taken the form of women, we would be horrified at the wickedness of the city and then move on. Because the angels were in the form of men, however, later readers of the story assumed that the men of Sodom must have been gay. After all, why would straight men threaten to rape other men? And if Sodom truly was a "gay city," it seemed natural to assume that must have been the reason for its destruction. Soon, words like "sodomy" and "sodomite" crept into the language based on the idea that Sodom's sin must have been homosexuality.

As I considered the passage, though, numerous questions immediately sprang to my mind.

For one thing, how was it possible that the *entire city* could have been gay? The text was very clear that *every man in the city, young and old,* participated in the attack. I already knew people couldn't *choose* their sexual orientation. I couldn't make myself straight even when I had been desperate to, and I seriously doubted that any straight man could voluntarily turn himself gay, even if he wanted to. But, that being true, how could so many gay men end up in one city? Was there something in the water? Were gay people traveling to Sodom in droves to settle there? If so, how did they find out about it? Even today, in the age of airplane travel and the internet, there are no *entirely* gay cities. And if that *had* been the case, why would Lot and his family have moved there? Something about the whole concept just didn't make sense.

That wasn't all. As I quickly discovered, Sodom wasn't alone. In Judges 19, I found the story of Gibeah, eerily similar to the Sodom story in almost every respect. In that story, a male traveler comes to the town of Gibeah and, like the angels, plans to spend the night in the square. A kind man warns him that it is not safe to do so and brings him into his house instead. Once again, an angry mob forms, and once again, they threaten to gang-rape the traveler.

What was going on here? Was the ancient landscape dotted with "gay cities" everywhere, populated entirely by men who raped other men?

The end of the Gibeah story held an important clue. In that story, the man's concubine—a woman—is finally sent out to the crowd, and the mob rapes and murders *her* instead.

So maybe the crowd wasn't gay after all. They might have been bisexual, but that was even less likely than all of them being gay. The most likely explanation was that at least most of them were straight. But why would straight men threaten to gang-rape a man?

As I was thinking about this, I remembered one of my history classes in school; we had discussed how rape had been used at times as a symbol of domination, with armies raping the (male) leader of a conquered enemy. I thought, too, about stories I had heard in the news of men being beaten and violently sexually assaulted with broom handles or other objects during fights.

Clearly, in some cultures and contexts—whether in ancient times or in modern-day prisons—male-male rape had been used or threatened as a method of violent humiliation and domination. The perpetrators in these cases were usually straight men, not gay men, and their interest wasn't sexual; it was to do harm.

Could this be what was happening in Sodom and Gibeah? I read through the passage again. Which made more sense: that the entire town was gay, or that the entire town was participating in an angry, violent attack against unwelcome outsiders? Could it be that this was the ancient equivalent of a lynch mob?

I considered the evidence.

Everyone in the city participated in the attack. It was a lot easier to believe that everyone would be whipped up in a frenzy of hate than to believe that everyone in the town was gay.

Their tone also suggested this was about violence, not sex. They tell Lot that if he gets in their way, "We'll treat you worse than them!" He urges them, "Don't do this wicked thing." This was clearly a threat of rape, not a request for consensual sex, and the threat to treat Lot "worse" suggested that the mob's goal was to inflict harm, not just to satisfy a sex drive.

Lot offers his virgin daughters to the crowd as a distraction, something that (in addition to raising a lot of moral questions) wouldn't make sense if he knew the men were gay. In response, the crowd points out that Lot came to Sodom as a foreigner and therefore has no footing to judge them, suggesting that the angels' outsider status was the real issue and that Lot should feel grateful that they had even allowed *him* into the city.

Clues like these, combined with the Gibeah story, made it seem likely to me that this was a story about a violent threat, not a story about a gay city. It certainly wasn't a story about consensual relationships.

Some Bible scholars have argued that Sodom's sin was "inhospitality." I laughed the first time I read that, because in light of passages about gang rape and murder, to say that the real problem in these cities was about not being *hospitable* sounds like a ludicrous understatement.

Here's what I think they mean.

This was a culture where travelers really did depend on the kindness of strangers. Throughout the Bible, we see that one of the signs of God's people is that they are generous with what they have. For instance, when Jesus tells the story of God separating out the righteous "sheep" from the unrighteous "goats" on Judgment Day, the sheep are those who use their time and resources to help those who are less fortunate. They clothe the naked; they feed the hungry; they visit those in prison. Jesus often entreats his disciples to be more generous than people expect, giving more than asked for and not expecting repayment. Likewise, Job cites his treatment of travelers as evidence of his own righteousness, saying that "no stranger had to spend the night in the street, for my door was always open to the traveler" (Job 31:32).

What we see in the stories of Sodom and Gibeah is the opposite extreme. These cities are not generous and welcoming to strangers; they are cities full of hate, mistrust, and prejudice toward them. These are cities that say to outsiders: *You're not welcome here! We don't want your kind here! If people like you set foot in our town, we will do the most violating things to you we can think of, to send a message to anyone else who might dare to come onto our land.* It's the same sentiment that underlies racism, hate between nations, and many other kinds of prejudice.

And in Genesis 19, God is having none of it.

The prophet Ezekiel reinforces this image of Sodom as a city without compassion. Speaking on God's behalf, Ezekiel says:

> Now this was the sin of your sister Sodom: She and her daughters were arrogant, overfed and unconcerned; they did not help the poor and needy. They were haughty and did detestable things before me. Therefore I did away with them as you have seen. (Ezekiel 16:49–50)

There are a number of important messages in the Sodom story, but none of them helped me decide what to do about my sexuality. I wasn't trying to choose between celibacy and threatening people with gang rape! I was trying to find out if it was okay for me to have a romantic relationship someday, and if so, what it might look like.

This passage wasn't helpful in my situation, but maybe one of the other passages on the subject would give me more specific guidance. Confused, I moved on to Leviticus.

LYING WITH A MAN

Leviticus 18:22 was certainly straightforward: "Don't lie with a man as with a woman." Period. End of story.

Except that it wasn't the end of the story. Leviticus is in the Old Testament, and as anyone who's been to Sunday school knows, Christians don't typically follow most of the commands in the Old Testament. We do follow some, though, so was this one of the ones we *should* follow or one of the ones we *shouldn't*?

In Leviticus 18–20, God gives Moses a list of rules for the Israelites to keep them separate from the polytheistic cultures around them: "You shall not do as they do in the land of Egypt, where you lived, and you shall not do as they do in the land of Canaan, to which I am bringing you. You shall not walk in their statutes" (Leviticus 18:3 ESV). These aren't just rules for their own sake; these are rules to keep the Israelites set apart for God. So do they apply to us, or not?

I read through the list of rules. Some of them were things that certainly seemed just as valid today as when they were written: Bestiality, incest, lying, stealing, and child sacrifice are all condemned in the passage, and Christians continue to condemn them today. But there were plenty of other rules that no Christian I know would preach today. Among other things, Leviticus 18–20 also condemns shaving, wearing mixed fabrics, getting tattoos, sowing different crops in the same field, and sexual activity during a woman's period.

Clearly, just because something was condemned for the Israelites in Moses' day didn't mean it was likewise condemned for Christians today. So if some of these rules applied today and others didn't, how could I figure out which was which? Most important, how could I determine which type the "don't lie with a man" rule was?

Growing up, I had considered that the Old Testament had two types of commandments. *Moral* commandments like those against murder or stealing would apply to all cultures and all situations. They would still be applicable to me today. *Cultural* commandments, like those requiring ritual sacrifice or forbidding certain foods, were only applicable at a time and place in the past. Today's Christians weren't obligated to follow the *cultural* rules anymore. It seemed to me a pretty good way of dividing up the Old Testament, one held by many Christians I knew, and I had never questioned it. So all I had to do was figure out if this rule was a *moral* commandment or a *cultural* one.

It would be great if it were that simple. As I discovered, it's not.

In this passage, for example, the rule against wearing mixed fabrics seemed pretty obviously cultural to me. I couldn't imagine God condemning a twenty-first-century Christian for wearing a cotton/poly blend. But how did I know it was cultural? Nothing in the passage identified it as such. In fact, nothing in the Old Testament ever differentiates between "moral" and "cultural" commandments.

The New Testament specifically overturns a few Old Testament laws, but the rule about mixed fabrics isn't one of them. Nowhere in the entire Bible does it say that the commandment against wearing mixed fabrics is cultural. So how did I know it was cultural? Sure, it seemed "obvious," but why? Well, because Christians don't follow that rule anymore. So why don't we follow that rule? Presumably because it was a cultural command. And how did we know it was a cultural command? Because we don't follow it anymore. But—

That approach only led to a circular reasoning loop. Based on that logic, those who believe that the "lie with men" rule should still apply today would identify it as moral, and those who believe it shouldn't apply would identify it as cultural. That didn't help me. I wasn't looking for a loophole to exploit; I wanted to know what God really wanted me to do!

I kept looking. Perhaps there was some other way of differentiating the commands that still should apply from those that shouldn't. Maybe, for instance, I could divide the rules into those pertaining to sex and those not pertaining to sex, and assume that all the sex-related rules were moral commands. This didn't quite work either, however. For one thing, there was nothing in the text to say that; I was just making that leap on my own because there were so many obviously moral commands about sex. For another thing, this didn't address the bigger picture at all; it still left all the non-sex-related commands ambiguous. And for another thing, one of the commands forbade a man from having sex with his wife during the time of her period, and that sounded like a good candidate for a cultural rule, not a moral one. It certainly wasn't something I'd ever heard a pastor preach on, and it didn't strike me as something that God would send people to hell for.

I considered another possibility. Perhaps it was all about the *language*; laws that used the word "unclean" (like dietary restrictions and sex during a woman's period) were cultural, and laws that used the word "sin" were moral. But the Old Testament sometimes used the words interchangeably (e.g., Leviticus 5:1–6), and neither word was used to describe male-male sex.

Ultimately, I kept coming back to the word "abomination." Male-male sex wasn't just condemned in this passage; it was called an "abomination." If anything made this sound like a moral command, that word did. I wondered why it was called that. Was that a sign that this was among the worst sins, something God absolutely detested? (Another translation of the Bible rendered this word as "detestable.") I looked up "abomination" and discovered that it was used to describe a number of things in the Old Testament. Among them: forbidden foods, something I knew to be cultural.

But here it got even more complicated. When I looked up the Hebrew text, I discovered that there were different words translated as "abomination." The "forbidden food" type of abomination was different from the "lying with man" type of abomination, and the word for the "lying with man" type of abomination was most often used for things connected to idolatry. But why?

Some scholars, arguing that the Bible doesn't condemn modern-day gay relationships, maintained that this passage was actually intended to condemn ritual cult prostitution, a form of idolatry in that culture that involved male–male sex. But hey, they were arguing in favor of accepting gay relationships, so they might be biased. What did the *other* side say? Pretty much the same thing, it turned out. Of the Bible scholars who argue for the traditional view (that gay sex is always a sin), the foremost authority is widely considered to be Robert Gagnon, an associate professor of New Testament at Pittsburgh Theological Seminary who has spent much of his career studying and writing in condemnation of homosexuality. On Leviticus, Gagnon writes:

> I do not doubt that the circles out of which Leviticus 18:22 was produced had in view homosexual cult prostitution, at least partly. Homosexual cult prostitution appears to have been the primary form in which homosexual intercourse was practiced in Israel.[1]

So scholars on both sides of the argument agreed that this probably had something to do with cult prostitution. That made sense to me, since the rest of the passage was about keeping the Israelites separate from polytheistic cultures. Many of the passage's other rules had similar theological significance: tattoos, for instance, weren't condemned just because God doesn't like ink on skin; they were apparently part of certain pagan rituals that God didn't want the Israelites associated with. (The verse condemning tattoos also condemns making "any cuts on your body for the dead," making the theological rationale more apparent.)

If only this passage had said, "Don't lie with a man...because it is connected to idol worship in our culture," I could have put it aside with confidence, knowing that it didn't refer to modern-day committed relationships. But it didn't. Instead, it used a word that *usually* refers to idolatry, but in a context that left the purpose unclear.

If gay sex was being condemned for its connection to idolatry and cult prostitution, that would explain the harsh punishment and the description of it as "abomination," and it wouldn't apply to modern-day relationships at all. But if gay sex was being condemned because gay sex is inherently sinful in all situations, then that condemnation would still apply today, even in a committed relationship.

I wasn't going to be able to solve this by looking at Leviticus in isolation. I had to consider it in light of the New Testament.

EXCHANGING NATURAL FOR UNNATURAL

In Romans 1, Paul writes about wickedness:

> For the wrath of God is revealed from heaven against all ungodliness and unrighteousness of men, who by their unrighteousness suppress the truth. For what can be known about God is plain to them, because God has shown it to them. For his invisible attributes, namely, his eternal power and divine nature, have been clearly perceived, ever since the creation of the world, in the things that have been made. So they are without excuse. For although they knew God, they did not honor

him as God or give thanks to him, but they became futile in their thinking, and their foolish hearts were darkened. Claiming to be wise, they became fools, and exchanged the glory of the immortal God for images resembling mortal man and birds and animals and creeping things.

Therefore God gave them up in the lusts of their hearts to impurity, to the dishonoring of their bodies among themselves, because they exchanged the truth about God for a lie and worshiped and served the creature rather than the Creator, who is blessed forever! Amen.

For this reason God gave them up to dishonorable passions. For their women exchanged natural relations for those that are contrary to nature; and the men likewise gave up natural relations with women and were consumed with passion for one another, men committing shameless acts with men and receiving in themselves the due penalty for their error.

And since they did not see fit to acknowledge God, God gave them up to a debased mind to do what ought not to be done. They were filled with all manner of unrighteousness, evil, covetousness, malice. They are full of envy, murder, strife, deceit, maliciousness. They are gossips, slanderers, haters of God, insolent, haughty, boastful, inventors of evil, disobedient to parents, foolish, faithless, heartless, ruthless. Though they know God's decree that those who practice such things deserve to die, they not only do them but give approval to those who practice them. (Romans 1:18–32 ESV)

Before I knew I was gay, I didn't pay any special attention to this passage. I didn't worship idols, I wasn't having gay (or straight) sex, and I'd already understood the basic concepts of humanity's sin and our need for a Savior. In my mind, this passage didn't really have anything to do with me.

Now, thanks to the discovery that I was gay, that had all changed.

This passage was one of the few passages in the New Testament to mention homosexuality, and it did so in a very negative light. I needed to understand what it was saying and what that meant for someone like me.

The passage described people who had turned from God, refusing to give God honor or thanks, and had worshiped idols instead. God had responded by giving them over to sexual immorality, resulting in their abandoning "natural" (heterosexual?) sex in favor of committing "shameless acts" with each other. At the end of the passage, Paul listed some of the many sins these people were involved in.

I had always glossed over it before, but now that this passage seemed directly relevant to my future, I discovered that I had a lot of questions about it. For example, this passage made it sound like God gave people over to homosexuality as a result of their turning from Him. Did that mean that *straight* people had become *gay* when they turned from God? Was being gay a punishment for turning from God?

I hadn't turned from God. I was sure I hadn't turned from God. I knew I wasn't perfect, but I certainly had never turned away the way this passage seemed to suggest. How could it say that my being gay was a punishment for turning from God? And if other Christians read this, no wonder they thought I was some kind of apostate.

Did it perhaps mean that they were *already* gay, but that they were celibate—until they turned from God and He gave them over to homosexual *behavior*? But that didn't seem to be what the passage was saying. It said the men had abandoned relations with women *after* they turned from God and *after* God gave them over to impurity. That made it sound like they had been *straight* before, not gay and celibate. Once again I was stuck with the same question as in the Sodom story: *Why would straight people choose to have gay sex?*

Or maybe I was looking at it all wrong. Maybe this was meant to refer more broadly to all of humanity—that because we, *humanity,* had sinned, God had allowed some kind of corruption of our natural sexual desire to affect us as a species. So perhaps my same-sex attractions were the result of humanity's fall in a broader sense, and not necessarily my own turning from God.

But if this was about all of us, then why did Paul keep saying "they": "*They* are without excuse," "*They* became fools," "God gave *them* up," "*Their* women exchanged natural relations," and so forth? It certainly sounded like he was referring to a specific *group* of people, not just humanity in general, and that this group of people had turned from God, worshiped idols, *and* been given over to some kind of unnatural sexual activity. But who were those people, and did they have anything to do with me? Was he talking about gay couples or was he talking about something entirely different? Whoever "they" were, clearly in Paul's eyes they were sinning. I didn't want to be like them. But what exactly was going on in this passage?

Then I noticed something else curious. When I had skimmed the passage initially, I had read the idol worship and the sexual behavior as two unrelated sins, mentioned to provide examples of wickedness. But as I read the passage more closely, I realized that in Paul's view, these two behaviors were somehow connected. Twice, in fact, he said that the dishonorable sex was a direct result of the idol worship:

[They] exchanged the glory of the immortal God for images resembling mortal man and birds and animals and creeping things. *Therefore* God gave them up in the lusts of their hearts to impurity, to the dishonoring of their bodies....

They exchanged the truth about God for a lie and worshiped and served the creature....*For this reason* God gave them up to dishonorable passions.

What was the connection between the idol worship and the dishonorable sex? I could understand saying that sin *in general* is a result of turning from God, which is what I had originally interpreted this passage to mean. But Paul had a long, separate list of sins at the end of the passage. If he intended to mention homosexuality as one of the sins that result from turning from God, why didn't he list it there with all the other sins? Why did he single it out and specifically connect it with the idolatry?

I began to research this question, and it didn't surprise me to discover that in Paul's day, as in the time of Leviticus, some idol-worshiping cults included sex (in sometimes bizarre ways) as part of their worship rituals. Cult temple prostitution, castration, and same-sex sex rites in honor of popular goddesses were all well-known practices of the time.

This explained Paul's connection of idol worship to shameful sexual behavior. With this new information, suddenly the whole passage made a lot more sense to me. The "they" was a reference to people who had turned from God, as represented by the idol worshipers. Paul was using them and their sexual rites as an illustration to make a point to his audience.

In some ways, it was like the strategy the prophet Nathan had used with King David in 2 Samuel 12. David had had Bathsheba's husband, Uriah, killed so that he could have Bathsheba. Rather than directly confronting David about his sin, Nathan told him a story about a rich man who stole from a poor man. After David became angry at the man in the story, Nathan revealed that the man in the story was in fact a representation of David.

Paul's strategy in Romans was similar. He began by talking about wicked people who had turned from God, then discussed how they had begun to worship idols, leading God to give them over to the dishonorable sex rites that accompanied such worship—rites that involved gay sex practiced by otherwise straight people, something Paul knew his audience would find objectionable. Furthermore, Paul said, these people had become caught up in all kinds of sins. And just as his audience was nodding their heads in agreement, ready to condemn these people to hell, Paul sprung his trap, catching them by surprise:

> Therefore you have no excuse, O man, every one of you
> who judges. For in passing judgment on another you condemn
> yourself, because you, the judge, practice the very same things.
> (Romans 2:1 ESV)

Paul's entire point in this passage was to show his audience that all of us are sinners in need of a Savior. The idolaters who engaged in shameful sex rites were a perfect illustration for the seriousness of turning from God, a way to get his audience agreeing with him before he unexpectedly turned the tables on them. Read in this light, the purpose of the passage was much clearer.

But it still left me asking, "What does this mean for me?"

If this was about sex rites during idol worship, that didn't seem to have anything to do with committed gay relationships. Even so, Paul's view toward the same-sex aspect of those rites didn't seem very positive at all, and he did call the sex acts (as the NIV put it) "shameful" and "unnatural." Perhaps he would have condemned the gay sex even if it weren't in the context of idolatry.

Then again, Paul also calls it "shameful" and "unnatural"—using the same Greek words—for a man to have long hair (1 Corinthians 11:14). Most Christians today understand that passage as referring to the cultural standards of that time, and it has far fewer cultural references than the Romans passage does.

I could argue this either way, but the bottom line was that this passage didn't give me much guidance about how to live as a gay Christian.

THE SINFUL *ARSENOKOITAI*

There was only one other passage in my Bible that seemed to mention any form of homosexuality. It was 1 Corinthians 6:9–11:

> Do you not know that the wicked will not inherit the kingdom of God? Do not be deceived: Neither the sexually immoral nor idolaters nor adulterers nor male prostitutes nor homosexual offenders nor thieves nor the greedy nor drunkards nor slanderers nor swindlers will inherit the kingdom of God. And that is what some of you were. But you were washed, you were sanctified, you were justified in the name of the Lord Jesus Christ and by the Spirit of our God.

In other words, all sinners must be washed and sanctified by Jesus in order to enter God's kingdom. In our sinful states, we cannot do so. This is true of any type of sin, and Paul lists several examples here: Theft. Greed. Slander. Drunkenness. Before we were Christians, our lives might have been characterized by these or other sins, but God wants to cleanse, forgive, and redeem us, at which point our lives will no longer be characterized by sin.

That much I understood. But *what* was a "homosexual offender"?

A friend of mine likes to joke, "The Bible condemns homosexual offenders, so stop offending the homosexuals." At the time, I wouldn't have found that very funny. This was no laughing matter to me. The options for my future, it seemed, would be determined by this short phrase.

Searches through several reference books taught me that "homosexual offenders" was a translation of the Greek word *arsenokoitai*. To my surprise, one reference book listed the same word as appearing in another passage, 1 Timothy 1:10. I turned to 1 Timothy 1:10 in my New International Version Bible, and, there, saw that the word was translated simply as "perverts." There's quite a difference between "homosexual offenders" and "perverts." I was even more intrigued: What did this word *arsenokoitai* mean?

In pursuit of the answer to that question, I spent countless hours in the library, read every book I could get my hands on from any perspective, and began studying Greek language and history. The answer that emerged was anything but clear-cut.

I soon discovered that this word was the source of significant debate among scholars. (No doubt, its significance to the gay debate in the church was one of the primary reasons.) Normally, scholars researching the meaning of a word in a particular passage look to other uses of the same word in other writings from that era. In this case, there are no other writings that use this word *arsenokoitai* in Paul's day or before Paul; the first surviving recorded usage of the word is in Paul's epistles. This might mean that Paul invented the word, or it might mean that the word was already in common use in his day and his epistles are simply the oldest documentation of it that has survived.

Arsenokoitai is a compound word, made up of the Greek words for "male" (*arsen*) and "bed" (*koite*). The same words appear in the Greek translation of the Leviticus passage, leading some scholars to speculate that Paul could have coined the term in reference to that passage.

Was Paul referring to Leviticus? If so, was he intending to refer to the cult prostitution apparently referenced by both Leviticus 18 and Romans 1? Or was he using the reference to condemn male-male sex in general?

Other scholars believe that *arsenokoitai* is intended to be interpreted together with *malakoi*, the Greek word translated as "male prostitutes" in the NIV and "effeminate" in the King James. The 1990 edition of the Catholic Study Bible, for instance, suggested that:

> The Greek word translated as "boy prostitutes" [*malakoi*] designated catamites, i.e., boys or young men who were kept for purposes of prostitution, a practice not uncommon in the Greco-Roman world. In Greek mythology this was the function of Ganymede, the "cupbearer of the gods," whose Latin

name was Catamitus. The term translated "practicing homosexuals" [*arsenokoitai*] refers to adult males who indulged in
homosexual practices with such boys.

This practice—married men having sex with boys on the side—was
common in Greek culture long before Paul and continued to be
practiced in his day. We would certainly condemn that today for a
number of reasons, but if *that* was what he was referring to, it didn't
tell me anything about the morality of consensual adult relationships
in today's society. The New Testament speaks negatively about tax
collectors, but we don't view that as a condemnation of modern-day
IRS agents; instead, we understand that it's referring to the corrupt
practices of the tax collectors of Jesus' day.

The NIV translation of these words was very similar to the
Catholic translation. Was that Bible right about what these words
referred to? (In 2011, the NIV altered its translation, removing the
phrase "male prostitutes" and retranslating the two words together
to mean "men who have sex with men.")

Was this passage a condemnation of corrupt same-sex practices in
Paul's day—either pederasty or idolatry? Or was it a condemnation
of all gay sex for all time? Even if I knew for sure how to translate
arsenokoitai and *malakoi*, I wasn't sure how to answer this question
beyond a shadow of a doubt. The passage didn't give me enough
context to be certain.

And so, it seemed, the entire Bible argument came down to this
one word. The Leviticus and Romans passages had a clear context
of idolatry, not committed relationships. If 1 Corinthians 6:9 was
condemning the same things, or something else like pederasty, then
the Bible didn't address committed gay relationships at all.[2] If *arsenokoitai*, however, was really a reference to all gay sex in every time
and place, then it shed light on the other passages as well, and any
other interpretation was just looking for loopholes.

I realized with frustration that neither answer was entirely satisfactory. I could make a convincing argument for either side, but whatever argument I made, how did I know I was right? If I got this wrong, I'd end up either trying to justify sin or unjustly condemning loving relationships that God never intended to condemn.

I tried reading the passage one way. Then I tried the other. They both sounded convincing, yet they both left me feeling thoroughly unconvinced.

THE WINE IN FRONT OF ME

I was disappointed. I had expected that studying these Bible passages was going to clearly answer my question, one way or the other. In my fantasy, there would have been some clear indication that the biblical authors had heard of people like me and had some kind of advice about how we should live.

If any of these passages had mentioned anything, pro or con, about committed gay relationships, or faithful Christians with same-sex attractions, or the importance of mandatory celibacy for people like me, I could have accepted it. But they didn't. Instead, every one of these passages seemed tainted by issues like idolatry and rape, leaving me in serious doubt as to whether they even applied to my situation at all.

On the flip side, if all of these passages had been as clearly irrelevant as the Sodom story, I could have felt satisfied that they *didn't* condemn gay relationships and that I could someday fall in love with a clean conscience. Sadly, it wasn't so simple; as much as I wanted to, I couldn't just brush aside that word *arsenokoitai*. Yes, there was debate about its translation, but the Greek word roots and possible Leviticus connection made a pretty powerful argument for translating it as "men who have sex with men." If that was true, I couldn't ignore it.

But did it really make sense to base such an important, life-altering doctrine—one that would tear relationships apart and destroy families—on one hotly contested word? And how could I ignore the culture in which Paul wrote his letter? If the *arsenokoitai* of Paul's day were married men having sex with boys on the side or participants in fertility rites, shouldn't that impact how we interpreted and applied the passage today?

I was even more confused than I had felt before. I realized that I could easily make a clear, compelling argument for either position. If I chose to pursue a relationship, I could simply focus on the cultural issues and the irrelevance of discussions of fertility rites to committed couples. If I decided to remain celibate, I could focus on the condemnation of the *arsenokoitai*, arguing that every clear instance of homosexuality in the Bible was condemned. I built both of these arguments in my mind, arguing them back and forth with each other like Bobby Fischer playing both sides of a chess board. Whichever way I argued, I always seemed to end up in a stalemate.

In the classic fantasy film *The Princess Bride*, the mysterious Man in Black challenges the villainous Vizzini to a deadly battle of wits.

Placing two goblets of wine on the table, the Man in Black invites Vizzini to determine which of the goblets is poisoned. Once he makes his selection, each man is to drink—and only one is to survive.

Vizzini prides himself on being a master thinker, and as he thinks through the possibilities, he finds himself drawn first to one goblet, then to the other:

"But it's so simple!" he says. "All I have to do is divine from what I know of you: Are you the sort of man who would put the poison into his own goblet or his enemy's? Now, a clever man would put the poison into his own goblet, because he would know that only a great *fool* would reach for what he was given. I am not a great fool, *so I can clearly not choose the wine in front of you!*"

And then, with barely a pause, he shifts direction: "But you must have known that I was not a great fool—you would have counted on it! *So I can clearly not choose the wine in front of me!*"

Back and forth he goes.

From his knowledge of the poison's origin he deduces that "*I can clearly not choose the wine in front of you!*"

But the Man in Black's penchant for reverse psychology proves that "*I can clearly not choose the wine in front of me!*"

And on and on.

"*...I can clearly not choose the wine in front of you!*"

"*...I can clearly not choose the wine in front of me!*"

I was beginning to feel like Vizzini. I could argue the passages back and forth to a dizzying degree. Maybe, I thought, I was looking at the whole thing too closely. Maybe I needed to accept my initial impression of these passages—that they condemned all gay relationships—and not think too much about it.

But *not thinking too much about it* was exactly the problem that had caused the church to be so unloving in the first place. We *needed* to think more about it. We *needed* to understand better. And this wasn't just about me; there were lots of happy, committed gay couples out there, some of whom had been together for decades, who truly loved each other. Was I going to be the one to tell them they had to break up if they wanted to be Christians?

I considered, too, what role my own biases played in this. I was attracted to guys, so, by definition, the idea of a God-ordained relationship with one was appealing to me. Did that desire for a companion disqualify me from being objective on this? Was I too blinded by my own loneliness to honestly evaluate what the Bible had to say? Perhaps I should stick with the "safe" position of celibacy, just to be certain. I would never want to let my own desires lead me to justify something sinful.

But, I realized, I also had an *opposing* bias in favor of continuing to believe what I always had believed. I had grown up believing without a doubt that gay relationships were sinful in all cases. As much as I wanted to fall in love, the idea that I had been wrong—and that my church had been wrong—on such a major issue didn't appeal to me at all. Even to *consider* changing my position on this was scary. However much my loneliness might push me in one direction, the security of my long-held beliefs pulled me in the other.

I briefly considered abandoning my quest to figure it all out and going back to just trusting my church and other Christians for answers. But other Christians were divided, too, and my church hadn't even understood yet that I didn't *choose* to be gay. How could they adequately advise me when they didn't even understand the key issue at stake?

"God, what do you want me to do?" I prayed. I half expected to hear an audible voice from the heavens answering my question.

Instead, I heard only silence. Where was God? When would He answer me?

CHAPTER 13

WHATEVER COMMANDMENT THERE MAY BE

After going through all the passages, I felt like I was back where I had started, confused and frustrated. Once more, I reviewed the evidence.

I was torn.

On one hand, yes, there was a potential explanation for each of these passages that meant it wouldn't apply to a modern-day committed gay relationship.

On the other hand, every explicit mention of homosexuality in the Bible was negative. Taken together, the most *obvious* sense of the passages was to condemn gay sex in all contexts. Even if there were other explanations, at some point it just started to feel like looking for loopholes rather than accepting the plain sense of Scripture. I wasn't interested in looking for loopholes.

On the *other* hand, context matters! The Catholic Church condemned Galileo for insisting that the earth revolves around the sun. Their rationale was based around a "plain sense" reading of several passages like Psalm 104:5: "[The Lord] set the earth on its foundations; it can never be moved." Today, the poetic imagery is obvious, but at the time, Galileo's interpretation of such passages as metaphors was seen as a weasely way of trying to avoid the plain sense of Scripture. Similar arguments were made about slavery, hair length, and women's head coverings. In each case, the church ultimately realized that the passages were relevant to a specific context or culture and did *not* apply in the same way to us today. Couldn't the same be true of same-sex relationships?

On the *OTHER* hand, if there was any doubt at all about this, as there certainly seemed to be, wasn't it the best thing to do—the safe thing to do—to count it a sin and stay celibate?

But on the other hand…

I thought of Tevye in *Fiddler on the Roof*, torn between his passion for his traditions and his love for his daughters, throwing up his hands and shouting, "No! There is no other hand!"

I couldn't do this anymore. I couldn't take the constant back and forth, and I was too afraid of talking myself into something wrong. I decided I would have to assume that God required celibacy unless God did something to change my mind—even though something about that approach didn't feel right in my spirit.

At the end of the battle of wits between Vizzini and the Man in Black, after debating at great length between the two goblets of wine, Vizzini attempts to trick the Man in Black into revealing the solution by surreptitiously switching goblets with him. Satisfied he's arrived at the only possible answer, Vizzini confidently drinks from his goblet—only to fall over dead.

"They were both poisoned," the Man in Black admits. "I spent the last few years building up an immunity to iocane powder."

After all that effort, and with all his cleverness, Vizzini had been looking at the puzzle all wrong. His assumptions were faulty, so he never asked the right question.

It wasn't until I stopped focusing on those few passages and went back to studying the Bible as a whole that it began to dawn on me that I had been doing the exact same thing.

I was asking the wrong question. I had been so focused on passages that mentioned homosexuality that I had completely missed the forest for the trees.

The passages I had become so fixated on are *not* the only confusing passages in Scripture. The more I studied, the more I began noticing other passages with the same sorts of problems. For instance, at a time when the term "Scripture" referred primarily to the Old Testament, Paul wrote to Timothy that "all Scripture is God-breathed and is useful for teaching, rebuking, correcting, and training in righteousness" (2 Timothy 3:16) and Jesus told his critics, "Do not think that I have come to abolish the Law or the Prophets [that is, the Old Testament]; I have not come to abolish them but to fulfill them" (Matthew 5:17). Yet both Jesus and Paul were accused by their opponents of disregarding the Old Testament Scriptures, and most Christians today feel comfortable ignoring many Old Testament laws. So are we supposed to follow those laws or not?

Even in the New Testament, there are passages I found distressing. For instance:

- Teach slaves to be subject to their masters in everything. (Titus 2:9)
- Women should remain silent in the churches. They are not allowed to speak, but must be in submission, as the Law says. (1 Corinthians 14:34)
- If a woman does not cover her head, she should have her hair cut off; and if it is a disgrace for a woman to have her hair cut or shaved off, she should cover her head. (1 Corinthians 11:6)

- Everyone must submit himself to the governing authorities, for there is no authority except that which God has established. The authorities that exist have been established by God. (Romans 13:1)

When examining this last passage, I came across a preacher who argued that civil disobedience such as sit-ins during the civil rights movement was a sin because it opposed "the authorities." But in that case, couldn't you also argue that Christians who helped the Jews escape the Nazis were violating this passage?

I don't know any Christian who would argue for the "plain sense reading" of all of these passages. Frankly, if they did, I would be concerned about them and their theology. I certainly don't believe that women have to cover their heads or stop talking the moment they enter a church, I don't think for a second that God approves of slavery, and I'm positive that the Christians who fought the Nazis are heroes.

Virtually all Christians recognize that there are passages in the Bible that can't be fairly applied with only a superficial reading. We need context and interpretation, and sometimes that means we need historical insight or other kinds of analysis that come only from a lot of study. For instance, many scholars argue that Paul's prohibition of women speaking in church was a cultural rule related to certain issues of the day. But many of the Christians who argue for a cultural interpretation of *that* passage would argue against the same kind of interpretation for the homosexuality passages.

So how do we know which passages are limited by their cultures and which ones still apply today? If we simply disregard as "cultural" whichever passages we don't agree with, the Bible becomes essentially useless as a moral guide. It's only reaffirming our own views, not challenging us on what we may have gotten wrong.

This leaves us with two options. One option is to throw out the Bible as a moral guide altogether, viewing it as simply a collection of flawed human writings and not expecting it to give us any divine perspective. That is, of course, the approach many non-Christians would take, but that wasn't acceptable to me as a Christian.

The other option is to have a clear, consistent biblical standard for interpreting the text, a principle we can apply to various passages that will help us to determine, fairly and consistently, how to translate them for our culture. This standard could help us make sense of difficult passages without reading our own beliefs into the text.

Such a standard would need to be able to differentiate God's eternal laws—such as those dealing with murder, theft, and adultery—from the cultural biblical rules Christians are no longer obligated to follow—such as those dealing with dietary restrictions and head coverings. It would give us a basic yardstick for Christian behavior, against which to measure all other actions and interpretations. And, ideally, it would give us a core touchstone by which to judge the many moral questions we face that aren't explicitly addressed in Scripture.

Paul offers just such a standard in his letter to the Romans. In the now-famous epistle, Paul lays out the central message of the Christian faith. People are sinful, he says, and even those who pride themselves on following God's law fall far short of God's expectations. Because none of us can be declared righteous based on our imperfect following of God's law, Paul explains, God offers us grace and a Savior in the form of Jesus, freeing us from the burden of the law without giving us license to sin.

Paul spends a lot of the letter addressing what this means for our relationship with God's law. He uses the term "law" seventy-four times in the letter's first twelve chapters; his final mention of the law comes in this passage:

> Let no debt remain outstanding, except the continuing debt to love one another, for he who loves his fellowman has fulfilled the law. The commandments, "Do not commit adultery," "Do not murder," "Do not steal," "Do not covet," *and whatever other*

commandment there may be, are summed up in this one rule: "Love your neighbor as yourself." Love does no harm to its neighbor. Therefore love is the fulfillment of the law. (Romans 13:8–10)

The first time I read this passage, I had to read it several more times to be sure I wasn't misreading it. Was Paul really saying that *whatever commandment there may be*—every commandment from God, including but not limited to the Big Ten—can be summed up in the rule to love one another? That sounded a little too "hippie liberal" for me. By that logic, couldn't someone use "love" as an excuse to justify, for instance, cheating on their spouse with someone more attractive?

No. Paul wasn't talking about that kind of "love." Paul used the Greek word *agape,* a term that suggested a selfless, unconditional, sacrificial kind of love, the kind of love that seeks others' good before our own. *That* kind of love is the fulfillment of God's law, and, according to Paul, it can be relied upon in any situation.

This didn't start with Paul, of course. Jesus had said that all the Law and the Prophets hung on the two greatest commandments: to love God and to love our neighbors (Matthew 22:34–40). In this context, focusing on interactions between human beings, Paul only mentioned the second of the two, with the first being implied.

But even so, how could Paul claim that *every commandment* could be summed up in the rule to love?

I considered this for a moment. If I truly love someone, and I'm living in love toward that person, I wouldn't kill them. I don't need a rule to remind me not to murder the people I love; living out my love for them precludes me from doing it anyway.

Similarly, if I'm living out God's pure *agape* love toward someone, I wouldn't steal from them. Stealing is an inherently unloving act. If I'm living in love toward my spouse, I wouldn't cheat on them. Cheating is selfish and unloving. If I truly love my brothers or sisters, I wouldn't covet the things they have; I'd be happy for them when good things come their way. That's what love is.

If I were truly filled with God's perfect *agape* love, and if I could live that love out in every moment of my life, I wouldn't need any other commandments written down, because I'd be automatically doing all the right things.

I thought about every example of sin I could come up with. In every single case, Paul was right: Truly living out God's *agape* love for others *always* led to doing the right thing. Sin always resulted from selfish desire in one form or another.

Surely, I thought, there must be more than that. In the past, I had thought of the Bible as a rule book for life. Yes, we're saved by grace, but I'd usually thought of righteous living in terms of following rules about what you could and couldn't do as a Christian. Yet Paul seemed to take the opposite view:

> Since you died with Christ to the basic principles of this world, why, as though you still belonged to it, do you submit to its rules: "Do not handle! Do not taste! Do not touch!"? (Colossians 2:20–21)

Well sure, but that was about *the world's* rules, right? What about God's law?

> Before this faith [in Christ] came, we were held prisoners by the law, locked up until faith should be revealed. So the law was put in charge to lead us to Christ that we might be justified by faith. Now that faith has come, *we are no longer under the supervision of the law.* (Galatians 3:23–25)

So if we're no longer under the supervision of the law, did that mean Paul was saying we get to sin if we want to?

> What then? Shall we sin because we are not under law but under grace? By no means! (Romans 6:15)

This confused me the first time I read it. It must have confused Paul's audience as well. How can we say that we're not under the law but at the same time say that we're not supposed to sin? How else can we know what sin is, except that it's a violation of God's law?

Paul very carefully explains the distinction:

> You, my brothers and sisters, were called to be free. But do not use your freedom to indulge the sinful nature; rather, serve one another humbly in love. For the entire law is fulfilled in keeping this one command: "Love your neighbor as yourself." (Galatians 5:13–14 TNIV)

Here Paul exposes two theological extremes. First, we are called to be free; we're not bound by the rules and regulations anymore, so the legalists are wrong. By the same token, we must not use that freedom to indulge our selfish desires—our "flesh"—so the hedonists are wrong. The middle way, the way of living out our freedom without sinning, is by serving one another humbly in God's *agape* love. If we live out that love in selfless service of others rather than indulging our own selfish desires, we will automatically do what God has called us to do. Sin comes from our own selfishness, not from selfless love.

And, once again, Paul reminds us that the command to love sums up the entire law.

This isn't just Paul's theology. Jesus applied the same principle.

One of the most important rules in the Jewish Scriptures (the Christian Old Testament) was the commandment to observe the Sabbath. From sundown on Friday to sundown on Saturday, Jews weren't supposed to do any work—no cooking, no lifting heavy loads, nothing at all. The day was supposed to be a day of complete rest dedicated to God.

Observing the Sabbath was a sign of allegiance to God (Exodus 31:13). It was one of the Ten Commandments (Deuteronomy 5:12–

15). God describes it as a "lasting ordinance" (Leviticus 16:31). Breaking the Sabbath was punishable by death (Exodus 31:14–15; Numbers 15:32–36). Over and over in the Scriptures, whether or not people are keeping the Sabbath is a sign of whether or not they are faithful to God (Nehemiah 13:15–22; Isaiah 56:2, 4, 6; Isaiah 58:13–14; Jeremiah 17:19–27; Ezekiel 20:12–16). Avoiding work on the Sabbath wasn't just any commandment; it was one of the most important commandments, like a litmus test for whether people were following God or living in sin.

So when Jesus healed people on the Sabbath, it was a big deal. Here he was, claiming to represent God, and yet he wasn't even following one of the most important of all God's commandments. Not surprisingly, this greatly upset the Pharisees.

It's easy for us to condemn the Pharisees from our perspective today. In the Bible cartoons I watched as a kid, the Pharisees were often depicted as one-dimensional villains, evilly stroking their beards as they plotted ways to oppose Jesus for no reason other than that he was the good guy and they were the bad guys. In fact, though, the Pharisees may have been more like us than we want to admit.

In many ways, these Pharisees were like the pre-Christian equivalent of today's most prominent preachers and Christian leaders. They were devoutly religious, they knew the Scriptures well, and they were very concerned with obedience to God. In addition to any political motives they may have had, one of their strongest objections to Jesus' ministry was that he seemed to be violating God's law and teaching others to do the same. If we'd been in their shoes, many of us modern Christians might have had the same concerns.

When Jesus publicly healed a man's withered hand on the Sabbath, the Pharisees were furious. Jesus knew this, and he made a point of letting the Pharisees see what he was doing. What fascinates me most, however, is Jesus' *justification* for his action.

Growing up, I always assumed that Jesus *wasn't* really breaking the Sabbath by healing someone, because perhaps God didn't count supernatural healing as "work" on the same level with cooking or heavy lifting. If I had been Jesus, that's the argument I would have made: "The Bible says not to *work* on the Sabbath. I'm not working; I'm healing. This isn't work for me."

Jesus doesn't make that argument. Instead, he asks something that seems like avoiding the question:

> Then Jesus asked them, "Which is lawful on the Sabbath: to do good or to do evil, to save life or to kill?" (Mark 3:4)

This used to puzzle me.

Students of logic would call this argument a "false dichotomy." Good or evil, saving life or killing aren't the only options. No one was asking Jesus to *kill* anybody, and he was healing a man's hand, not saving his life.[1] He surely could have waited until the next day to heal the man; there was no reason he *had* to do it on that particular day. The question was about the morality of healing on the Sabbath, and Jesus seemed to be avoiding it.

From a rule-following perspective, Jesus' argument makes no sense. But from a love-your-neighbor perspective, it makes perfect sense. What's the most loving thing to do: to help someone in their time of need, or to pass them by? If given the choice between the loving option and the unloving option, isn't it always right to do the loving thing? If love is the fulfillment of the law, shouldn't that take precedence over everything else?

The Pharisees were obsessed with following the Scriptures to the letter. In their zeal to obey God's law, they had become legalistic, debating questions like what would or wouldn't count as "work" on the Sabbath. If Jesus had defended his actions by saying "Healing isn't work," he would have been validating their legalistic letter-of-the-law approach to the whole issue. Instead, he suggests there's something much bigger at stake here: an underlying principle that is greater than the letter of the law.

On another occasion, Jesus and his disciples are walking through a grain field, and as they do, they pick some kernels to eat. Once again, the Pharisees are incensed. The Sabbath law forbade harvesting grain, and according to the Pharisees' strict interpretation, this included even picking a few kernels to eat.

> Some of the Pharisees asked, "Why are you doing what is unlawful on the Sabbath?"
>
> Jesus answered them, "Have you never read what David did when he and his companions were hungry? He entered the house of God, and taking the consecrated bread, he ate what is lawful only for priests to eat. And he also gave some to his companions." (Luke 6:2–4)

Notice what Jesus doesn't say. He doesn't say, "We're only picking grain, not harvesting, so we're not technically breaking the rule." That's what I would have said, and it's the sort of nitpicky argument the Pharisees were used to having.

Instead, Jesus gives them an even *clearer* example of a violation of God's law—and from the Scriptures, no less! In 1 Samuel 21, David is on the run from King Saul, and the only food he is able to get is the "bread of the Presence," which he is forbidden by God's law to eat, but he eats it anyway. Jesus approves this, arguing that sometimes violating the letter of the law is necessary in order to do the right thing and support the spirit of the law.

After healing on the Sabbath on another occasion, Jesus makes another argument to the Pharisees:

> Then he asked them, "If one of you has a child or an ox that falls into a well on the Sabbath day, will you not immediately pull it out?" And they had nothing to say. (Luke 14:5–6 TNIV)

Over and over, Jesus provides examples of the spirit of the law superseding the letter of the law. It's clear that pulling a child out of a well *is* work; there's no getting around that. It's equally clear that it would be the right thing to do, even on the Sabbath. What loving parent would allow their child to lie in a well overnight in order to follow the letter of the Scriptures?

When the Pharisees challenge Jesus about breaking the Sabbath, he doesn't argue with them about whether the Sabbath law "still applies." Nor does he argue with them about whether healing or picking grain is *really* a violation of the law (even though he would have a good case that it's not). He doesn't fall into the trap of debating about, for example, how much grain someone can pick before it counts as harvesting. These are exactly the sorts of arguments Christians often get into about homosexuality, debating to what extent certain passages apply to us today and whether they condemn a particular behavior in a particular situation or not. They are the arguments I had been agonizing over for months, feeling torn between different almost-convincing explanations.

Instead, Jesus gives the Pharisees examples of even more drastic violations of the law that would still be the right actions to take in their circumstances. Then he says:

> The Sabbath was made for man, not man for the Sabbath.
> (Mark 2:27)

Considering how important a part of the law the Sabbath was, we might interpret Jesus' words this way: "The law was made for people; people weren't made for the law."

Or, as Paul put it, "The law was put in charge to lead us to Christ." Christ did not come to lead us to the law.

Throughout his ministry, Jesus emphasizes the spirit of the law over the letter of the law, and often this means that Jesus' way is more difficult. When the law says not to commit adultery, Jesus says not to commit it even in your heart. When the law says to give and pray and fast, Jesus says to do these things for the right reasons and avoid doing them for praise from people. On the other hand, sometimes Jesus' way gives the freedom to set aside legalistic restrictions in favor of doing the loving thing, like pulling a child out of a well even when it violates the Sabbath law.

It is this approach that gets Jesus accused of abolishing the Law and the Prophets, and why he says:

> Do not think that I have come to abolish the Law or the Prophets; I have not come to abolish them but to fulfill them. (Matthew 5:17)

If Jesus had said that he *did* come to abolish the Law and the Prophets, we might just write all this off as proof that Old Testament laws such as the Sabbath law don't apply to Christians. But we still do follow some Old Testament laws (like the Ten Commandments), and Jesus said he came not to abolish, but to *fulfill* them. What can he mean?

From a Christian perspective, everything in the Bible—Old and New Testaments—points toward Jesus. The sacrifices, the rituals, the rules—all of these are just shadows of the reality in Christ (Colossians 2:17). What Jesus brings us isn't just a new set of laws; he brings us something completely different from what we had before.

If you've ever had to supervise young children, you know that sometimes kids need things spelled out for them. "Hey, Billy! You know the rule: Don't hit!"

"Well you didn't say 'Don't kick.'"

"Don't kick either, Billy. Hey! What did I say?"

"You said 'Don't hit' and 'Don't kick.' You didn't say 'Don't push.'"

"Don't hit, kick, *or* push."

As adults, we understand the purpose behind these rules. We

don't need to be told not to hit or kick or push; we understand that the point is to be kind to one another, and that these rules are a way of approximating that for children. We know that the rules don't really cover everything, and that there may be times when the rules must be violated in order to follow their spirit (say, to push someone out of the way of a truck). Rules have a purpose, but they don't exist for their own sake.

Medicine bottles tend to have a lot of rules on them. They're there for our protection. But have you ever had a doctor tell you to disregard the rules? If so, which did you follow—the rules or the doctor?

Once, when I was sick, the doctor advised me to take an over-the-counter medication in a way that contradicted the instructions on the bottle. "On the bottle it will tell you to take only two tablets," she said. "But for the next week, I want you to take four instead." I followed her advice. Why? Because I trust the doctor. She knows why that rule is on the bottle, and she knows that in certain circumstances, it makes sense to disregard it. On my own, I would never make that decision, but led by someone who understands the underlying purpose of the rules and has my best interests at heart, I have the freedom—even the responsibility—to do so.

I believe the Holy Spirit functions in that capacity for us as Christians. Christians usually understand the Holy Spirit as the "Helper" Jesus promised to send, the indwelling of God in the hearts of all believers. The Holy Spirit knows the purpose of God's laws and can guide us in interpreting and applying them to our situations, superseding the letter of the law when appropriate, and helping us to fulfill God's ultimate desire for us on earth: not to be slaves to a set of rules, but to live out God's unconditional *agape* love in every moment of every day.

That's why Paul says:

> If you are led by the Spirit, you are not under law. (Galatians 5:18)

Of course, anyone can *say* they're being led by the Spirit. Thankfully, the Bible gives us a reference for what it should look like when we are. Jesus tells us that bad trees bear bad fruit and good trees bear good fruit (Luke 6:43–44), so while we can't judge people's hearts, we *can* see the results of their actions.

Meanwhile, Paul tells us that every commandment from God can be summed up in the rule to love one another. As I mentioned, I could easily see how this was true for every sin I could think of: murder, theft, adultery, coveting, and so forth. Sin *always* results from a failure to act out of God's perfectly selfless love, and in the end, it always bears bad fruit.

With these standards in mind, it became much easier to interpret Scripture's difficult passages consistently. Yes, there were slaves in Bible times, but doesn't selfless *agape* love demand their freedom? Rules about head coverings and hair length had a purpose in Paul's culture, but if they have no ultimate bearing on our commission to selflessly love God and our neighbors, then, led by the Spirit, we can safely set them aside today.

I then tried applying these standards to the question of homosexuality. Undeniably, there were many types of homosexual behavior that were driven by selfishness, not by *agape* love. Behaviors like rape, idolatry, prostitution, and child exploitation were all clear examples of the results of selfish, fleshly motivation, not love for God or others. They were sinful, and their bad fruit bore that out.

But suppose two people loved each other with all their hearts, and they wanted to commit themselves to each other in the sight of God—to love, honor, and cherish; to selflessly serve and encourage one another; to serve God together; to be faithful for the rest of their lives. If they were of opposite sexes, we would call that holy and beautiful and something to celebrate. But if we changed only one thing—the gender of one of those individuals—while still keeping the same love and selflessness and commitment, suddenly many Christians would call it abominable and condemned to hell.

As I read and reread Romans 13:8–10, I couldn't find any way to reconcile that view with what Paul tells us sin is. If every commandment can be summed up in the rule to love one another, then either gay couples were the one exception to this rule, and Paul was wrong—or my church had made a big mistake.

A TERRIFYING PROPOSITION

The more I studied the Bible, the more I found myself coming to the conclusion that my church had gotten this issue wrong.

Because of Paul's teachings about grace and sin, and because of the way Jesus read and applied Scripture, I could no longer justify condemning a loving, committed, Christ-centered relationship based solely on gender. The bad fruit I saw coming out of my church's current approach and the good fruit I saw in Christ-centered gay couples I met only further reinforced this for me.

The standards Jesus and Paul applied—the same standards that allowed me to put aside culture-based biblical rules about food or hair length or head coverings—didn't just *allow* me to do the same on this issue; they *required* it. To do otherwise was being inconsistent.

As I considered this, I realized that my view had completely changed. Studying the Bible had convinced me of something I would have thought impossible only months before: that God would bless gay couples. For a lot of gay Christians, coming to that conclusion would have been a happy ending. For me, it was a terrifying proposition.

Yes, if my studies had reinforced the traditional view, I knew I'd have to endure the loneliness of celibacy, but at least that had felt like a "safe" position within established Christian tradition. Coming to a conclusion that supported gay relationships was uncharted territory. If I was wrong about this, I was moving in a sinful direction, and if I told anyone else what I believed, I could unwittingly lead people into sin. That was something I just couldn't risk! I would much rather be single and celibate—even if God didn't require it—than risk sinning against God and leading others down a sinful path.

And yet, the more I studied these passages and the more I prayed about this, the more I found it impossible to return to my former way of thinking. It was like the famous illustration that appears to be an old woman when viewed one way and a young woman when viewed another way. At first, you may only see one image, but once you've seen the other one, you can't go back and unsee it. Try as I might, I could never go back.

Still, I was terrified of being wrong, especially since I had such a personal stake in the matter. How could I ever be sure that I wasn't just seeing what I wanted to see? Maybe, I thought, I should say I still believed gay relationships were sinful, even though that now seemed to me in conflict with the Scriptures. I didn't want to risk being wrong.

But there was another thought I just couldn't shake: What if I was *right*? What if the majority of Christians had interpreted these passages incorrectly? What if we had allowed our own prejudices to cloud our judgment? What if we were turning people away from God by misapplying the Bible? If so, that wouldn't just be a grave injustice; it would be a sin against God!

Now I had a real dilemma.

Studying the Bible had brought me to a conclusion that was different from the one I had learned growing up. And if I was wrong and I spoke out, I could be sinning and leading others into sin. But if I was right and I *didn't* speak out, then I was allowing the church to be an active participant in a terrible sin, one that was not only destroying lives and families, but was also turning countless people away from the unconditional love of Christ.

The early church dealt with a similar dilemma. Today, Christians debate whether *gays* can be members of the church and if so, whether they have to be celibate. Then, Christians debated whether

Gentiles could be members of the church and if so, whether they had to be circumcised. Circumcision was required according to the Scriptures, and a split formed between those who believed it was still required and those who believed it no longer was. Not surprisingly, many of the Gentiles were on the side of not requiring circumcision anymore. I don't blame them!

Paul argued against requiring circumcision, but he went even further than that:

> Mark my words! I, Paul, tell you that if you let yourselves be circumcised, Christ will be of no value to you at all. (Galatians 5:2)

Paul didn't just believe circumcision wasn't *necessary*. He believed that doing it in order to be on the "safe" side was actually a *sin*. It was putting oneself back under the law and nullifying the grace that comes from Christ.

By that standard, I realized, there was no "safe side" on this issue. If I *supported* gay relationships and was wrong, I would be sinning by encouraging people to do something wrong, but if I *opposed* gay relationships and was wrong, I would be sinning by putting myself and others back under the law and making Christ "of no value."

Either way, these were big stakes, and I couldn't afford to keep quiet. I had to do my best to live according to what I believed, remaining open to God's leading and trusting in God's grace if I made a mistake.

And I had to speak up about the biggest thing the church was missing.

CHAPTER 14

LIGHTNING ROD

G race. We had missed the point of grace.

In his book *What's So Amazing About Grace?*, evangelical author Philip Yancey takes the church to task for failing to embody the very grace we sing about. He tells the story of a prostitute in Chicago, enduring horrible conditions and desperate for help. A friend of Yancey's asked whether she had considered turning to a church for support.

"'Church!' she cried. 'Why would I ever go there? I was already feeling terrible about myself. They'd just make me feel worse.'"

This, Yancey points out, is a far more common problem than most Christians would like to admit, and it has colored the world's view of Christians:

> These characterizations of Christians are surely incomplete, for I know many Christians who embody grace. Yet somehow throughout history the church has managed to gain a reputa-

tion for its ungrace. As a little English girl prayed, "O God, make the bad people good, and the good people nice."[1]

Whether I was right or wrong in my interpretation of Scripture about gay marriage, one thing was clear: We Christians were failing to show grace to the gay community the way Jesus would. At the very least, Christians ought to be listening to their gay friends, seeking to understand them, to know their joys and their struggles. If we couldn't do that much, how could we hope to be vessels for God's lavish grace and unconditional love?

I was sure most Christians were under the impression that they were extending grace. Nevertheless, even I as a fellow Christian was experiencing grace from them only rarely. If I, who was actively seeking grace from the church, wasn't finding it, then it almost certainly wasn't being felt by those gay people who had turned their backs on the church.

Jesus radiated grace and compassion in such a way that people came to *him* to hear his views on things. By contrast, we Christians were so focused on preaching our views on things that we were driving people away, turning them off to church, Jesus, and everything we had to say. If we didn't fix this soon, the damage to the church's reputation might be irreversible.

I had started this journey in search of answers for my own life. I had continued it because I wanted to fit in and be understood. Now I was moving into a completely new chapter: This was about stopping the misinformation cycle so the church wouldn't treat anyone else with such unintentional ungrace. And maybe, just maybe, helping to save the church from itself.

But why should anybody listen to me? I was a nobody. I wasn't a preacher or a theologian or a scholar. There were lots of things about the Bible I didn't understand and lots of theological questions I didn't have answers to. I did have a different take on the Bible passages in question, but I wasn't ready to go public with that yet.

There was just one thing I had that qualified me to address this subject, and it was something no one could take away from me: my story.

I typed up a short version of my story—growing up in the church, wrestling with my sexuality, and ultimately realizing I was gay—and posted it to a Christian internet group I was part of. The responses I got were surprisingly positive. One guy, who had only days before been railing against the evils of homosexuality, wrote to me to tell me that he had been deeply moved by my story and was now having to reconsider his approach to the issue.

Encouraged, I built a simple website for myself and posted my story there as well, sending the link to several of my close friends as a way of helping them better understand me. Those friends, too, sent me positive responses, indicating that I had made them rethink things.

What happened next stunned me. One by one, emails started trickling in from people I'd never met before. Many of them were closeted and scared gay Christians who had somehow found my website, and, with it, the first story they'd ever read from someone whose experience was similar to theirs.

At first, most of the emails were from teenagers and young adults, many of them going through the very same emotions I had been through. They wrote about feeling scared and alone, wanting to serve God but being afraid of rejection at the hands of the church. They wrote about how emotional it was for them to find my story and know there was someone else out there like them, someone who loved God like they did and knew what it felt like to be attracted to the same sex. They asked for my advice on coming out to their parents and their pastors. They wanted to know if I thought there was any chance that, someday, they could fall in love. I tried my best to offer encouragement without claiming to have the answers.

Then other emails began to come in from people of all ages. A mom wrote to ask about how to respond to her gay son. A pastor wrote, saying that I was the only person in the world he'd told about his true feelings; he was afraid of losing his congregation if they knew. A seventy-year-old woman wrote, saying that all her life, she'd never told anyone her secret—not her husband, not her kids, not her grandkids. She wanted to encourage me not to make the same mistakes she had. "Tell the truth," she urged.

Then came the email I can never forget. "I was going to kill myself tonight," it said. "I told God He had one more chance to give me a reason not to. Somehow I found your website.... You will never meet me, but tonight you saved my life."

As the emails continued to pour in, a few of us began meeting regularly in an internet chat room, where we discussed the challenges of being gay in the church. I encouraged the others to write out their stories and post them online too.

Meanwhile, on campus, tensions between GALBA and CCF were at an all-time high. GALBA students had showed up to protest CCF's latest ex-gay speaker, and the resultant shouting match had pleased no one on either side. One of my GALBA friends and I began meeting with two CCF members to discuss a better way for CCF to address the relevant issues. From what I could tell, it seemed that CCF's members and leadership were split about how to handle the question, but eventually they agreed to host a symposium to discuss the subject.

There were some conditions: The symposium would be planned and hosted entirely by CCF; GALBA was to have no involvement. (This was all just as well, since I'm not sure GALBA would have wanted any involvement anyway.) At the symposium, three speakers would be given ten minutes each to tell their stories, followed by Q&A with the audience. I was to be one of the speakers, to represent a gay Christian viewpoint; my friend Jordan, a CCF leader, was to represent a straight Christian viewpoint; and a representative of an ex-gay organization was going to come to campus to represent an ex-gay viewpoint.

I groaned inwardly at the inclusion of the final speaker. CCF had already had multiple ex-gay speakers come to campus. If the goal of this symposium was supposed to be building bridges between CCF and the gay students on campus, the dialogue could have taken place between a representative of each of those communities. There was no reason to bring an out-of-town ex-gay leader to campus to add to the mix. This arrangement was a reminder of the underlying Gays-vs.-Christians dynamic—we were being set up as competing points of view rather than simply an opportunity to understand a group of students on campus.

Reservations aside, I knew this was a huge step forward for CCF, and I jumped at the chance. The three of us sat onstage in front of an auditorium full of CCF students. It was the first time I had spoken in front of so many people. With only ten minutes to speak, I knew I didn't have time to represent the concerns of GALBA or talk about Bible interpretation; instead, I just focused on telling my story as I had told it now to so many others. The Christians sat transfixed, and afterward, most of the questions were for me.

"You've really never been attracted to a woman?"

"Has it been difficult to hold on to your faith through all this?"

"What are some practical things I could do to better support the gay students on campus?"

This last question caught me by surprise. It was exactly the right question to ask, and yet I suddenly realized I didn't have a good answer ready. I tried my best to answer off the top of my head, while mentally filing this goof away. *Next time I speak to a Christian audience,* I thought, *I'll have some practical tips ready.*

When the symposium ended, I was suddenly the man of the hour. CCF members lined up to thank me and to tell me how much my story meant to them.

One wide-eyed girl shook my hand as if I were her favorite movie star. "When you apologized for going over by a couple of minutes, I just wanted to say, 'Don't apologize! Keep talking! Keep talking!' I could have listened to you all night."

That bit of praise felt a little overboard to me, but I realized what she meant. It wasn't that I was such a compelling speaker; I had been nervous and awkward. The big deal was that the story I had to tell was a story these kids had never heard before. For some, I was telling their story, though they might never admit it. For others, I was telling the story of their friends or family members. Fundamentally, I was telling the story of people the church had wronged, and that mattered to them.

I went to bed that night with my mind racing. This was the way to change the world: combat the misinformation with personal stories.

Lights, Cameras, Activist

Our campus had a closed-circuit TV station, accessible in all the dorm rooms. Perhaps the most popular show aired at midnight, a campus issue discussion/call-in show hosted by two conservative Christian students. As GALBA was gearing up for a week of activities to bring attention to its cause, we got a call asking if we'd like to discuss our plans on the show. I volunteered along with Martin, a fellow GALBA member, and that evening, we were miked up and staring into TV cameras as midnight hit and the show went live.

This was it. If anyone on campus didn't know I was gay by now, they were about to.

Sitting there under the bright lights and fielding questions from the hosts and the disembodied voices of the show's callers, it hit me that I was in way over my head. The hosts began by asking us about GALBA and our upcoming activities for the week, but the questions quickly turned to topics like the long-term impact of gay couples adopting or how we could know definitively if a certain historical figure was gay.

I didn't have answers to these questions. I couldn't speak for the American gay community. I was just Justin, a Southern Baptist college student who had figured out he was gay only a few years earlier. Yet in a lot of people's minds, merely admitting that I was gay was a political statement.

Lesson learned: Being out didn't make me an expert on all things gay. It only made me an expert on my own story. Like it or not, though, people were going to ask me those kinds of questions. If I was going to keep speaking out, I was going to have to study, and I was going to have to learn how to set boundaries and graciously decline to answer questions outside of my area of expertise.

A hundred miles away, my parents were fast asleep when the phone call came, startling them from their slumber.

My mom answered.

"Do you have a son named Justin Lee?" the voice on the other end asked.

Her heart dropped. She was sure something horrible had happened. People don't call you in the middle of the night and ask you about your child unless something is wrong.

"Yes," she said, fearing the worst.

"Did you know he's a homosexual?" the caller asked.

Never have I been more glad that I told my parents the truth before starting college than I was when she told me about this conversation the next day. I can only imagine how it would have affected them and my relationship with them if this had been how they'd learned the truth.

Thankfully, they already knew.

"Who is this?" my mom asked.

"I'm a student at your son's school," he said. "I'm watching him on TV right now."

I hadn't told her I was going to be on TV.

Mom was confused, worried, and probably more than a little irritated that I hadn't told her I was going to do this. But she was *not* going to let someone speak badly of her son. As the anonymous caller proceeded to disparage me, telling her how disgusted he was that I would call myself gay while claiming to be a Christian, she stuck up for me, telling him that he didn't know what he was talking about, and that she was proud of me for being honest. Whatever disagreements she and I had, in this moment, she was my mother. And that was all that mattered.

Later, my parents and I realized that the caller must have gotten my home phone number from the campus directory, where that information was listed for every student. But we never knew who the mysterious caller was, leaving me wondering who on campus would harass my parents in the middle of the night, and what else they might do.

The incident shook me up. I realized that taking an unpopular stand could cost not only me, but my family as well. In spite of that, it brought my mom and me closer together. I knew she didn't want me going on TV and taking public stands. When I had first come out, she had begged me not to tell anyone about my sexuality. She worried it would follow me forever, and that people would only see me as a gay man, no matter what I might otherwise accomplish. Even so, she never fussed at me for that late-night campus TV appearance. She was angry at whoever would say such horrible things about me. We didn't stop disagreeing after that, but it reminded us both that we were family before anything else. We were all going to get through this together.

Shaken but undeterred, I continued speaking out and telling my story whenever I could. I made more campus TV appearances, published my story in a book of campus essays, and helped organize another seminar on homosexuality and Christianity, this one with GALBA's help. The more I told my story, the more positive feedback I got. There were always detractors, but in general, other Christians seemed genuinely moved by my story, and many of them thanked me for changing their attitudes toward gay people.

All this time, emails kept pouring in from around the world, and I spent more and more of my time answering them, offering to pray for people and letting them know they weren't alone.

Like it or not, I was becoming a lightning rod for the gay/Christian controversy, not only on campus but around the internet. Other people were turning to me as an authority, even though I was still very aware of how much I had to learn. I studied the Bible regularly and devoured every theological work I could find on the subject, but I always found myself with more questions than definitive answers. What I knew for sure was what I had experienced, and that was what I told people about.

The Gay Christian Network

By the time I graduated, I was receiving more emails than I could answer from gay Christians in need of support and someone to talk to. I knew I couldn't keep being the sole support system for all these people, so I prayerfully considered ways they could support each other.

I bought some message board software, configured it for our needs, and launched an internet community space for my newfound gay Christian friends to gather and support one another. We called it the Gay Christian Network, or GCN.

As I responded to emails from gay Christians, I mentioned this new online safe space to them. Soon, there were about a dozen of us posting messages each day, praying for each other, chatting, becoming friends, rediscovering how good it felt to be part of a community that loved you as you were.

Then there were a hundred of us.

Before long, there were a thousand.

As this little pet project of mine grew, I realized how deep the need was for this kind of connection, drawing people from very different places in life. People who were wrestling with the burden of lifelong celibacy showed up, as did people who had been in committed same-sex relationships since before I was born. Some came looking for friends. Some came looking for love. Some came looking for God. Some came because they wanted to offer their support to others. Most came because they were desperately in need of that support.

We were all over the world. We crossed all denominational lines. We were diverse in age, gender, and race. Some of us hadn't decided yet whether we thought it was okay for gay Christians to be in committed, consummated relationships. Those of us who *had* made up our minds didn't all fall on the same side. Yet in the midst of all our disagreements, we were united by two things: our passion for Jesus Christ and our conviction that the church needed to do a much better job of supporting gay people.

For the first two years, I paid all the organization's expenses out of my own pocket. I designed and maintained the website, wrote the computer code to make it work, approved and followed up on new member registrations, moderated discussions to ensure everyone was heard, answered all the emails that came in, and so forth, all while working a full-time job. As the community continued to grow, it got to be overwhelming. So great was the need for this kind of resource that I found myself requesting fewer hours at work and spending every moment of my free time just trying to maintain the website.

After a while, people began asking spontaneously whether they could write me checks in gratitude and to support the future of what they had come to see as an important ministry. I didn't want the burden of handling people's money without some kind of oversight, so after further prayer and reflection, I suggested something else: We should incorporate. People pitched in the money for a lawyer and filing fees, and a year later, the Gay Christian Network was officially a 501(c)(3) nonprofit organization.

As we became a nonprofit, our focus changed. No longer was GCN going to be my little pet project; now it was about all of us. Together, we had the power to do much more than provide prayer and encouragement to individual hurting gay Christians. Together, we could work to help the church understand how it was missing the mark. Our goal, then, was to help transform the church into an institution that would be doing the kind of supportive ministry work we had so needed and found lacking—and in so doing, to make the existence of our own organization someday no longer necessary.

Until then, we would keep providing that one-on-one support that people needed and working to bring about the day when GCN would be an anachronism.

Up until starting GCN, my primary focus had been on *gay* men and women in the church. Soon, I was meeting people who were bisexual and transgender,[2] and learning from them about some of the other kinds of experiences that can make people feel like outcasts. We welcomed them into our group and began using the common acronym "LGBT" (lesbian, gay, bisexual, and transgender) to talk about challenges all of us shared. I also began meeting a lot of straight Christians who cared deeply about these issues and wanted to be part of helping make change. We welcomed them, too, with open arms.

Change came quickly. What began as an internet project morphed into something more. People were forming strong bonds with their new friends from the website, and it wasn't long before they were talking about getting GCN members together in person for local Bible studies and social events. Then someone asked: What if we set a date and place for a national gathering?

The first GCN conference was on January 8–9, 2005, at a small church in Dallas, Texas. Forty people attended, not just from across the United States but from other countries as well. A volunteer named Danny and I pulled together a bare-bones agenda, but we didn't really know how to plan a conference, and the end result was about the least polished, least professional event you can imagine. Nothing started on time, the audio system didn't work, and it wasn't until I was set to take the stage with a video presentation that I discovered I had forgotten the video cables.

In the end, none of that mattered. We began singing songs of worship, and in that moment, every one of us knew we were home. Some people raised their hands in praise; others swayed back and forth; still others stood quietly and mouthed prayers. Something I cannot describe filled the room—an overwhelming experience of the peace and joy and warmth of the love of God—the moving of the Holy Spirit in all of us in a way that took my breath away and reduced people to tears. This was undeniably God's work.

We set up an open mike for people to share the things God was doing in their hearts that weekend. One after another, people came forward to tearfully pour out their gratitude for the existence of a group like this. A young man's voice cracked as he told us all this was the first time he had felt the Holy Spirit in his life since coming out and being forced to leave his home church. Another man broke down as he shared how GCN members had been there to pray with and support him after his partner of fifteen years had died in a hiking accident. A Southern Baptist woman beamed with joy at the experience of being in such a community of support and seeing God work in so many lives. A recording of testimonies from that first conference still sits on our organization's website to this day, a reminder of where we began.

The next year, the conference doubled in size. Then it doubled again. Soon, hundreds were attending each year from all over the world for worship, speakers, and fellowship. Talented volunteers ensured that things felt much more professional in time, but underneath it all was that same powerful experience of God's love working in our lives. And we were amazed.

SIDE A AND SIDE B

Before I even built the GCN website, I knew I had to make a critical decision about how this new group would handle differing opinions. I had once believed that gay relationships were sinful and that I would have to be celibate in order to serve God. I no longer believed that, but I had gay friends who still did. How was GCN going to respond to people like them?

One of the websites that had proved helpful to me in my journey was a now-defunct internet discussion group called Bridges Across the Divide. Bridges Across wasn't a Christian group, but it had been started by two Christians with very different views on homosexuality—Maggie, a straight mother who supported her gay daughter's committed relationship, and Steve, an ex-gay man who viewed such relationships as contrary to God's will. The two had begun a dialogue about how people with such opposing viewpoints could understand one another and work together for respect and peace in the midst of the culture war.

As others joined the conversation from both sides, the group discovered a problem: There was no easy way of referring to the two positions.

Maggie's position might be called "pro-gay," but did that make Steve "anti-gay"? That didn't sit right, and since there were celibate gay people who agreed with Steve, it didn't make sense. They might call them "liberal" and "conservative" views, but those terms already had too much political and theological baggage to be particularly helpful. (What of those who agreed with Maggie but had conservative political and theological stances?) Similar problems plagued every pairing of terms they could think of.

Eventually, the group settled on something completely different: "SideA" and "SideB." They explained the terms this way on their website:

> SideA: There are people from many backgrounds who for religious or other reasons believe that homosexual relationships have the same value as heterosexual relationships.
>
> SideB: And there are those of many faiths who disagree, believing that only a male/female relationship in marriage is the Creator's intent for our sexuality.

In essence, SideA holds that gay sex (like straight sex) is morally acceptable in the right circumstances. SideB holds that gay sex is inherently morally wrong.

Each of these groups might have many subgroups. For instance, two SideA people might disagree on what the "right circumstances" are. One might say that gay sex is only acceptable within a same-sex marriage, while another might argue that it only matters that the partners are consenting adults. Similarly, two SideB people might disagree on how a same-sex-attracted person should live. One might argue for ex-gay ministries, while another might strongly oppose that and push for celibacy instead.

SideA and SideB were just broad terms, but they gave the group a way to talk about the issues. Eventually, the terms began to pop up in other places as well, with people discussing whether they held a "Side A" or "Side B" (now usually with the spaces) view of homosexuality.

The Bridges Across project made a huge impression on me. As I read and participated in some of the conversations the group was having, I was struck by the respectful tone of the dialogue between such different people. I saw Christian ex-gay leaders having productive conversation with gay Wiccans, and that floored me.

I also saw the limitations of such dialogue. In order for this kind of thing to be successful, it seemed that the group had to be small and intimate enough for people to really get to know and trust each other. If the group got too large, the respectfulness of the dialogue seemed to suffer. Personalities made a difference; so, too, did the existence or nonexistence of shared values between people.

Bridges Across functioned primarily as a training ground, bringing people from different viewpoints together to dialogue and take what they learned to their respective walks of life. As an organization, Bridges Across didn't really do work "in the world." The success of their dialogue made me wonder, though: Could this model of bridge-building be practically applied to other kinds of organizations as well?

All this was already in my head when I started GCN. I wanted *all* my gay Christian friends—celibate or not—to feel welcome, safe, and respected in this new space. I wanted to model for the church and the world that it is possible to live in loving, Christian community in the midst of significant theological disagreements. We developed some basic rules: Both "Side A" and "Side B" people would be welcome at GCN, and within this space, both sides would agree not to try to convert or talk down to one another. GCN was to be a neutral zone, a place for people to put the culture war aside and know they were among friends.

Being a group that supported gay Christians was shocking enough to a Gays-vs.-Christians world, but the idea that we welcomed both Side A and Side B was more than some people outside the group could take. I received regular hate mail from people on both sides, accusing us of everything from being secretly in league with Exodus to being secretly in league with the devil. Some people, upon visiting GCN's online community and realizing that people from "the other side" were welcomed, immediately left and didn't come back. Potential supporters offered to provide funding for the project, but only if we would get rid of the people from the side they didn't agree with, or at least officially disavow that view. We refused.

Yet for every person who condemned us or left in protest, there were five or ten more who told us that our bridge-building approach was the very reason they had come. Amazingly, this experiment was working. People were getting along and loving one another across the divide. Yes, we had our setbacks, but we had far more successes. In our human, fallible way, we were discovering what it means to be the Church.

News of what we were doing made it out to the media, and then things really exploded. The *New York Times* called. *Dr. Phil* called. CNN called. Reporters wanted to come interview me in our office, and I was embarrassed to tell them that we didn't even have an office; I was still working out of my apartment. I did TV, radio, and newspaper interviews for markets across America. It was amazing; we were this little nonprofit with hardly any money at all, no staff, and no office, but the media was fascinated by us. Gays and Christians are supposed to be enemies. Side A and Side B are supposed to be enemies. Yet here we were, cats and dogs, living alongside each other and supporting one another in good times and bad.

A new command I give you: Love one another. As I have loved you, so you must love one another. By this everyone will know that you are my disciples, if you love one another. (John 13:34–35)

Over the last few years, GCN has become a safe haven for many thousands of LGBT Christians and a leader in the movement to educate Christians about LGBT issues. We've produced pamphlets, videos, and podcasts, and put on conferences and retreats. I've been invited to speak to Christians across the country and overseas as well. Recently, I interviewed dozens of young gay Christians for a

GCN documentary called *Through My Eyes* to help straight Christians understand what it's like to be gay in the church. We have an office now, and a small staff—and from time to time we field phone calls from people like Cindy, the mom with the gay son I mentioned at the beginning of this book.

We're all still learning and growing and changing each day, and we still don't do everything perfectly. We never will. But I've now had the opportunity to meet so many amazing Christians and churches who are committed to fixing the mistakes we Christians have made and getting this right. They've proven to me that the Holy Spirit is still alive and well in the church, and that underneath all the ugliness our fallen humanity has brought to the name of Christ, there is plenty of hope for the future.

Christians will not all agree on this issue anytime soon. But living together in loving Christian community is possible, even in the midst of that challenging disagreement. It's not easy, and we will all make mistakes. But it's what God calls us to.

It is, I believe, even more than our doctrine, the thing that most demonstrates our commitment to Christ.

CHAPTER 15

THE WAY FORWARD

Two millennia ago, a man called Jesus of Nazareth changed the world forever.

Born in the humblest of circumstances, he devoted his life to the service of others. He socialized with outcasts and sinners. He had compassion for those who were hungry and sick. He preached about God's plans for our future, but he preached even more about grace, humility, and forgiveness in the here and now. His followers rightfully proclaimed him a king, yet *he* was the one who washed *their* feet. He lived every moment as a servant, and then he gave up his life for the sake of those who killed him.

I believe that man was and is the Son of God. I am a Christian because of *him*, and I believe that we as Christians are called to follow in his footsteps. When we do, we make the world a brighter place. When we fail, we can destroy lives. Tragically, our treatment of LGBT people is one place where we've failed over and over again, and the neighbors Jesus taught us to love are the ones who have paid the price for our sins as a church.

Nearly every day, I hear a story about someone whose life has been torn apart by this culture war, and far too often, the Christians in their lives either left them to fend for themselves or took an active role in making their lives worse. That's not the way of Jesus. If we're going to call ourselves his followers, we have to do better.

There are seven things I believe we must focus on if we want to create a better world for the next generation and see the church become what God has called her to be.

1. CHRISTIANS MUST SHOW MORE GRACE, ESPECIALLY IN THE MIDST OF DISAGREEMENT.

When I discussed homosexuality with my high school friend Sean over fifteen years ago, I thought that "love the sinner, hate the sin" was the perfect summary of Christian grace in the midst of disagreement. Now, I cringe when I hear people say that.

The basic point of the phrase is true. But "love the sinner, hate the sin" feels very different depending on which side of the table you're sitting on. To the person doing the "loving," it feels very generous: *Even though this person is a sinner, I'm going to treat them with love and compassion!*

However, it doesn't feel very generous at all when someone is saying it about you. Yes, I know I'm a sinner, as we all are, but something about the phrase feels condescending and dehumanizing, as if I'm now "the sinner" rather than the person's friend or neighbor, and "loving" me has become the new project they've taken on out of obligation to God rather than a genuine interest in my well-being. For this, it seems, I am supposed to feel grateful, as if this were a great imposition on someone who could easily have passed me by and left me in my sinful state.

When someone says they're "loving the sinner," it sounds as though the person being referred to is a "sinner" in some sense that the speaker is not. That's not a biblical picture. According to the Bible, all of us are sinners, equally fallen in God's eyes, and all of us have been shown so much grace by God that we have absolutely no right to look down on anyone else.

Baptist author Tony Campolo has an interesting response to the phrase:

> I always am uptight when somebody says…"I love the sinner, but I hate his sin." I'm sure you've heard that line over and over again. And my response is, "That's interesting. Because that's just the opposite of what Jesus says. Jesus never says, 'Love the sinner, but hate his sin.' Jesus says, 'Love the sinner, and hate your *own* sin. And after you get rid of the sin in your own life, then you can begin talking about the sin in your brother or sister's life.'"[1]

Jesus was known for his grace and mercy. His friends were widely known as outcasts and sinners, yet he treated them as his friends, not as "sinners" or projects. When other people were ready to stone a woman caught in adultery, he stood in her defense. When he met another woman with a live-in boyfriend and a long string of husbands, he acknowledged her situation without lecturing her about it. Jesus knew that most of the people he encountered were already painfully aware that "people like him" looked down on them as sinners. Rather than adding to their shame, Jesus met them as friends, treating them as equals even though they were in no way his equals, and showing them love and grace even when they didn't deserve it.

If anyone had a right to lecture people about their sin, it was the sinless Son of God. If even he could meet sinners as equals, how much more should we Christians—all sinners ourselves—treat as equals the people we encounter in our lives?

Jesus saved his lecturing and anger exclusively for the self-righteous and those who put barriers in the way of others trying to come to God. When greedy and unscrupulous money-changers set up shop in the only space reserved for Gentiles to worship, Jesus turned over their tables in disgust. His most famous frustration, however, was with the self-righteous Pharisees.

As I mentioned earlier, I believe the Pharisees of Jesus' day had a lot in common with today's Christian leaders. Whenever Jesus addresses the Pharisees in the Bible, I think we Christians need to sit up and take notice to see if in some ways he may be talking to us. In Matthew, he says of them:

> Do not do what they do, for they do not practice what they preach. They tie up heavy loads and put them on men's shoulders, but they themselves are not willing to lift a finger to move them....
>
> Woe to you, teachers of the law and Pharisees, you hypocrites! You shut the kingdom of heaven in men's faces. You yourselves do not enter, nor will you let those enter who are trying to.
>
> Woe to you, teachers of the law and Pharisees, you hypocrites! You travel over land and sea to win a single convert, and when he becomes one, you make him twice as much a son of hell as you are....
>
> Woe to you, teachers of the law and Pharisees, you hypocrites! You give a tenth of your spices—mint, dill and cummin. But you have neglected the more important matters of the law—justice, mercy and faithfulness. You should have practiced the latter, without neglecting the former. You blind guides! You strain out a gnat but swallow a camel. (Matthew 23:3–4, 13–15, 23–24)

What the Pharisees lacked—and what we Christians have all too often lacked—is grace. We must never let our theological disagreements get in the way of showing God's unconditional, overpowering grace to everyone we meet.

When CCF leader Warren invited me out to lunch only to preach at me, I didn't feel any grace. A year later, he and his wife moved to another position, and a new couple, Brent and Jennifer, took their places. By this point, it was common knowledge within the group that I was gay, so I knew it was only a matter of time before Brent and Jennifer found out. I was tired of feeling like a victim, waiting for other people to figure things out, so during one of my first conversations with them, I found an excuse to mention my involvement with GALBA. Sure enough, Brent responded almost immediately by asking me to meet him for lunch, just as Warren had done before him, "just to talk."

I accepted the offer, but this time I came prepared. The day of the meeting, I made a list of the questions I thought he was likely to ask, and I rehearsed short, simple answers to all of them so that I could explain myself before he could interrupt. I bookmarked all the relevant passages in my Bible and packed it into my backpack. Then, with a deep breath and a silent prayer, I was off to meet Brent for lunch.

As Warren had done before him, Brent started out with small talk: "How are you?" "How are your classes going?" "Do you have plans for the future?" I sat there stiff as a board, keeping an eye on the time and keeping my answers short, making sure we'd have plenty of time to talk about the real issue at hand.

About halfway through lunch, there was a lull in the conversation. I was worried we wouldn't have time if we didn't get a move on, so I spoke up: "So, Brent, what did you have in mind to talk about today?"

"What do you mean?" he asked.

"Well, I mean, you invited me to lunch. I assume you had a reason for inviting me. What did you want to talk about?"

He looked confused. Then—what? Hurt? Offended? I couldn't

tell. "I didn't have anything in particular in mind," he said simply. "I'm new to the group, so I'm trying to get to know everyone, and you're active in the group, so I just wanted a chance to meet you and have lunch."

As soon as the words came out of his mouth, I knew it was true. I had assumed he was just the same as Warren, and with all my emotional armor on, it had never occurred to me that he might just be a nice guy who wanted to get to know me for me, not because he wanted to preach at me. In my haste to keep him from stereotyping me, I had stereotyped him.

That was over ten years ago, and Brent still stands out in my mind as one of the examples of straight Christians in the world who know how to love people like Jesus loved, not with an air of condescending paternalism, not proud of themselves for "loving the sinner," but with genuine humility and caring. If only all Christians were like Brent.

But with every negative encounter gay people have with Christians, it gets that much harder for the Brents of the world. I went into the conversation with Brent ready for a battle because my past experience had led me to believe that that was what I was going to get. When Christians try to mask a condescending attitude with politeness and faux friendliness, gay people begin to suspect that all supposedly friendly Christians are really hiding judgmental attitudes toward them. Eventually, they try to avoid Christians altogether.

This effect is so strong that it even affects committed Christians who are gay. My friend Michael recently confessed to me that he sometimes catches himself wanting to avoid "the sort of people who like going to church" even though he also likes going to church. Michael is a deeply devout Christian, but he's heard so many anti-gay remarks from other Christians that he finds himself dreading conversations with Christians *even though he's one of them!*

Aaron, another gay Christian friend of mine, shared with me that his experiences with other Christians were seriously damaging his faith. In a recent chat online, he wrote to me, "With all that I've been going through these last few years, I'm having trouble trusting Christianity. Like I don't know if I can ever trust a pastor ever again." Gay people are not pulling Aaron away from the church. Christians are.

Tragically, the lack of grace in the church has cost some people their faith entirely. I've seen it happen over and over, not just with gay people, but with those who care about them. In 2010, Catholic author Anne Rice, herself the mother of a gay son, made headlines when she publicly renounced her faith, at least partly due to the church's treatment of people like her son. "I quit being a Christian," she said, adding, "I remain committed to Christ." I know many people who can't even say that.

Many people on both sides have imagined that this fallout is a result of the disagreement over the morality of gay relationships. It isn't. That disagreement is important, but Christians are able to disagree on many theological and moral issues without causing this kind of turmoil. What makes this issue unique is the level of venom and ungrace people are feeling from the church, and it is that—not merely the disagreement—that people are responding to in such strong ways.

So what can we do? We can show grace. We can make grace the centerpiece of everything we do as Christians.

There's no step-by-step guide for being gracious. There's not a list of rules to follow. Grace is about letting the Holy Spirit work through us to show people understanding and love instead of judgment. When people wrong us, we can be merciful and forgiving instead of trying to get even. When it comes to gay people, the church can remember that they're already well aware that Christians think they're sinners; no one needs to remind them. In every moment of every day, we can treat people with God's *agape* love.

Rather than loving the sinner and hating the sin, we can love everyone and hate our own sin.

2. WE MUST EDUCATE CHRISTIANS.

Whether you're a Christian or not, whether you're straight, bi, or gay, this is something you can help do.

If the yeast of misinformation is one of the most powerful forces working against us, then better education is the antidote.

As I've reiterated throughout this book, Christians are not bad people. They're good people. Many of them have just been misinformed on this issue. If they really understood what it was like for gay people, they would change their attitudes in a heartbeat. It's up to us to help them understand.

In many cases, we'll have to start at the very beginning, explaining that people don't choose to be gay and that there's a difference between people's behavior and their orientation. Those seemingly simple concepts are at the heart of a lot of misunderstanding on this issue, and it's easy for people to skip over them in their rush to get to the Bible debate. Education like this can't be rushed, however; we have to take things one step at a time to make sure we all understand the dilemma even though we may not agree on the solution.

One of the most powerful ways of educating people is by sharing our stories. If you're a parent of a gay person, share what that's been like. If you're a pastor wrestling with questions because of people you know in your congregation, share that experience. Whoever you are, you have a story. When we're able to be vulnerable about our pain as well as our joy, that vulnerability has great power to open hearts and change minds. Jesus often modeled how apparent weakness and humility can actually bring tremendous strength, and that's definitely true here.

Some gay people are worried about sharing the painful parts of their journeys because they don't want to come across as victims. I definitely understand that fear. But I believe it's important for us to be honest about the good *and* the bad in our stories. Pretending we haven't been hurt—if indeed we have—doesn't help people understand us. Being honest about our emotions, our mistakes, our pain, our confusion, and everything else allows people to see us as the human beings we are instead of seeing us as just an issue.

In addition to sharing our stories, we can educate in all kinds of ways. A church might plan a forum on the issue. A pastor might preach a sermon. A family member can share resources from the internet. You might even give someone a copy of this book. We need to take every opportunity to help the church understand the issues better. In so doing, we might just save the church and save lives.

3. WE MUST MOVE AWAY FROM AN "EX-GAY" APPROACH.

Too many churches have relied in the past on ex-gay ministries to be the "solution" to the gay "problem." In these churches, if a person comes out or admits to struggling with their sexual identity, they're usually pointed to an ex-gay or "sexual brokenness" ministry for healing. As we've already seen, this simply doesn't work.

I could share hundreds and hundreds of stories of people who poured their hearts into ex-gay programs, prayer, and other types of therapy, only to discover that neither they nor the others in their programs ever became straight. It wouldn't matter; people would still keep asking me, "Yes, but how do you know it could never work for *anyone*? Maybe this time will be the exception."

It's true that I can't make any promises about what a particular person's experience will be. I can tell you, though, that of all the people who try to become straight through prayer and therapy, only a tiny percentage ever claim to have succeeded. And in most of those cases, there are significant reasons to doubt that they really changed from gay to straight.

But, some wonder, if there's even a tiny chance that an ex-gay ministry might work for some people—or even just for one person—isn't that a reason for Christians to support them?

I get asked this question a lot, especially by Christians who disagree with my biblical support of gay relationships but who still want to be compassionate to gay people. Asking people to be single and alone for the rest of their lives seems harsh, so they reason, isn't it worth at least trying to become straight, even if the possibility of success is remote? And if so, shouldn't churches promote ex-gay ministries as an option for those who want them, if for no other reason than to provide hope that at least some people could become straight?

The motive for supporting ex-gay ministries is often noble, and the Christians who point others to them are usually well intentioned. So they're often surprised by the vehemence with which many gay people—including celibate gay Christians—oppose these efforts.

The truth is, in spite of the good intentions, promoting ex-gay groups can have some serious negative consequences for both the church and the gay people those Christians are trying to reach.

It's very clear that ex-gay ministries do not work for the vast majority of people, and from the evidence I've seen, I think it's doubtful that they have changed anyone's orientation. Yes, some people have claimed that they went from gay to straight, but many of them later admitted this wasn't true, and there's a lot of motivation for people to claim a change that isn't actually happening. In most cases, even those who have married a member of the opposite sex will admit that they haven't actually gone from gay to straight, that even if they never act on their feelings, they remain attracted to the same sex.

What's much more common, as I shared in the stories of Terry and James, is for people to convince themselves that they've changed, marry a member of the opposite sex, and only later realize that they're still gay. At that point, they've dragged other people into a bad situation with them. I've heard countless stories of lives ruined this way, with husbands, wives, and kids all suffering devastating consequences.

Even for those who don't marry, the false hope of change can function like a drug, providing an initial high followed by a terrible crash. As people begin to recognize that their orientation is not changing, they often sink into deep depression, realizing they've wasted years of their lives working for something that was a lie. For people who already started off feeling ostracized and disordered, this can be an absolutely crushing blow. Many blame themselves, beating themselves up for not having enough faith, and in some cases even becoming suicidal. Others blame God or the church; I've lost track of the number of people I've seen lose their faith entirely as a result of their experiences in ex-gay groups. These people end up many years later just as gay as they were to begin with, but now with deep emotional scars and a distrust of anything the church says. If gay Christians as a group have been hurt by the church, those who have gone through ex-gay ministries are often wounded far more deeply.

In spite of their public claims, ex-gay ministries are often much more effective at taking away faith than at taking away attractions. Churches need to know this before they send people in that direction.

These ministries don't only have a negative impact on those who go through them; they also affect the churches and Christian groups that recommend them. Even when the ex-gay groups do publicly state that they can't promise that gay people will become straight—something they don't stress nearly enough—churches frequently fail to hear the warning. When churches host or recommend an ex-gay ministry, they typically feel they're addressing the "gay issue"—and, as a result, offer no support for the many gay Christians who don't want to spend years of their lives trying to change their attractions, or who have already done so and found it ineffective.

Individual Christians, too, tend to offer very little support to their gay friends and family members if they think those people could go to an ex-gay group and become straight. The very existence of the ex-gay group is enough to make many straight Christians think that any gay person *not* in such a group must be "choosing" to be gay. As a result, these Christians try to push their loved ones into ex-gay therapy or look down on them for "not trying to change."

For these and other reasons, ex-gay groups—though usually very well meant—tend to create toxic environments for gay people in churches and Christian society. Gay people know this from experience; this is why so many gay people get emotional about them and feel unsafe in churches where such groups are promoted.

The bottom line is, ex-gay ministries don't do what many people think they do. The people who started them a few decades ago had high hopes, but we now know more than we did then. Sexual brokenness groups can be helpful for people wrestling with addictions or recovering from past abuse, but they aren't a solution to the struggles facing gay people in our churches, and they have the potential to cause a tremendous amount of harm. As Christians, we must move away from an ex-gay mentality and look at real, workable solutions that will allow gay Christians to live openly and honestly.

4. Celibacy Must Be a Viable Option.

In the past, many people assumed that there were only two options for Christians who were attracted to their own sex: Either go to an ex-gay ministry to be "healed," or accept oneself as gay and pursue a consummated same-sex relationship.

There is, however, a third option: Be celibate.

Members of the other two groups are often reluctant to promote the idea that one can be openly gay and celibate. Many ex-gays object to the idea because they don't like the term "gay"; if we admit that a celibate gay person is still *gay*, then it becomes obvious that same-sex-attracted "ex-gays" aren't really ex-*gay* after all. Other gays, meanwhile, may view "Side B" celibate gays as sitting in judgment of non-celibate gays, and they may worry that promoting celibacy as an option only encourages churches to expect and require it for *all* gay people.

I believe, though, that both sides need to work to ensure that celibacy is a viable option for gay Christians and that celibate gay Christians are fully welcomed and supported.

In previous chapters, I explained how my own biblical study led me to the conclusion that God does *not* require gay people to be celibate. I still believe that, and growing numbers of other Christians are coming to the same conclusion. However, at this point in time, that view is still the minority view in the church, and I think it's important for all Christians—including those who disagree with me—to have the support and understanding of their brothers and sisters. Celibacy is an extremely difficult path. It can be lonely and disheartening. Gay Christians who believe this is God's call for them need tremendous support from their church families.

Because most churches currently teach that gay sex is contrary to God's will, we'd expect that at least *those* churches would support their gay members in living a celibate life. In practice, unfortunately, that is usually not the case. Most of the time, such churches either ignore the issue altogether or only support an ex-gay approach. As one celibate gay Christian woman I know recently wrote, "My experience with a lot of churches is that they will say, 'Gay people should be celibate,' but then leave you out in the cold to figure out what that means." Her frustration is echoed by many other celibate gay Christians I know; they're doing what their churches taught them to do, but their churches aren't giving them any help in doing it. In many cases, they're even looked down on because they didn't "change."

If churches are going to teach that gay Christians must be celibate, then at the very least they must provide ongoing, tangible support for them in their journey. These celibate gay Christians need avenues for companionship and love. They need to be able to be open about their lives, not to have to hide the fact that they're gay for fear that someone will misunderstand. Even with all the support in the world, many wouldn't be able to make it. So how can anyone be expected to do so when they are given no help and are even reviled for their honesty?

In some ways, it's a symptom of a larger problem. Many American churches have fallen into the cultural trap of idolizing dating and marriage relationships, to the point that even *straight* single Christians beyond a certain age begin to feel like second-class citizens. American culture tends to obsess over romantic relationships—just turn on the radio, watch TV, or go to the movies for proof—and people who make it to midlife without having married must face the perception that something is "wrong" with them.

The church has the power to be a family to single people and to give them a place to feel fully welcomed and included. All too often, we fail to do that. Even when churches offer special classes or programs for single adults, many of them only consist of some combination of general Bible knowledge and teachings designed to prepare people for meeting their future spouse; few of them adequately address the unique needs of single people *as* single people. Many churches don't seem to know how to support a single adult who isn't planning to get married.

I've talked to many single Christians who find the church a challenging place to be at times. But for single *gay* Christians, there are even bigger hurdles. A forty-five-year-old single straight woman may feel overlooked or misunderstood at her church, but she doesn't have to worry about being condemned for being *straight*. Single gay Christians face the difficulties of singleness alongside potential condemnation for their orientation. And while all single people face challenges in our culture, the challenges faced by people who are single by choice or because they haven't yet found the right person are different from the challenges faced by those who eagerly desire companionship but believe God requires celibacy *even if they should fall in love in the future.*

Earlier in this book, I shared some of the many worries I had about the possibility of a future as a single gay Christian—among them, worries about loneliness, companionship, and the challenges of handling aging and sickness alone. These are all worries that the church has the ability to help address. They are the sorts of things churches are perfect for. Yet over and over, instead of offering the kind of everyday support celibate gay Christians need, we've focused only on preaching at them. We're dropping the ball where it really counts.

Without church help in determining how to handle the challenges of celibacy, some gay Christians have had to do their best to work things out on their own. Some have formed special covenant friendships—loving but non-sexual relationships to meet their need for companionship without engaging in any kind of sexual activity. Even this, however, can earn them condemnation from other Christians. In 2009, after hearing of two women who entered such a friendship, Exodus International president Alan Chambers wrote that it was an obviously sinful relationship and an attempt at what he called "diet homosexuality." "If I was going to go as far as these two women have I would just go all the way," he said.[2]

But if even a covenant friendship isn't good enough for the church, then how should these women live? Mr. Chambers seems to suggest they should get back into an ex-gay program and just keep trying to change—not a surprise, given that he's the head of such an organization. However, that is simply not a realistic or compassionate solution based on the evidence. Other Christian leaders may have other ideas, but right now, the church as a whole isn't giving much help to women like them. It's amazing they're able to stay strong in their faith in spite of it all.

Seeing the lack of support for celibate gay Christians in the church, I decided from the beginning that GCN needed to welcome and embrace them. This surprised a lot of people. Most gay and gay-friendly groups don't have any tangible place for "Side B" celibate gays.

I believe they must be welcomed and supported in following their consciences. They face many of the same challenges and prejudices that "Side A" gay people face, along with unique struggles of their own. They are making very difficult decisions for their own lives in the face of seemingly impossible obstacles. They deserve our support and respect, and if we each want people to respect our own views and right to follow our consciences, I believe we must give the same to others.

It's also important that people know this option is available to them if they want it. There are many gay Christians out there who don't believe it would be right for them to be in a gay relationship, so they think their only option is to spend their lives in ex-gay therapy. Celibacy is a challenging path, but it gives people in that position the opportunity to be honest and admit that they're gay while staying true to their beliefs. That can be incredibly healing.

5. WE MUST SHATTER THE MYTH THAT THE BIBLE IS ANTI-GAY.

As long as people believe the Bible is anti-gay, they will continue to believe the church is anti-gay as well, and the war between gays and Christians will continue.

So far, neither side has done a very good job of challenging the notion that the Bible is anti-gay, leaving many people to believe they must choose either to follow the Bible *or* to love their gay friends.

Outspoken Christians on the traditional side have been so eager to oppose sexual immorality that they've frequently come across as hostile to gay people. Bible references and words like "abomination" have become firmly linked in our cultural mindset to these ungracious Christian attitudes, giving the impression that the Bible is the source of such hostility.

Often, gay and gay-friendly groups unintentionally *reinforce* this view. When ungracious Christians quote the Bible to support their anti-gay rhetoric, many in the pro-gay world respond by attacking the Bible's legitimacy as a moral guide, calling it a fallible, 2,000-year-old human work. All this does is reinforce the idea that the Bible must really be anti-gay and that the only way to truly support gay people is by not believing the Bible.

In a variation on this theme, some pro-gay Christians will argue that others are reading the Bible "too literally" and that if they would stop taking it so literally then they would understand that it's not really anti-gay. This doesn't help either. When these Christians say not to take the Bible "literally," what they usually mean is that the Bible should be read in *context* and that we should not "proof-text" by pulling passages out of their historical, cultural, and biblical context. I wish they would say so, using words like "context" to explain their position. Instead, when they say not to take the Bible "literally," what the other side *hears* is that they don't take the Bible *seriously* and don't believe it means what it says or that it can be trusted for moral guidance. Once again, this comes across as a concession that the Bible really is anti-gay and that loving gay people requires abandoning a view of it as God's Word.

Of course, there are many who do see the Bible as a bunch of hogwash or don't agree with the way certain Christians read it. But if those are the only arguments against anti-gay attitudes in the church, then we are creating the perception that the Bible is hostile to gay people and that Christians who *do* take it "literally" should be hostile to gay people too.

That's simply not the case, and we need to make that known. In Chapter 13 I showed why I believe that even a very conservative reading of the Bible is consistent with support for gay relationships. Many other gay and straight Christians have come to this conclusion while still viewing the Bible as the authoritative and trustworthy Word of God.

But Christians need not agree with my conclusions in that chapter. Even with a more traditional reading that condemns gay sex, the Bible never condemns gay *people* for who they are and what they feel. We may disagree on whether the Bible can be reconciled with same-sex marriage, but we should be able to agree that the Bible is not homophobic and does not justify the unkind attitudes some Christians have become known for.

It is *not* because of the Bible that some Christians are ungracious to gay people. That attitude is absolutely contrary to what the Bible says.

Churches on both sides need to hammer this point home. Christians should know that there are different interpretations of these passages in the church and that whatever the correct interpretation may be, it is certainly not necessary to dilute or throw out the Bible in order to have a loving, welcoming approach to gay people.

6. OPENLY GAY CHRISTIANS MUST FIND THEIR PLACE THROUGHOUT THE CHURCH.

I spent years thinking that something was wrong with me because I was gay and that in order for God to use me, I'd have to become straight. I now realize God's been able to use me even more because I'm gay.

In a culture that sees gays and Christians as enemies, gay Christians are in a unique position to bring peace and change minds. We're Christians who know firsthand what it's like to feel like outcasts and to be hurt by the church, and that gives us important perspective that the church needs. We've become very aware of our reliance on God's grace at a deep, personal level in a way that many Christians haven't. We've had to fight for our faith, questioning everything and making us rebuild our faith from the ground up, truly claiming it for ourselves and not just accepting what we were always taught. We've had to evaluate what works and what doesn't in the church, and that's made us stronger and made our faith stronger. We've had to learn to put our ultimate trust in God instead of in the human institutions of the church.

When it comes to sharing our faith, we have more credibility because of what we've been through, and we know the reasons many people outside the church are so resistant to our culture's version of Christianity. If Christians in our culture are killing Christianity, the gay Christians just might be the ones who are able to save it.

For these and dozens more reasons, I think God wants to use gay Christians—along with bi Christians, and trans Christians, and others in similar situations—to help the church become what she's supposed to be. That means that we who are gay and Christian must accept the calling and take our place in the church, working in the various ways we're led to make the world and the church a better place. It also means that straight Christians must work to ensure that gay Christians are welcomed and supported at all levels of the church, and that their unique experiences and insight are honored.

This is easy to say, but making it happen raises some significant challenges. What happens, for instance, when a "Side A" gay couple in a committed relationship attends a "Side B" church that believes such relationships are sinful? Is it possible to welcome someone you believe to be sinning, without compromising your moral stance?

Churches continue to wrestle with this question. Some have responded as my old church did, telling gay Christians they are welcome to attend only as long as they are celibate. Their rationale for this comes from 1 Corinthians 5, where Paul chided the Corinthian church for failing to take a stand when a man in their congregation became well known for having an incestuous relationship with his own stepmother. The relationship was one that was universally recognized as sinful not only within the Christian community but also throughout the whole society. Paul described it as something that "does not even occur among pagans."

Paul had good reason to be concerned: Not only was the church failing to offer the moral guidance it should; this man's behavior risked seriously harming the reputation of the church in the broader culture. In Paul's day, this "Christianity" was a mysterious new thing most people didn't yet understand, and false rumors about what Christians believed dogged the church for centuries. As Denver Theological Seminary professor Bruce Shelley notes:

> [One] cause of persecution of early Christians were the slanders disseminated about them. Once these were started, they could not be halted. The suspicion that the Christian gatherings were sexual orgies and cover for every kind of crime took hold of the popular imagination with a terrible vehemence.[3]

As the church was just starting to make its mark, it was vital that Christians distance themselves from the appearance of condoning sin, and Paul advised them to do so. In some ways, though, that situation was the exact opposite of the situation faced by the American church today, where the prevailing view of us is that we are unkind, judgmental, and homophobic, and where distancing ourselves from gay people only damages our reputation even more.

There's another critical difference here. Paul was describing a situation where there was essentially universal agreement that the behavior in question was sinful: The church knew it, the culture knew it, and presumably the man knew it as well but simply didn't see any need to repent. Paul hoped that by taking a strong stand against his sin, the church could demonstrate the seriousness of the problem and move him to repent. That does not, however, describe the modern-day situation about gay relationships. There is widespread disagreement—both within the culture and within the church—about the morality of these relationships, with honest, sincere, committed, Bible-believing Christians on both sides of the argument. The gay couple attending church is likely doing what they believe to be the right thing, not living in open and sinful rebellion, and as I've tried to demonstrate in this book, the questions are difficult, complex, and hotly disputed among Christians.

Paul's advice for situations like these is completely different from his advice in 1 Corinthians 5. In Romans 14, Paul addresses a similar, hotly disputed question of the day, the question of whether it was participating in idolatry for Christians to eat food that had been sacrificed to an idol. Because of the widespread availability of such food in that culture, it had become a major issue. Some Christians argued that eating such food was idolatrous and sinful, while others argued that it was acceptable if one did it with the right heart. In his response, Paul wrote:

> Accept the one whose faith is weak, without quarreling over disputable matters. One person's faith allows them to eat anything, but another, whose faith is weak, eats only vegetables. The one who eats everything must not treat with contempt the one who does not, and the one who does not eat everything must not judge the one who does, for God has accepted them. Who are you to judge someone else's servant? To their own master, servants stand or fall. And they will stand, for the Lord is able to make them stand.
>
> One person considers one day more sacred than another; another considers every day alike. Each of them should be fully convinced in their own mind....
>
> You, then, why do you judge your brother or sister? Or why do you treat them with contempt? For we will all stand before God's judgment seat....
>
> Therefore let us stop passing judgment on one another. Instead, make up your mind not to put any stumbling block or obstacle in the way of a brother or sister....

So whatever you believe about these things keep between yourself and God. (Romans 14:1–5, 10, 13, 22)

When everyone was in agreement, Paul encouraged the church to take action. But when there was serious disagreement within the Body of Christ, Paul encouraged people to follow their consciences and allow other believers to do likewise. I believe the situation we're facing today is the latter type.

Of course, no matter how welcoming a "Side B" congregation is, many gay couples will feel unable to attend a church that cannot honor their relationship as blessed by God. Two years ago, GCN sponsored a Christian dialogue on gay issues that was held at a church with a traditional ("Side B") viewpoint. One of the pastors from that church spoke movingly of his desire to reach out to and welcome the gay community, even though he and his church officially considered gay relationships to be sinful. He pointed out that although that was the official view of the church, it was not a regular sermon topic, and he felt the environment of the congregation was warm and loving for *all* people, regardless of their background. We had discussed some of the hurt that gay people have faced at the hands of the church, and this pastor was clearly brokenhearted over the pain. He wanted to do his part to change things.

In response, a partnered gay man spoke up. "I hear your earnestness," he said. "I see that you want to welcome me. But I have to tell you that I just couldn't sit Sunday after Sunday in a church where my relationship with my partner—the most important person in my life—is viewed as something sinful. Could you be a member of a congregation that said your relationship with your wife was really just living in sin? My integrity and respect for my partner and myself won't allow me to do that."

The exchange continued for quite some time, and it impacted all of us. That couple won't be attending that church, but the honest conversation that took place—with grace and love on both sides—helped to build a vital bridge of understanding that may transform how both sides see the issue.

Each gay person has a different perspective. Celibate gay Christians may well feel at home in that church, and I know many gay couples who have chosen to attend churches because of other things about the church or about its theology, in spite of a lack of support for their relationship. Others say that's just something they could never do. Each of us must make our own decision, and each church must carefully examine the issue and decide what sort of place there is for gay Christians in the congregation.

Ultimately, I believe it is incumbent on those of us who are gay Christians to graciously take our places in the church wherever God calls us, and to lovingly prod the church to explore these difficult questions. We need not apologize for being different; this is something the church needs right now, and it is the role God has called us to.

7. WE MUST LEARN HOW TO EFFECTIVELY DIALOGUE.

By "we," I mean everyone who cares about this issue, whatever side they're on, gay or straight, Christian or not. This book is only a small piece of the larger conversation that needs to happen in the church and in our society. My experience is but one of the many, many unique experiences people on all sides have had. We each have a different perspective, and moving forward will require us to talk to one another, and, more importantly, to listen to one another.

For parents, this means listening to your kids. If you find out your child is gay, don't make assumptions about what that means. Allow them to tell you. Listen to their stories, and seek first and foremost to understand what they are feeling. Don't push them into "reorientation" therapy they don't want; it's only likely to damage their faith and their relationship with you. Let them know that you love them, and don't ever push them away. They may do things you don't approve of, but they need to know that they can still come to you when things go wrong.

For gay people, this means being patient with your Christian friends and family members. They haven't had your experience and they don't know what it's like to be you. If you've only recently come out to them, they haven't had much time to process it, and they may say things they later realize they didn't mean. Remember that ignorance is your enemy, and the best way to battle ignorance is by gently and patiently sharing your story: fear, joy, pain, and all. They may not receive it, and it may be many years before they understand. Don't pin your self-esteem on their approval, but don't give up hope, either. Even when they don't agree, you may still be able to maintain a positive relationship with them with a little effort.

For pastors and churches, this means encouraging loving, open-minded dialogue not only within your congregation, but with other congregations as well. Churches that have found success in welcoming gay people should reach out to other churches in their communities and work together to foster conversation among those who disagree. Churches without a substantial gay population should look for opportunities to get to know the local gay community and engage them in dialogue—not to preach at them, but to listen to and learn from them.

For all of us, productive dialogue means reaching out to people whose views and experiences are different from our own and having the patience to really listen to them with a goal of better understanding them and their worldview. This is difficult for many of us; we want to tell people why they're wrong and change their minds. Ironically, that approach is also the *least* likely to actually change anyone's mind. To have any hope of changing someone, we often have to stop trying to force them to change, focusing instead on building a bridge of understanding.

Have you ever answered the phone in the middle of a busy day only to discover that the person on the other end was a telemarketer? Telemarketers often use friendly words, asking, "How are you doing today?" as if they had a genuine interest in you as a person. But it becomes quickly apparent through their actions that they have no interest in you personally; the show of compassion is just a trick to keep you on the phone long enough to hear their sales pitch.

It's incredibly annoying, and it's not limited to telemarketers. A character in the movie *Fight Club* suggests that only when people think you're dying do they actually *listen* to you "instead of just waiting for their turn to speak."

But real, healthy dialogue, as management consultant Stephen Covey reminds us, requires that we "seek first to understand, *then* to be understood." We can't skip the first step in order to get to the second. If we approach people as telemarketers, asking questions only for an excuse to pitch our own ideas to them, they'll sense our lack of real interest, and they won't care about anything we have to say.

Healthy dialogue doesn't wait until people are dying—physically, emotionally, or spiritually—before really listening. Healthy dialogue necessitates that we focus first and foremost on seeking to *understand* other people, learning everything we can about them—how they feel, what they believe, and why—and then making sure *they* feel fully understood by us before we ever attempt to help them understand *our* point of view. Sometimes it can be helpful to restate what you're hearing the other person say, and see if he or she agrees that you've gotten it right. Sometimes you have to wait for the other person to ask about your views before he or she is ready to hear them. Sometimes you might end up waiting a long time.

It's vital, too, that we take time to learn the other person's language. This is especially true for Christians entering into their first dialogue with the gay community.

For example, the term "homosexual" is widely considered offensive when used to describe people ("How do homosexuals feel about this question?"). Technically, the word is accurate, but it was long used in a clinical context and has been most recently used by gay-rights opponents, so Christians seeking loving dialogue with the gay community would be much better off to use the word "gay"—or the broader term "LGBT"—as a sign of respect. (In 2008, one anti-gay group intentionally set up the news feed on their website to change the word "gay" to "homosexual" in all news articles, knowing this would anger the gay community. The joke was on them when, in an article about sprinter Tyson Gay, he was automatically renamed "Tyson Homosexual" by their computers, resulting in the humorous headline, "Homosexual eases into 100 final at Olympic trials"!) Likewise, the word "lifestyle" (as in "the gay lifestyle") sounds disparaging to many gay people and has strong associations with the ex-gay movement. Gays, like straights, live many different kinds of lifestyles, so instead of "the gay lifestyle," it's usually better to be specific: "people in committed same-sex relationships."

Dialogue means we must set aside our own prejudices and language preferences for the sake of communication. It often requires finding ways to work within the other person's value system. If the thing you value the most is your commitment to the Bible, I'm not going to get very far if I ask you to throw that out in order to address my own concerns. In order to work within other people's value systems, though, you have to know what their values are, and that's why it's so important to seek to understand them first and foremost.

We must be willing, too, to seek common ground and shared interests. Perhaps you and the other person have very different views on some things but both share a concern for the emotional health of gay people who feel hurt by the church. If so, that's a starting point. You can find ways to build on that without having to compromise on your most deeply held values.

This kind of gracious dialogue is hard for a lot of people. It feels wishy-washy to them, as if it requires that they stop thinking the other side is wrong.

However, it's not as if there are only two ways of relating to a person—either agree on everything, or preach at them about the things you disagree on. We already know this. Every day, we all interact with many people in our lives, and we probably disagree with the vast majority of them on a lot of things: politics, religion, sex, relationships, morality, you name it. Very few of my friends share my theological beliefs, and yet I don't feel compelled to bring those differences up time and time again, making them feel self-conscious about them. If I did, I'd probably lose those people as friends. Most of the time, I'm not even thinking about our differences; I'm just thinking about who they are as people and the many reasons I like them.

Grace sees people for what makes them uniquely beautiful to God, not for all the ways they're flawed or all the ways I disagree with them. That kind of grace is what enables loving bridges to be built over the strongest disagreements.

Gracious dialogue is hard work. It requires effort and patience, and it's tempting to put it off. All of us have busy lives and a lot of other issues to address.

But for anyone who cares about the future of the church, this can't be put off. The next generation is watching how we handle these questions, and they're using that to determine how they should treat people and whether this Christianity business is something they want to be involved in. Moms like Cindy are waiting to know that their churches are willing to stand with them in working through a difficult issue. And gay Christians everywhere, in every church and denomination, are trying to find their place in the world.

Will we rise to the challenge? Will we represent Jesus well? Or will we be more like modern-day Pharisees?

A SHINING EXAMPLE

When I was still in college, at the height of my struggles to figure out my place in the world, our campus was visited by Baptist minister and author Tony Campolo, the one with the quip about loving the sinner and hating your own sin. Dr. Campolo believes that the Bible limits sex to the marriage of a man and a woman. His wife, Peggy, holds the opposite view; she supports same-sex marriage, and the two of them have delivered a number of joint public presentations in which they discuss their differences of opinion and how they're still able to love each other and respect each other's faith in spite of such a significant theological disagreement.

I had read about the Campolos and their presentations, so when I heard Dr. Campolo was going to visit the CCF weekly meeting while he was on campus, I knew I had to be there.

The room was busy with activity when he entered the room. The meeting hadn't started yet, so he walked around, greeting people warmly. I realized this was my chance to meet him and thank him in person for his work building bridges in the church on the issue that was changing my life.

I nervously made my way through the crowd in his direction. Then he turned around, and I found myself standing face to face with him.

"Dr. Campolo," I blurted out, "my name is Justin Lee. I'm part of the gay student group on campus here, and—"

I had intended to tell him that I was also a member of CCF, that I had been studying the Bible debate, and that I respected him and his wife for their willingness to talk publicly about the need for greater understanding and patience. All of that was in my head, but I didn't get that far.

Before I could get another word out, he was giving me a warm embrace, saying, "Well, I'm glad you're here!"

I was stunned. This man knew nothing about me except that I

was gay. He didn't know if I was a Christian, if I was having sex, or anything else about my life. He didn't ask. He simply made me feel welcome and unconditionally loved.

Nearly speechless, I managed to tell him that I was a Christian who had been struggling with what it meant to be gay and Christian.

"Tell me all about it!" he said, leading me to two chairs in the corner of the room and inviting me to sit next to him. For the next few minutes, he ignored the crowd just to hear my story. He didn't offer any advice or judgments, and he didn't ask whether I shared his view that gays should be celibate. He just listened and affirmed me. He made me feel important and heard as a human being. He showed me love. And when he had to get up to speak to the crowd, I realized that it didn't matter whether he and I agreed theologically or not. He loved me as I was, just as Christ would.

In that moment, I knew one thing for certain. No matter what theological views Christians might ultimately hold on gay marriage, sex, or relationships, if all Christians loved as Dr. Campolo loved me in that moment, this world would be a completely different place.

May it be so, and may we be the ones to make it happen.

NOTES

CHAPTER 1. BATTLE OF THE CENTURY

1 David Kinnaman and Gabe Lyons, *unChristian: What a New Generation Really Thinks About Christianity…and Why It Matters* (Grand Rapids: Baker Books, 2007) 92.
2 Matthew 11:19 (ESV).
3 Romans 3:9–31.
4 Matthew 18:23–35.
5 Luke 18:9–14 (TNIV).
6 Dan Savage, "In Your Image," *Savage Love* (14 October 2010).
7 Jonathan Merritt, "An Evangelical's Plea: 'Love the Sinner,'" *USA Today* (20 April 2009) 11A.
8 Steve Clapp, et al., *Faith Matters: Teenagers, Religion, & Sexuality* (Fort Wayne, IN: LifeQuest, 2003) 93–110.

CHAPTER 4. THE TRUTH COMES OUT

1 Luke 15:11–32.
2 E.g., John 3:19–21; Ephesians 5:8–13.

CHAPTER 5. WHY ARE PEOPLE GAY?

1   For the sake of simplicity, I'm not addressing some of the more complicated gender questions in this section, and I will be using the terms "sex" and "gender" interchangeably.

2   Irving Bieber, et al., *Homosexuality: A Psychoanalytic Study* (New York: Basic Books, 1962) 310–313.

3   Gilbert, Elizabeth, "Queer and Loathing," *SPIN* 12.3 (June 1996): 78.

4   Joseph Nicolosi and Linda Ames Nicolosi, *A Parent's Guide to Preventing Homosexuality* (Downers Grove, IL: InterVarsity Press, 2002) 86.

5   Simon LeVay, *Gay, Straight, and the Reason Why: The Science of Sexual Orientation* (New York: Oxford University Press, 2011) 271–272.

CHAPTER 6. JUSTIN IN EXGAYLAND

1   Colin Cook, "Church Funds Program for Homosexuals," *Spectrum* 12.3 (1982): 46–48.

2   Ann Japenga, "It's Called Change Counseling: Troubled Pioneer Maintains His Faith in Program," *Los Angeles Times* (6 December 1987).

3   Virginia Culver, "Sessions with Gays Criticized: Former Minister's Counseling Methods Brought Reprimands," *Denver Post* (27 October 1995).

4   E. Mansell Pattison and Myrna Loy Pattison, "Ex-Gays: Religiously Mediated Change in Homosexuals," *American Journal of Psychiatry* 137.12 (December 1980): 1553–1562.

5   Alan Chambers, "Pray the Gay Away?", *Our America with Lisa Ling* (March 8, 2011).

6   Exodus altered these paragraphs on their website just as this book was going to press, but they continue to refer people to "Exodus member ministries" across North America that use similar language.

CHAPTER 7. THAT THE MAN SHOULD BE ALONE

1   Donald Trump, *Piers Morgan Tonight* (9 February 2011).
2   Roger Ebert, "All the Lonely People," *Chicago Sun-Times Online* (5 November 2010).

CHAPTER 9. THE POISONED YEAST

1   Stephen Covey, *The 7 Habits of Highly Effective People: Restoring the Character Ethic* (New York: Fireside, 1990) 30–31.
2   Bruce Bawer, *A Place at the Table: The Gay Individual in American Society* (New York: Touchstone, 1993) 47.

CHAPTER 10. FAITH ASSASSINS

1   Philip Yancey, *What's So Amazing About Grace?* (Grand Rapids: Zondervan Publishing House, 1997) 31.

CHAPTER 11. THE OTHER SIDE

1   Bawer 18–19.

Chapter 12. Back to the Bible

1 Robert A. J. Gagnon, *The Bible and Homosexual Practice: Texts and Hermeneutics* (Nashville: Abingdon Press, 2001) 130.

2 I did read Bible commentaries that suggested romantic relationships between figures such as David and Jonathan or the centurion and his servant, but I wasn't convinced that these were romantic/sexual relationships or that there was enough there on which to hang a theological argument about sexual morality.

Chapter 13. Whatever Commandment There May Be

1 The Pharisees, by contrast, did have murder in their hearts.

Chapter 14. The Lightning Rod

1 Yancey 11, 32.

2 The word "transgender" can refer to a variety of situations where a person's gender identity differs from what is commonly expected for their biological sex.

Chapter 15. The Way Forward

1 Tony Campolo, *Bridging the Gap: Conversations on Befriending Our Gay Neighbours,* DVD, New Direction Ministries of Canada, 2009.

2 Alan Chambers, "The New Homosexuality?", *Charisma* (10 March 2009).

3 Bruce L. Shelley, *Church History in Plain Language, Updated 2nd Edition* (Nashville: Thomas Nelson, 1996) 41.

ABOUT THE AUTHOR

Justin Lee is the founder and executive director of the Gay Christian Network (GCN), a nonprofit, interdenominational organization working to increase dialogue between gays and Christians and support people on both sides wrestling with related issues.

A passionate Christian from a conservative evangelical background, Justin thought he knew everything there was to know about the Christian approach to homosexuality—until unexpected events turned his world upside down and forced him to reconsider everything he believed. His journey to better understand both sides of the issue without abandoning his Christian faith or love of the Bible turned him into an internationally recognized authority on bridge-building between the church and the LGBT community. Today, his organization works with individuals, families, and churches to stop the debate from tearing people apart.

Justin's work has garnered national attention and praise from gays and Christians from across the theological spectrum. He has been featured in numerous print, radio, and television venues, including *Dr. Phil*, *Anderson Cooper 360*, the Associated Press, and a front-page article in *The New York Times*. He is the director of the 2009 documentary *Through My Eyes*, about the debate's impact on young Christians; and co-host of the popular long-running podcast *GCN Radio*. Justin lives in Raleigh, North Carolina.